THE JUNIOR COLLEGE:
Progress and Prospect

THE CARNEGIE SERIES IN AMERICAN EDUCATION

The books in this series have resulted from studies supported by grants of the Carnegie Corporation of New York, and are published by McGraw-Hill in recognition of their importance to the future of American education.

The Corporation, a philanthropic foundation established in 1911 by Andrew Carnegie for the advancement and diffusion of knowledge and understanding, has a continuing interest in the improvement of American education. It financed the studies in this series to provide facts and recommendations which would be useful to all those who make or influence the decisions which shape American educational policies and institutions.

The statements made and views expressed in these books are solely the responsibility of the authors.

Books Published

Clark · The Open Door College
Conant · The American High School Today
Glenny · Autonomy of Public Colleges
Henninger · The Technical Institute in America
Medsker · The Junior College: Progress and Prospect
Pierson · The Education of American Businessmen

In Preparation

Cleveland · The Overseas American
Corson · Governance of College and University

The Junior College:

PROGRESS AND PROSPECT

LELAND L. MEDSKER

Vice-Chairman
Center for the Study of Higher Education
University of California, Berkeley

McGRAW-HILL BOOK COMPANY, INC.

1960   New York   Toronto   London

THE JUNIOR COLLEGE: Progress and Prospect

II

41305

Foreword

Rooted distantly in the educational institutions of England and Western Europe, American higher education has adapted itself in manifold ways to the peculiar social, economic, political, and cultural conditions and needs of its own society. In this process it has created two unique institutions, found nowhere else in the world. They are the two-year junior college, increasingly called the community college, and the four-year liberal arts college. These two innovations, the one bringing higher education to the students' own doors, and the other offering a general education instead of the professional studies traditionally associated with the university, have been primarily responsible for the unprecedented expansion of college enrollment in this country.

Of all types of higher institutions, the junior college has experienced the most rapid growth in the last half century. And if the plans of many states materialize, it will be expected to absorb a large part of the explosive increase in college attendance that lies just ahead.

The widespread contemporary interest in the junior college is often based less on a philosophy of education, less on a consideration of the characteristics of students and their educational needs, than on the search for a means of containing tomorrow's stampede of students toward college doors, and serving them at minimum cost. But educational planners who are sensitive to the diversity of students' interests and abilities, and equally sensitive to diverse social, economic, and cultural needs, will put much heavier burdens on the two-year college. They will require it to conduct a highly differentiated educational program. Dr. Medsker is therefore thoroughly justified in saying, as he does in the early part of this volume, that "No unit of American higher education is expected to serve such a diversity of purposes, to provide such a variety of educational instruments, or to distribute students among so many types of educational programs as the junior college." In a system of higher education that prides itself on its diversity, junior colleges will not be mere centers for the accommodation of hordes of students. "Community colleges," as the Regents of the State of New York have expressed it, "have a meaning and competence in their own right."

It would be possible, of course, to use the first year or two of education beyond the high school, whether in junior colleges or four-year institutions, primarily for the purpose of sifting out the students who are capable of attaining a baccalaureate degree. There are those who believe that, in a society in which the many insist on going to college, the first responsibility of higher institutions is to eliminate those who are unfit for advanced college or university work. This can be done, and perhaps done most effectively, by putting all students through a conventional lower-division curriculum, failing a large proportion of them, and offering no curricular alternatives to those who fall by the wayside.

Others believe that it is the responsibility of higher institutions to adapt their educational processes to students whose abilities, interests, and goals require different kinds and levels of schooling. This does not mean that all institutions should provide all types of education, but that in a comprehensive educational plan, varied types of education would be somewhere available. In such a diversified system, the junior college presumably should play a distinctive role.

The proponents of the junior college as a distinctive institution have charged it with heavy responsibilities. Among the functions which are usually ascribed to it, the following are particularly significant in a diversified educational system: (1) providing terminal curricula of two years and less in length; (2) providing curricula preparatory to advanced undergraduate education in four-year institutions; (3) providing general education for all students, terminal and preparatory; (4) aiding students to make educational and vocational choices that are consistent with their individual characteristics; and (5) offering a wide range of general and special courses for adults.

Presumably, one of the *unique* functions of the community college is to provide terminal technical, semiprofessional, or general curricula of two years or less in length adapted to the needs and characteristics of students and to the needs of the community or region. But has this function been more professed than performed? In answering this question, Dr. Medsker discovered that fewer terminal curricula have been offered than one might have expected, and that when they have been given too few students have elected them.

Here, as in many other phases of American higher education, perception and conception of educational and social prestige have determined educational choice. Students prefer the program which leads (for many fewer than the number who enter it) to four-year colleges and universities. The junior college struggles against this bias, and probably against expectations which parents and even some junior college teachers (see Chapter 7) also hold. The way in which the community at large visualizes the role of the junior college also affects its character and destiny. These expectations again pose a fundamental question with respect to the junior college: Is it a really unique institution serving special functions which other institutions cannot serve effectively or do not serve at all? This is the basic question to which Dr. Medsker addresses himself in this study of some 75 two-year institutions in 15 states. His evaluation includes not only the extent and effectiveness of the performance of the terminal function, but also the other accepted functions of the junior college.

While the number of junior colleges has grown considerably in some states, and there are plans for considerable expansion in others, this is by no means the uniform pattern. In certain states, particularly Indiana, Wisconsin, Ohio, and Pennsylvania, state universities have established two-year extension centers as a means of decentralizing higher education. The question then arises as to whether lower-division university branches or local community colleges are more likely to meet the diverse needs of young people and the community.

In dealing with this question, Dr. Medsker observes that not all the advantages lie with either arrangement. But his most telling finding is that with relatively few exceptions the freshman-sophomore programs of the university branches are restricted to transfer courses closely paralleling those in the parent institution. While this may be useful in setting comparable academic standards and in facilitating the movement of qualified students from the centers to the central campuses, it does not contribute to the development of a broadly diversified scheme of post-high school education.

In at least one of the states with the pattern of extension centers, the state university has opposed the establishment of community colleges. The opposition has been based on grounds both of expediency and educational standards. It has been said that existing institutions can expand central enrollments and establish branches more expeditiously and efficiently than new colleges can be created. And it has been pointed out that the established institutions can assure the maintenance of high academic standards from the new centers' beginning.

No doubt these arguments have been advanced sincerely. But one would think that, with the prospect of overpowering numbers, the large state universities might take a leaf from California history and policy by urging a larger proportion of students to take the first two years of a four-year program in community junior colleges, particularly since the California junior colleges (and those in certain other states as well, as indicated in Chapter 5) have demonstrated that they can successfully prepare students for upper-division work. Apparently, many state universities still wish to enroll as many freshmen and sophomores as possible. The reason, one suspects, is that they do not wish to share state funds for post-high school education with junior colleges, which ordinarily enjoy partial state support. The size of the enrollment still talks when legislators are considering university appropriations! Even so, self-interest might, in the long run, mean encouraging the development of community colleges that would permit the university to become more selective and to concentrate on purposes and programs of university level and character.

Additional information on the influence of different types of public higher institutions on college attendance from varying socioeconomic and ability levels will be available later as a result of another study also directed by Dr. Medsker and supported by the United States Office of Education.

Dr. Medsker's description and evaluation of the junior college is part of an extensive series of investigations conducted under the broad title of "The Diversification of American Higher Education" at the Center for the Study of Higher Education of the University of California at Berkeley under a subvention from the Carnegie Corporation of New York. The purposes of these investigations are to provide a more adequate description of the diversity than now occurs, and to lay a part of the groundwork for more effective differentiation of educational opportunities. Obviously, the studies had to be selective rather than exhaustive. They were grouped around these topics: (1) the diversity of student characteristics, not only in academic ability, but also in social and cultural background, attitudes, beliefs, values, and basic characteristics of personality; (2) the junior college as an instrument for diversifying educational opportunities and distributing students among appropriate educational programs; and (3) the state-wide coordination of higher education as a means of providing, with reasonable economy and efficiency, a pattern of educational institutions and programs commensurate with the characteristics and needs of students and the requirements of the commonwealth.

These studies were planned with the assistance of a group of consultants and an advisory committee. The consultants were Dr. John G. Darley, then Professor of Psychology and Associate Dean of the Graduate School at the University of Minnesota; Dr. Lyman Glenny, Associate Professor of Political Science at Sacramento State College; Dr. Leland L. Medsker, then director of East Contra Costa Junior College, now Vice-Chairman of the Center; Dr. Floyd Reeves, Consultant to the President of Michigan State University; and Dr. James Reynolds, Professor of Junior College Education at the University of Texas.

The advisory committee was composed of the following: Dr. Jesse P. Bogue, then Executive Secretary, American Association of Junior Colleges; Dr. William S. Carlson, then President, State University of New York; Dr. Henry Chauncey, President, Educational Testing Service; President C. W. de Kiewiet, University of Rochester; Dr. Samuel B. Gould, then President, Antioch College; Dr. Walter E. Hager, then President, Wilson Teachers College; Monsignor Frederick G. Hochwalt, Director, Department of Education, National Catholic Welfare Conference; President Douglas M. Knight, Lawrence College; President John D. Millett, Miami University; President J. L. Morrill, University of Minnesota; Dr. G. Kerry Smith, Executive Secretary, Association for Higher Education of the National Education Association; Dr. Dael Wolfle, Administrative Secretary, American Association for the Advancement of Science.

The study of state-wide coordination of higher education has been published under the title, *Autonomy of Public Colleges: The Challenge of Coordination*, by Dr. Lyman Glenny (McGraw-Hill, 1959). The studies of student characteristics will appear in due course. The present volume by Dr. Medsker is one of two books on the junior college. The second, already published, is *The Open Door College: A Case Study*, by Dr. Burton Clark. This is a study of the way in which a specific two-year institution, the San Jose Junior College, developed a particular role and character by interaction with its environment.

T. R. McConnell, CHAIRMAN
CENTER FOR THE STUDY OF
HIGHER EDUCATION
UNIVERSITY OF CALIFORNIA
BERKELEY, CALIFORNIA

Contents

Introduction

The relative newness and the rapid growth of the two-year college have given rise to many questions. Though much is known and much has been written about this type of college, recent objective data are lacking. For example, not since 1940 has a comprehensive attempt been made to determine how many students entering junior colleges later transfer to four-year colleges. As a result, no up-to-date information is available to answer the question of whether the two-year college is primarily a transfer or a terminal institution. Furthermore, the few studies on academic performance and retention of students who have transferred have been isolated undertakings. At no time have a number of colleges and universities cooperated in a study under a uniform design in an effort to determine the extent to which and how well the two-year college serves as a transfer institution. Specific information has also been lacking on how and to what extent the two-year college has implemented certain of its other commonly expressed objectives. Likewise, no study has been made to determine whether the attitudes of teachers in two-year colleges are in harmony with the expressed objectives of these colleges. Few analyses exist of the organizational and financial patterns of the two-year college and of its relationship to other segments of higher education. Yet such information would seem indispensable to the many official and unofficial bodies engaged (or to be engaged) in planning for post-high school education.

It is understandable, then, why a study on the diversity of American higher education would include a special investigation of the two-year college and its activities. Only by doing so would it be possible to depict the total diversity of institutions, programs, and students which characterizes higher education. To this end the more specific objectives of this phase of the diversification study were:

I

1. To observe and report on the patterns of control, finance, and administration of the two-year college in different states, and its relationship to other segments of higher education

2. To describe the functions of the two-year college as they are actually discharged, with an attempt to compare the functions performed with the claims commonly made by this institution

3. To make such evaluations of two-year institutions as are possible within the limitations of the study and to identify some of the problems which they must face in the immediate years ahead

The Nature of the Study

Such a study necessitated a consideration of the two-year college throughout the nation. Accordingly, certain data about its development in the various states were assembled. However, there are more than 600 two-year colleges scattered through most of the states, which made it impracticable to investigate every one. The more intensive investigation was therefore limited to 15 states, selected to provide examples of the various organizational, financial, and control patterns. Some states were included because they illustrated locally controlled junior colleges, others because of the prevalence of state or regional junior colleges, and still others because they used extension centers of four-year colleges. Three states were chosen because no public two-year colleges existed, or only a few, although the need for them had been a subject of much discussion in the state for several years.

The states finally selected were California, Georgia, Illinois, Iowa, Massachusetts, Minnesota, Mississippi, New York, North Carolina, Ohio, Oklahoma, Oregon, Pennsylvania, Texas, and Wisconsin. According to the 1956 *Junior College Directory*, 342,[1] or 58 per cent, of all two-year junior colleges in the country were in these states; these states also accounted for 216, or 66 per cent, of the nation's public junior colleges and 126, or 48 per cent, of all private junior colleges. The total freshman and sophomore enrollment in these states amounted to 76 per cent of all such enrollments in junior colleges in the country.

Florida, Indiana, and Washington were later added to the list of states to be investigated because of certain developments of the two-year college movement there; however, studies in these 3 states

[1] Excluding evening junior colleges in California.

were more limited than in the other 15—no studies were made of individual institutions.

From the 342 two-year colleges in the 15 states, about 20 per cent of the individual institutions, considered characteristic in size, program, and control, were selected for intensive study. The institutions were selected after consultation with persons familiar with junior colleges in each of the states. In all, 76 colleges, hereinafter referred to as "cooperating institutions," participated in the study, some of them only in certain phases. They are listed in Appendix M.

Some four-year colleges were also invited to take part in the study. Through their cooperation it was possible to obtain the data on the performance of junior college transfers reported in Chapter 5. These institutions, which are listed in Appendix N, were selected because of the relatively large number of students transferring to them from junior colleges. Most of them were located in the 15 states.

It was early decided, with the concurrence of the advisory committee to the general study of the diversification of American higher education, that the study of the two-year college should include the compilation of both factual data and observations made by the director of the study who would spend some time in each of the states and at the cooperating institutions. The field work was considered important as a method of expediting, supplementing, and checking the objective data and as a means of obtaining opinions and points of view on the role of the two-year college and its problems in each state.

As a first step in obtaining data in the selected 15 states, a questionnaire type of instrument referred to as the original check list was mailed in the spring of 1956 to each of the 342 institutions. This instrument, returned by 243 institutions, not only furnished important data but also helped to identify colleges that could logically be invited to participate more intensively.

After the participating institutions were selected, each was asked to collect certain data on provided forms, according to a uniform design developed by the director of the study. In addition, the director spent one or two days on each campus assisting in the compilation of data and gathering information by interviews with staff members and by the examination of available publications. The director also spent considerable time in each state interviewing officials in state agencies and often in the state university.

Data collected from the institutions and through field observation were assembled and analyzed in the office of the Center for the Study of Higher Education in Berkeley. The result of this work is the present report.

The Problem

The two-year college was designed to play a special and a strategic role in American higher education. This it does in a variety of ways: It is perhaps the most effective democratizing agent in higher education. It decentralizes post-high school opportunities by placing them within reach of a large number of students. It makes higher education available at low cost to the student and at moderate cost to society. It offers a wide range of educational programs not found in other colleges.

The junior college plays a special role, too, as a distributing agency. It offers a constructive way for many students to terminate formal education, and it is a means of identifying students capable of more advanced training. Once the secondary school discharged this function but as the social and economic conditions made more formal schooling desirable, either simply as a maturing experience or as a means of better civic and vocational education, it was inevitable that, for many students, these functions should be performed by an extension of common schooling.

Furthermore, the American technological economy requires many persons trained at an intermediate level—not full-fledged engineers or scientists but high-level technicians or semiprofessionals. This has necessitated the upgrading of industrial personnel either by more advanced technical, scientific, and managerial training or by more advanced general education.

No unit of American higher education is expected to serve such a diversity of purposes, to provide such a variety of educational instruments, or to distribute students among so many types of educational programs as the junior college.

A study like the present one raises many questions: How fully is the junior college meeting its wide range of responsibilities? What are the abilities, family backgrounds, and motives of the students attending the junior college? How extensive are the efforts of the junior college to meet the educational needs of its students? Is it still predominantly a preparatory institution despite its long espousal of semiprofessional and general education for the student who will not continue formal education beyond the fourteenth year? Has it taken technical education seriously? If it offers terminal programs, do students take advantage of them? If in fact there are many "concealed terminals" and few "announced" terminals, if it attains legitimacy, primarily by duplication of the first two years of a four-year institution—what are the forces that reinforce this practice and handicap the development of its terminal function? Do they include the motives of the students, the desires of the parents, the wishes of community organizations, the attitudes of the junior college teaching staff? To the extent that the junior college *is* a preparatory institution, how successful are its students in the colleges and universities to which they transfer?

Questions of a different nature also need to be asked. Are student personnel services in the junior college sufficient in quantity and quality to enable it to discharge its distributive responsibility? What are the financial-support problems of the junior college? How do the services of the junior colleges compare with those of extension centers? How does the junior college fit into state-wide systems of higher education?

Such questions bring into sharp focus the overriding question: What is the role of the two-year college in higher education both now and in the future?

The Report

This report was prepared with three groups of readers in mind: first, the laymen and educators interested in the functions and problems of the two-year college; second, those already taking part in the work of the junior college or preparing to become teachers or administrators in it; third, those concerned with state-wide planning and coordination of higher education.

For the benefit of all three groups the introductory chapter presents briefly the growth and the present emphasis on the two-year college, enumerates the socioeconomic forces that have given rise to its existence, and evaluates the junior college's response to such forces. The chapter serves as an overview of the two-year college movement and as a summary of its strength and weaknesses.

Chapter 2 describes the students who attend two-year colleges. The following chapters consider the programs offered by these colleges; the extent to which students transfer to four-year colleges; the performance and retention of transfer students; the efforts by the two-year colleges to counsel students; the faculty and the extent to which its attitudes toward the purpose and function of the junior college are in harmony with the commonly expressed goals of the institution.

Since the two-year college has developed under widely different patterns and has encountered various problems in the different states, it was considered essential to review its status in each of the states included in the study. Chapter 8, therefore, contains a section discussing the extent to which a junior college system has evolved in each state, together with its pattern of organization, its source of financial support, and the problems it currently faces.

The final chapter projects the two-year college into the immediate years ahead—the major problems it will most likely encounter are discussed, and certain conclusions pertaining to its organization and financial support are drawn.

An Explanation of Terms

A few terms in the report warrant a word of explanation. The phrase "two-year institution" or "two-year college" was substituted for "junior college" in order to have an all-embracing term that could also include technical institutes and freshman-sophomore extension centers. Nevertheless, the term "junior college" often appears in the report as a synonym for "two-year college" merely to reduce repetition. Thus, when the term "junior college" is used without qualification, it is to denote the wide range of two-year colleges rather than institutions that happen to be called junior colleges.

The terms "transfer" and "terminal," applying to students and curricula, appear frequently in the report. Transfer courses or curricula are those designed for acceptance for credit in senior institutions. Transfer students are those who expect to continue or have continued their studies in a four-year college. The word "terminal" is sometimes objected to on the grounds that education never terminates and that neither students nor educational programs can properly be classified as terminal. It cannot be denied, of course, that education should be continuous throughout life. But some term is needed to describe the student who does not expect to continue his formal full-time collegiate training beyond the junior college or who does not continue beyond that point. By the same token, a term is needed to describe educational programs that serve primarily students who do not expect to transfer. Since the word "terminal" rightly or wrongly has become entrenched in the literature, and since no one has coined a more apt single word to describe the students and programs referred to above, it is used without apology in this report.

Acknowledgments and Appreciation

It is evident that this study is the result of the work and devotion of many people and agencies. It is not practicable to enumerate them all. To the cooperating institutions and their chief administrators as well as to the many other staff members in each college, the author acknowledges his indebtedness. The same is true of the senior institutions and their representatives who participated in the study of transfers, and of the representatives of the different state agencies in the several states. Acknowledgment is made to the members of the advisory committee for their guidance in the design of the study, and to Jesse P. Bogue, S. V. Martorana, and James W. Reynolds for their helpfulness in periodic consultations. Many others contributed by reading and evaluating the manuscript.

Special gratitude is due to the Carnegie Corporation for financing the study. All members of the research and clerical staff in the Center for the Study of Higher Education at Berkeley were of great assistance, particularly James W. Trent, research assistant for this particular study, who paid relentless, painstaking, and efficient attention to both the details and the larger aspects of the study. Herbert Maccoby, research consultant in sociology, was exceedingly helpful in the execution of the study on staff attitudes. Finally, I am deeply indebted to T. R. McConnell, chairman of the Center for the Study of Higher Education. His insight into higher education and research, his understanding of the problems in so large an undertaking, his encouragement, and his advice were invaluable for the conduct and conclusion of the study.

CHAPTER 1

Realization, Expectation, and Examination

Twice within a decade two presidential bodies have pointed to the potential place of the junior college in American higher education. In late 1947 the Commission on Higher Education appointed by President Truman, after estimating that at least 49 per cent of the population had the mental ability to complete 14 years of schooling with a curriculum that should lead either to gainful employment or to further study, said:

> As one means of achieving the expansion of educational opportunity and the diversification of educational offerings it considers necessary, this commission recommends that the number of community colleges be increased and that their activities be multiplied.[1]

Less than 10 years later the Committee on Education beyond the High School appointed by President Eisenhower said in its *Second Report to the President:*

> The expansion of the "2-year college" has been one of the most notable developments in post-high school education in twentieth-century America. . . . These [institutions] respond to the increasing demand for a greater variety of more accessible training and education, while at the same time helping other colleges and the universities to concentrate a greater proportion of their energies

---

[1] *Higher Education for American Democracy: A Report of the President's Commission on Higher Education,* Harper & Brothers, New York, 1948, vol. 1, p. 67.

than would otherwise be possible on upper division, graduate, and professional work. . . . Community colleges are not designed, however, merely to relieve enrollment pressures on senior institutions. They have a role and an integrity of their own.[2]

Such statements are not rare. Many other agencies and commissions have during the past decade referred to the junior college as an important contributor to diversity in American higher education and have recommended that additional junior colleges be established.

But the rise of the two-year college to national recognition and the youthfulness, the different organizational patterns, and the multiple responsibilities of this in-between institution that exists nowhere outside the United States have led to many questions. This study attempts to answer some of them, particularly whether these institutions really strengthen American higher education; whether they achieve their objectives; which are the best patterns of organization, finance, and control; how their programs can be integrated with those of other institutions; and what conditions are necessary if they are to perform a unique function.

The purpose of this chapter is twofold. First, it is to summarize the development and present status of the two-year college. Since much has been written on this aspect, only information sufficient for background purposes is included. Second, by referring to some of the data and observations reported in the following seven chapters, the role performed by the junior college is summarized briefly. In effect, therefore, the chapter serves as a summary of the entire report to provide a general view of the two-year college. Further summary statements, particularly as they relate to the projection of the junior college into the next decade, are made in Chapter 9.

FROM CONCEPTION TO RECEPTION

The junior college is a product of the twentieth century, but the idea for it was germinated earlier by such university presidents

[2] The President's Committee on Education beyond the High School, *Second Report to the President,* U.S. Government Printing Office, 1957.

as Folwell of Minnesota, Tappan of Michigan, and Harper of Chicago. These men advocated what has been termed the "bifurcated university"—a university in which work of the freshman and sophomore years would be turned over to the secondary schools, and the university would thus begin its work with the junior year. Of the three men, Harper made the most progress toward the stated goal by setting up a system of affiliated colleges—all in connection with an academy or a public high school—for the purpose of conducting the normal lower-division work. It was Harper, too, who coined the term "junior college" to describe such lower-division units. Professor W. H. Cowley[3] of Stanford University in commenting on the proposal made by the proponents of the bifurcated university has called attention to the fact that they did not envision the two-year unitary college as it is known today. Implied in Cowley's remarks was the fact that the advocates were more concerned about eliminating lower-division work in the university than about the virtues of attaching the first college years to the secondary schools.

Although the idea of the completely bifurcated university did not meet with general acclaim, the plan of offering lower-division work either in private institutions or in local public school systems began to be implemented on a limited scale around the turn of the century. The consistent growth of the institution can be observed by examining the 1959 *Junior College Directory*.[4] A look at the data for three arbitrarily chosen years will show the change in numbers of colleges (by type of control) and enrollments in them. In 1921–22 there were 207 junior colleges. Although only a third were tax-supported, this group accounted for more than half of the total enrollment of more than sixteen thousand students. By 1938–39 the number of junior colleges had increased to 575. By then there were 258 public and 317 private institutions, although more than 71 per cent of the students enrolled were in the public colleges. In 1957–58 the total number of institutions had increased

[3] W. H. Cowley, "The Junior College—Whence and Whither?" unpublished manuscript, Stanford University, Stanford, 1955.

[4] Edmund J. Gleazer, Jr., "Analysis of Junior College Growth," *Junior College Directory*, American Association of Junior Colleges, Washington, 1959, pp. 44–52.

to 667 of which 391, or 58.6 per cent, were public and 276 were private. Almost 90 per cent of the total enrollment was in the public institutions in 1957–58.[5]

The relative importance of the two-year colleges is reflected in their share of the total enrollment in all higher institutions in the United States. Table 1-1 shows that for *all* higher institutions, public and private, the two-year colleges accounted for 12 per cent of the total enrollment of degree-credit students in the fall semester, 1958, and for 24 per cent of the degree-credit students who that year were enrolled in college for the first time. In terms of enrollments in public higher institutions only, the two-year colleges enrolled 17 per cent of the total college enrollment and 31 per cent of students enrolled for the first time. Since the U.S. Office of Education, the original source of these data, defined degree-credit students as those "whose program consists wholly or principally of work which is creditable toward a bachelor's or higher degree . . . ," it is evident that many students in junior colleges not working toward a baccalaureate degree would not have been included in the enrollment figure reported. The proportion of students enrolled in public two-year colleges was particularly high in California, Colorado, Illinois, Michigan, Mississippi, Oklahoma, and Texas.

Many forms of the junior college have developed, private and public. Though the private two-year colleges have in recent years declined in relative numerical importance and in the proportion of students enrolled in them, they constitute an important segment of post-high school education both in terms of students enrolled and in their freedom to offer special services and programs. At present they vary greatly among themselves. Some are church-related, whereas others are independent. Some have general programs, others specialized ones. Some are primarily residential, others mostly accommodate local students. Some are well financed

---

[5] Enrollment data in the *Directory* are cumulative for the year and thus include any student served by any junior college for the year reported; they do not reflect the enrollment situation as of a given date. Also, they include special students and students enrolled in classes for adults. With the rapid growth in service to adults reported in Chap. 3, particularly in public junior colleges, a report of total enrollments may not give an accurate picture of regular lower-division enrollment or allow an accurate comparison between public and private institutions.

and have good facilities, others need funds for capital outlay and operation.

With the American concept that public education is a function of the state, it is not surprising that public two-year colleges have developed in different ways and in different degrees in the various states. In some states few or no public colleges exist; in other states they are numerous. The principal types that have developed are (1) the locally controlled and supported junior or community college with or without state aid, (2) the junior college or technical institute fully controlled and supported by the state, and (3) the two-year extension center of a four-year college or university. In several states no one of these types is in use exclusively, but two or more types are in operation in the same state.

Table 1-1. Relation of Total and First-time Enrollment of Degree-credit Students in Junior Colleges to Enrollment in All Colleges, 1958*

	Total enrollment	Per cent in junior colleges	Public institutions	Per cent in junior colleges	Private institutions	Per cent in junior colleges
Total enrollment:						
In all colleges, fall, 1958	3,258,556		1,912,232		1,346,324	
In junior colleges, fall, 1958	386,511	12	331,671	17	54,840	4
First-time, fall, 1958:						
In all colleges	723,178		479,114		301,961	
In junior colleges	175,406	24	146,739	31	28,667	9.5

* SOURCE: *A Fact Book on Higher Education,* Office of Statistical Information, American Council on Education, Washington. Original data from the U.S. Department of Health, Education, and Welfare, Office of Education.

The different patterns of public two-year institutions in the different states are shown in Figure 1. Some type of public two-year college is found in 41 states. In 14 states the sole pattern of organization is the local junior college under the jurisdiction of either a local school system or a separate junior college district.[6]

[6] "Local" as used here means any political unit within the state—usually a county, a municipality, or a school district serving a given area. Local junior colleges are also found in combination with other types in 12 other states. Approximately 70 per cent of the public two-year colleges in the county are of the local type.

Fig. 1. Location of Public Two-year Colleges in the United States.

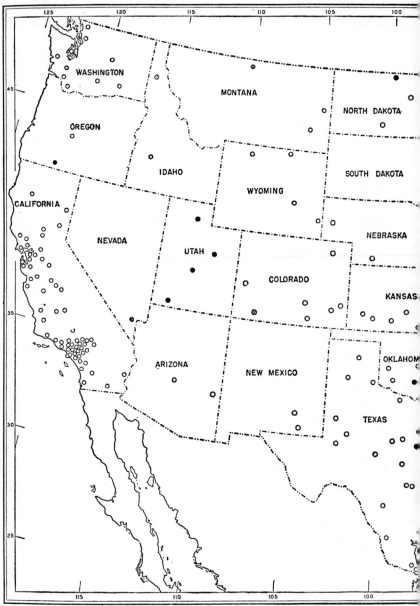

SOURCE: Data from *Junior College Directory*, 1959

95 90 85 80 75 70

MAINE

:SOTA

WISCONSIN

MICH.

NEW
YORK

VT.

NH.

MASS.

CONN.

R.I.

IOWA

MICHIGAN

PENNSYLVANIA

40

ILLINOIS

INDIANA

OHIO

MD.

N.J.

DEL.

MISSOURI

WEST
VIRGINIA

VIRGINIA

35'

KENTUCKY

ARKANSAS

TENNESSEE

NORTH CAROLINA

SOUTH
CAROLINA

ALABAMA

MISS.

GEORGIA

ALASKA:
THREE LOCAL JUNIOR COLLEGES

30

LOUISIANA

FLORIDA

25

SCALE

100 200 300 400 MILES

200 400 600 KILOMETERS

CONIC PROJECTION

WEST LONGITUDE

90 85 80 75

In only 1 state does the fully supported state junior college prevail exclusively; in 8 states extension centers of four-year colleges or universities constitute the only type of two-year unit, although in 4 of these states only 1 such extension center exists; 17 states have different combinations of the various types of two-year institutions.

In some respects the declared purposes of public two-year institutions are even more diverse than their organizational patterns. The majority of them claim to be comprehensive junior colleges; they stress lower-division work for students who expect to transfer to higher institutions and in addition offer programs for those who do not plan to transfer. Most of them also stress their role in adult education, in special community services, in guidance, in remedial work for students entering with educational deficiencies, and in general education.

This breadth of service earned many junior colleges the designation "community colleges." In fact, within the past decade this name has come to be used generically to describe a college which, in addition to offering conventional courses leading to a baccalaureate degree, also plays a major role in the educational, cultural, and civic activities in the community. The term connotes a close interrelationship of the college and the life of the community: the college looks to the community for suggestions in program-planning and the community looks to the college for many different services to many different people.

The development of the two-year college—particularly the local junior college—has been accompanied by numerous problems. In many states post-high school programs were started as more or less extralegal operations without the benefit of definite enabling legislation. Such legislation came slowly, often in the face of opposition on the grounds that junior colleges would compete with existing four-year colleges and necessitate unwarranted additional taxes. Even after enabling legislation was passed, in many states the full or the greater part of the financial burden for junior colleges was for years borne by the local community. During this time the state often gave substantially more aid to the local community to support elementary and high schools than to support the junior college. At the same time the state supported in full the public four-year colleges and universities, thus in effect making the junior college the only segment of public education for which it assumed no or only limited financial responsibility. In many states, too, there was no plan for giving over-all leadership to the junior college and few state-wide plans to integrate it with other segments of post-high school education. Interest, in general, was limited except in the communities which operated junior colleges.

But despite its slow-developing history, there are indications of an increasing acceptance of the two-year college idea. The growth in the number of such institutions and in the number of people enrolled in them, recent legislative action in several states providing for increased state aid to junior colleges, and the tendency for many state and national bodies to recommend the establishment of junior colleges all indicate that the American people regard these institutions as a practical means of decentralizing higher education.

SOCIOECONOMIC FORCES AFFECTING THE JUNIOR COLLEGE MOVEMENT

The two-year college is the result of the social and economic forces which created it and shaped its character. Without doubt one of the forces is the growing belief that educational opportunities beyond the high school must be equalized. Any society which puts a premium on higher education for all who can profit from it and which recognizes the college as an aid in developing talent of many kinds and degrees must make sure that economic and social barriers do not result in the development of an educational elite. In recent years the number of scholarship and loan programs for the lowering of economic barriers has increased. But even the availability of financial aid does not eliminate all economic differences among students. Low-cost education which provides the opportunity for the student to live at home and often to continue in part-time employment in the community may be a greater inducement to many students than a scholarship or a long-term loan.

There are also academic and social barriers to a post-high school education. Some high school graduates are not eligible to enter certain four-year colleges or pursue certain academic programs, yet they too have talents worthy of development. In the long run their desire to participate in a post-high school program will probably mean that pressures will be exerted upon society to make it possible for them to do so. Besides, there are young people from lower social groups who, though they may be able and also may be eligible for financial aid, would be reluctant to move into a conventional four-year college situation. Yet they may be inclined to enter a local two-year college with many of their social peers. For all such reasons the two-year college has been regarded as an agency that provides opportunity and motivation for many students to begin some post-high school experience that would otherwise have been unobtainable.

Two additional factors have a bearing on the extent to which the junior college equalizes educational opportunity. One factor is the deep and inherent American desire to move from one social class to another. The attempt at social advancement often is made by engaging in the same activities as those of a higher class, including college attendance. The presence of a local public college which charges minimum or no tuition affords the means by which many in a lower socioeconomic class may attend college and thus increase their chance of moving upward on the social scale. Havighurst and Neugarten characterized certain types of higher institutions in terms of the social class from which students are usually drawn. Among the types described was "opportunity college," which the authors linked with the junior college. Of this college the authors wrote:

> Opportunity college . . . is always characterized by low costs, easy admission standards, and a predominance of students from working-class families. . . . Opportunity college is primarily a place for youth who desire social mobility. . . . Students tend to think of attaining mobility more by learning middle-class vocational skills than by learning middle-class social skills.[1]

The other factor is the faith which the American people have come to place in higher education. The percentage of people enrolling in American colleges and universities to the total college-age population rose from 3 per cent in 1900 to 32 per cent in 1955. The greater the extent to which people in general covet the opportunity for themselves or their children to attend college, the greater is the demand for institutions most likely to make college a reality.

[1] Robert J. Havighurst and Bernice L. Neugarten, *Society and Education*, Allyn and Bacon, Inc., Englewood Cliffs, N.J., 1957, p. 255.

During the half century of increased interest in full-time college attendance, adults also become increasingly interested in improving themselves through enrollment in part-time educational programs. Many agencies provide organized opportunities for adults to return to school part time, and no one agency has a monopoly on this service. The experience has been, however, that a junior college in a community frequently becomes a popular medium of adult education. Enrollment of special and adult students in junior colleges in the nation increased from approximately 21,000 in 1936 to more than 400,000 in 1957. Although it is unlikely that many junior colleges were originally established as adult agencies, the idea of having a local college providing adult programs has doubtless been a factor in its establishment and general popularity.

Another force affecting the importance of the junior college is ever-increasing social and technological developments and their many by-products. These have helped to make the public aware that the more complex the society, the greater the need for education. At the same time the task of transmitting the cultural heritage becomes heavier, and the responsibility for improving it grows greater. Besides, occupational patterns change as a result of the technological developments. These changes have included an increase in the number of jobs involving new combinations of applied science, engineering, or business coupled with broad social and aesthetic understandings. In many instances technological changes have decreased the number of jobs that do not require specialized vocational training, and they have tended to postpone the normal age at which young people enter the labor market. They have contributed to the need for a new type of collegiate institution to prepare men and women for an increasingly complex occupational structure in an increasingly complex society.

A social force that affects the future of the junior college is the increased number of people who will reach college age in the next decade. The pronouncements made by many nationwide agencies and state study groups concerning the need for additional junior colleges have in part been based on the expected large number of students who will demand college opportunities. However, some agencies recommending the junior college have pointed out that it has merits other than becoming a mere center for the accommodation of additional students. "Community colleges," said the Board of Regents of the State of New York, "have a meaning and a competence in their own right."[8]

The foregoing discussion of the social forces points to the conclusion that the two-year college has been established to meet certain of society's basic needs. The following discussion will attempt to determine the extent to which the junior college has met those needs.

THE CONTRIBUTION OF THE TWO-YEAR COLLEGE

The junior college has responded in numerous ways to the forces giving rise to it. Its contributions to American higher education may well account for its growth and recognition, and these contributions are outlined in the sections to follow.

The Junior College as a Democratizing Agency

The public junior college in particular has made democratization of higher education possible by various means. In most states, it has kept its tuition rates low and in some states no tuition is charged. The establishment of an increasing number of junior colleges has brought them close to the homes of many potential students, thus again reducing the total cost of attendance. An earlier study[9] by Koos, of almost twelve thousand high school graduates of 61 high schools situated in 12 states of the Midwest, South, and Far West, showed that in school systems with junior colleges the median percentage of graduates entering college was almost two and a half times larger than that for systems without junior colleges. For the higher socioeconomic groups it was about one and a half times larger, and for the lower socioeconomic groups about three and a half times larger. Additional data from the same study showed that even among higher socioeconomic groups more high school graduates entered junior colleges where no tuition was charged than where tuition was charged.

The tendency of the junior college to serve students in lower

[8] *Statement and Recommendations of the Board of Regents for Meeting the Needs in Higher Education in New York State,* New York State Department of Education, Albany, N.Y., Dec. 21, 1956, p. 113.

[9] Leonard V. Koos, "How to Democratize the Junior College," *School Review,* May, 1944, pp. 271–284.

social brackets was further identified by Clark in his study of the San Jose City College.[10] He found that the students attending the institution represented almost a cross section of the socioeconomic distribution of the San Jose community.

In another study Koos showed how proximity of a junior college increases college attendance. He found that approximately 44 per cent of the high school graduates entered a local public or a state junior college in the home community, but that the percentage of graduates entering fell sharply with increasing distance of high schools from the location of the college.[11] A study made in Chicago[12] showed that, even in a city with good public transportation facilities, the proportion of high school graduates entering the branches of the city college from high schools in close proximity to the junior college branches ran as high as 50 per cent, whereas the proportion of graduates entering the college from high schools geographically far removed from the branches was as low as 6 per cent.

Democratization of education may also be achieved by making it possible for students to enter some type of college when their academic background may preclude their entrance to other colleges with higher admission standards. This situation is well illustrated by a recent study[13] in California which demonstrated that in 1955 only 11.4 per cent of the graduates of California high schools were eligible to enter the University of California and that 56.4 per cent did not meet entrance requirements of either the university or the state colleges. It follows, since requirements in private colleges are ordinarily as high if not higher than in public colleges, that the only post-high school opportunity available to more than half of California's high school graduates is the state's junior colleges. This is not to imply that only students who cannot be admitted to other

[10] Burton R. Clark, *The Open Door College: A Case Study*, McGraw-Hill Book Company, Inc., New York, 1960.

[11] Leonard V. Koos, "Local versus Regional Junior Colleges," *School Review*, November, 1944, pp. 525–531.

[12] Benjamin C. Willis, *Report on the Chicago City Junior College to the Chicago Board of Education*, Chicago Board of Education, May, 1956, p. 26.

[13] Liaison Committee of the California State Board of Education and the Board of Regents of the University of California, *A Study of the Need for Additional Centers of Public Higher Education in California*, California State Department of Education, Sacramento, Calif., 1957, table 30, p. 126.

institutions attend California junior colleges—many enroll who would easily meet admission requirements elsewhere.

The fact that junior colleges do enroll students with great diversity of background means they are busily concerned with what is referred to, for want of a better term, as "remedial work." The salvage function in its broad aspects—affording students the opportunity to complete required courses not taken in high school, to earn grade-point averages sufficiently high to demonstrate competence to do college work, and to increase basic skills in the fundamental subjects such as communication and mathematics—makes the junior college an important contributor to equality of educational opportunity.

The Junior College and Diversity in Higher Education

The junior college adds an additional type of institution to the already diverse American scene. In addition, the two-year college is extremely diverse within its own ranks: it is either public or private, and within each of these groups there is great variety in terms of control, purpose, and size.

The junior colleges offer a great variety of educational programs, which broaden the total scope of offerings available at the college level. Despite the deficiencies of certain junior college programs which are discussed in the following section, there are potential and actual educational outlets in the two-year college which are not found elsewhere. While there is much yet to be accomplished in the formulation and implementation of terminal programs, most junior colleges declare the terminal function to be one of their important purposes and make many such programs available.

The remedial programs and community services, including adult education, which are offered by most two-year colleges also add to diversity.

The Successful Record of the Junior College Program

In many ways the junior college has made an enviable record in terms of the quality of its program and the success of students who have enrolled in it. The commendable academic record made by junior college transfers to higher institutions is a testimonial of the preparation given the students. Though it was not possible in this study to survey the success of students who were prepared by the junior college for occupational pursuits, a number of reports on follow-up studies of terminal students done by individual junior colleges were reviewed. They, too, tended to indicate the successful performance in industry of the students with junior college preparation.

That the junior college has satisfied a community need is illustrated by the extent to which it has become a community center, with its facilities in full use from early morning until late evening. As one visits the campuses of these institutions throughout the country and witnesses the full utilization of plant, the day-long coming and going, the large parking lots often overflowing into off-campus streets, the libraries full with students, and the general seriousness of purpose reflected by the staff and students, one is compelled to conclude that these are institutions with vitality— a conclusion usually confirmed by a discussion with lay people in the community.

LIMITATIONS OF THE JUNIOR COLLEGE

All educational institutions are subject to continuous criticism for their failure to become all that is expected of them. The junior college is criticized on two counts: (1) failure to meet some of its claims and (2) failure in some instances to achieve an identity of its own.

Failure to Meet Claims

The junior college has claimed many exceptional achievements and has made good on many of them. Other claims—that emphasis is placed on the terminal student; on student personnel services, particularly counseling and guidance; and on general education— have not been fully realized.

Lack of Emphasis on Terminal Education. One of the most important claims on which the junior college has rested its case is that it appropriately meets the needs of the many students who will not transfer to higher institutions. While the terminal function was not one of the original purposes of the junior college, this emphasis developed gradually as faculties realized that many students entering and graduating from their institutions did not transfer but went directly into employment or homemaking. The discussion of this function was accelerated in the 1930s and 1940s, and has been highlighted in the numerous reports on the junior college since 1950.

Chapter 2 contains a discussion of the transfer and terminal functions of the junior college and the question of whether one role tends to be more dominant than the other. Data from a study of the 1952 entering class in 63 two-year colleges are presented. These show that, although there was a wide range in the percentages among the individual institutions, only about a third of the entering students later transferred to four-year colleges. Thus, for two-thirds of the students the two-year college constituted the last full-time formal education. They were the terminal students, regardless of how they classified themselves while they were in junior college. Yet the same group of institutions reported that ordinarily at least two-thirds of the entering students expect to transfer. Furthermore, an analysis of enrollments for the academic year 1956–57 indicated that two-thirds of the students were enrolled in transfer programs. It seems paradoxical that only one-third of the entering students should transfer in comparison with the two-thirds who originally planned to transfer.

This situation is not easily explained. Differences between the stated intentions of junior college students and what they later do are largely the result of circumstances outside the control of the junior college or of the students themselves. Entering students tend to classify themselves as transfer students because there are cultural and traditional values attached to the standard lower-division program; students are frequently loath to admit, even to themselves, that they are not candidates for the baccalaureate degree. In many instances, the parents also feel strongly about the matter and exert direct or indirect influence on the students. Clearly, the junior college has difficulties in effectively emphasizing the terminal function.

Cause for concern arises from two facts: (1) the prevalence of the claims made by the junior college that one of its chief functions *is* to prepare students for technical or semiprofessional pursuits, and (2) the discrepancy between the number of students enrolled in technical-terminal programs and the number who actually become terminal students. In other words, the contention that the junior college devotes much of its energy to the terminal program is substantiated neither by the objective data revealed in the study nor by the observations made in the majority of the institutions visited. Exceptions to this general tendency are discussed in Chapter 3.

There are, of course, broad questions of philosophy and social values which arise in connection with this problem. In the rapidly developing age of automation the question of what constitutes the best preparation for employment has not been clearly answered. While the staff in junior colleges must share the responsibility for lack of clarity about the role of the junior college in occupational training for the automatic age, others, including industrial and professional groups, are equally responsible. It is difficult to visualize the extent to which the entire occupational structure will change in the next few years, but almost certainly a premium will be placed on high-level technicians of all kinds, on well-qualified clerical and sales workers, and on candidates for advanced types of service occupations. Aside from the specific technical training for such fields, a more general curriculum may possibly constitute the best background for a worker in a complex social and technological world.

Inadequacy of Student Personnel Services. Since the beginning of the junior college movement it has been recognized that students in two-year colleges are at a crucial age, needing professional counseling assistance to make sound educational and vocational decisions. Further, it has been recognized that men and women of junior college age desire help in understanding themselves and in making plans that are in harmony with their characteristics. In fact, so much has been said about the responsibility of the junior college to organize the best possible guidance program and to coordinate it with the many other personnel services—including a student activity program, a good records system, a student financial aid program, and a continuous study of student characteristics— that it might be assumed the rendering of these services is one of the strong points of the two-year colleges.

These services are, in fact, one of the strong points in some of the colleges, but unfortunately not in all. A review was made of the institutions' concern for student personnel work, the organization, administration, and cost of personnel services, the concept of counseling and the implementation of the counseling program, the extent of personnel research activities, and the nature of the student activity program. It was possible to identify certain strengths and weaknesses and to suggest improvements.

Some institutions lacked planning and direction, made insufficient allowance of staff time for counseling, included very little by way of a research program on the characteristics and outcomes of students, and made only negligible attempts to evaluate the activities that were being carried on. There was general evidence that administration and boards of control had not put student personnel services on a par with instruction and that all too often insufficient budget appropriations had been made to ensure a full range of such services.

If the junior college is to provide the first post-high school experience for a large number of high school graduates and to channel them into avenues consistent with their characteristics and their likelihood of success, much will depend on the quality of the counseling program. The failure of the junior college in this important responsibility could well mean that the growing dependence on this institution is in error.

Deficiencies in General Education. Another unfulfilled claim of the junior college is its commitment to general education. The information gathered in the process of the study revealed that in the majority of two-year colleges relatively little had been done to meet the objectives of general education. For example, only a few colleges had developed special integrated courses as a means of helping students obtain a comprehensive background in interdisciplinary fields. Most colleges relied on conventional academic courses to meet the needs of general education. This method in itself is not necessarily to be criticized. The shortcoming lay, however, in the fact that in many colleges neither the faculty nor the administration appeared to be concerned whether or how the conventional courses were meeting objectives of general education. Furthermore, in many colleges which claimed to rely on conventional courses as a means of achieving a general education there was no assurance that students would necessarily experience a broadened education. Frequently certain limited statutory requirements plus one or two locally required subjects were all that was specified for graduation. Beyond that, the student was expected to satisfy requirements for his major and to elect other subjects to complete the two years' work. Only a few colleges attempted to effect a sampling of electives to introduce the student to the various disciplines.

Presumably, the junior college is no more responsible for fulfilling the objectives of general education than any other type of college. However, since most of its students do not go beyond the two years of college, providing some breadth of background for them, under the limitations of the two-year period, is particularly important in the junior college.

Slowness in Achieving an Identity

Though it would seem that the attention paid the junior college in recent years would indicate that it has fully achieved an identity of its own, many debatable issues still exist. For example, is public education through the fourteenth grade the birthright of every American child? Is the public junior college an extended secondary school, or is it a part of higher education? Should junior colleges be fully state-supported, fully locally supported, or jointly supported? Should they be autonomous units responsible to either local or state boards of control, or should they be organized as extension centers or branches of a parent college of university? Are local junior colleges best controlled through unified districts or through separate junior college districts?

States vary among themselves not only in the interpretation of the nature of the two-year college but also of its role in higher education. In fact, not even all of the staff members of the junior colleges are in agreement on the purposes, practices, and best organizational pattern of the two-year college.

FURTHER EXAMINATION

Any institution must always bear close examination and evaluation. With the eyes of the nation now on the junior college, it is doubly important to describe it accurately—both its weaknesses and its merits. The purpose of such an evaluation is not to condemn the institution or to reduce its effectiveness, but to assist it in rendering even greater service. No type of institution is without deficiencies and problems, and the junior college could not possibly be an exception.

Much of this examination must come from within and it is therefore hoped that boards of control, administrators, and teachers connected with any type of two-year college will double their efforts at self-evaluation as they consider the national recognition now given this institution.

Inquiries by outside agencies may be helpful because such agencies can compile data from many sources and thereby present a broad perspective.

CHAPTER 2

The Junior College Student

The junior college student is the first topic for discussion in this report because what happens in a college is conditioned in part by the students who attend it. Obviously, the opposite theory could be advanced, namely, that certain types of colleges attract certain students and that the college plays a greater role in determining the characteristics of its students than the students play in shaping the character of the college.

There are arguments in support of both theories. For example, one might expect that the selective private junior college and the nonselective public junior college would have different student bodies. Even among public institutions, differences in location, selectivity, cost to the student, and other factors influence the kinds of students who enroll. Nonetheless, most discussions about the two-year college assume that the functions which this institution performs are the result of the students who attend it.

Increasing attention is being given to the study of college students. Several investigations have been completed or are in process at the Center for the Study of Higher Education in Berkeley which yield valuable information on the intellectual, interest, and personality patterns of college students. More needs to be done in ascertaining subjective factors such as motivation. Also, much more information is needed on the relationship of the various characteristics to the performance of students.

Illustrative of the movement to look at college students more closely is a study completed by Max Wise for the Commission on the College Student of the American Council on Education.

In comparing present college students with college students in the past, the report of this study comments:

> College students today range from young to old, able to mediocre, idealistic to practical, naive to sophisticated, rich to poor; they are of all races, of all faiths—and of no faith. They are both full-time students and part-time students; they are both self-supporting and still dependent on their families. All these go to college, each for his own purpose. As the numbers of students continue to increase, so does the range of their individual differences.[1]

Diversity is found among junior college students as well as among college students in general, although junior college students do not necessarily have the same characteristics as their counterparts in four-year colleges.

ACADEMIC APTITUDE

The aptitude level of junior college students is a subject of much discussion. Some contend that only the less able students attend junior college and that it is a college of last resort for the student who cannot be admitted elsewhere. Others have stated the corollary that four-year college students are intellectually superior to junior college students, and the implication has been that *all* four-year college students are superior to *all* two-year college students. Neither contention is correct.

The available facts indicate that the average academic aptitude level of students entering two-year colleges *is* somewhat below that of those who enter four-year colleges. However, there is a wide range of abilities among two-year college students, and many of them are superior in ability to many students in four-year institutions.

Information on the aptitude of junior college freshmen was assembled from several sources. Two of these were published norms on college aptitude tests—one the American Council on Education Psychological Examination (ACE) and the other the College Qualification Test (CQT), published by The Psychological Corporation. The latter organization published norms for four-year college freshmen in 1957 and followed in 1958 with norms for junior college

---

[1] W. Max Wise, *They Come for the Best of Reasons—College Students Today*, American Council on Education, Washington, 1958, p. 2.

freshmen. Scores on the CQT have also been expressed in terms of equivalent ACE scores, thus permitting a comparison of groups taking either test. Another source was a study recently completed by the Center for the Study of Higher Education at Berkeley on the ability levels of students entering all types of American colleges and universities. In this study the ACE or equivalent scores were obtained on entering freshmen (1952) in 200 American colleges drawn from a stratified random sample of the approximately 1,800 institutions of higher education, including junior colleges, in the United States. The data obtained permit a comparison of the ability of junior college students with that of students in different types of four-year colleges and further permit comparison by region and by type of institutional control. Normative data from the three sources were supplemented by data from two additional studies: (1) an analysis of the ACE scores of the entering students in 31 of the two-year colleges which cooperated in the study of the 1952 class, and (2) a study of ACE scores on some five thousand students who entered 13 California junior colleges in the fall of 1952, spring of 1953, and fall of 1953.[2]

The mean scores from the sources enumerated above are shown in Table 2-1, either in terms of or as converted to ACE scores of the 1952 edition. The data from the different sources agreed remarkably. Three of the studies showed the mean score of junior college entering freshmen to be 94; the other two showed 93. The mean scores on the tests administered to *college* freshmen in both two-year and four-year institutions were between 10 and 14 points higher than the means for *junior college* freshmen. The mean score of freshmen entering four-year colleges only, as discovered by the Berkeley study, was 107, or 13 points higher than for students entering two-year colleges.

A study[3] completed in Minnesota shows the extent to which the junior college draws its students from the total ability distribution of the high school class. This study summarized the aptitude, as measured by the ACE, of the June, 1952, high school

---

[2] This study was undertaken under the auspices of the California Junior College Association in cooperation with the Educational Testing Service.

[3] John G. Darley, "Factors Associated with College Careers in Minnesota," unpublished manuscript, Center for the Study of Higher Education, Berkeley, Calif., 1959, table 5.

graduates in Minnesota who entered Minnesota colleges the following September. In the state's 10 junior colleges, 40 per cent of the entering men and 35 per cent of the entering women came from the bottom half of the high school class. About 32 per cent of the men and 38 per cent of the women came from the top quarter, and 28 per cent of the men and 27 per cent of the women came

Table 2-1. Aptitude of Freshmen Entering Two-year and Four-year Colleges
(According to 1952 ACE or mean equivalent scores)

Source of data	Entering freshmen in 2-year colleges		Entering freshmen in both 2-year and 4-year colleges		Entering freshmen in 4-year colleges	
	No.	Mean	No.	Mean	No.	Mean
ACE norms[a]	5,304	94	43,348	105	—	—
CQT norms[b]	7,837	93	21,482	107	—	—
Berkeley Center study of 200 colleges*	12,173	94	60,539	104	48,366	107
Berkeley Center study of 31 two-year colleges†	6,199	94	—	—	—	—
California junior college study‡	4,784	93	—	—	—	—

* A study of ACE equivalent scores of entering students in 200 American colleges drawn from a stratified random sample of the approximately 1,800 higher institutions, including junior colleges, in the United States.

† A study of the ACE or equivalent scores of students entering 31 junior colleges in 1952.

‡ A study of ACE scores on approximately 5,000 students who entered 13 California junior colleges in the fall of 1952, spring of 1953, and fall of 1953. Study completed by the California Junior College Association in cooperation with the Educational Testing Service.

SOURCE a: American Council on Education, Norms Bulletin, Psychological Examination for College Freshmen, 1952 ed., Educational Testing Service, Los Angeles, Calif., 1953.

SOURCE b: George K. Bennett et al., College Qualification Tests Manual, 1957, and Supplement, 1958, The Psychological Corporation, New York, 1957.

from the second quarter. The junior colleges were found to attract a somewhat more able student body than the state colleges in Minnesota but a considerably less able group than entered the College of Liberal Arts of the state university.

How do transfer and terminal students in junior colleges compare in aptitude? Transfer students are generally considered the more able, and the data in Tables 2-2, 2-3, 2-4, and 2-5 confirm this to some degree.

The data in Table 2-2 are from three of the sources used in Table 2-1. Those from the Center's study of 31 two-year colleges relate to students entering these colleges in September, 1952, who either did or did not subsequently transfer to four-year colleges. In other words, they were the *actual* transfer and terminal students.

Table 2-2. Aptitude of Junior College Transfer and Terminal Students (According to 1952 mean ACE or mean equivalent scores of students at time of admission as freshmen)

Source of data	No. of colleges	Mean ACE scores			Mean ACE scores		
		Men			Women		
		Total	Transfer	Terminal	Total	Transfer	Terminal
Berkeley Center study of 31 two-year colleges*	31	95	102†	92†	93	101†	90†
CQT norms[a]	20	95	99	88	89	93	85
California junior college study‡	13	93	97	82	92	97	85

* A study of the ACE or equivalent scores of students entering 31 junior colleges in 1952.

† The mean scores of freshmen who did or did not transfer, irrespective of how they were classified in junior college. Other scores are of students classified as terminal or transfer while enrolled in junior college.

‡ A study of ACE scores on approximately 5,000 students who entered 13 California junior colleges in the fall of 1952, spring of 1953, and fall of 1953. Study completed by the California Junior College Association in cooperation with the Educational Testing Service.

SOURCE a: George K. Bennett et al., *College Qualification Tests Manual, 1957,* and *Supplement, 1958,* The Psychological Corporation, New York, 1957.

Table 2-3. ACE Scores for Junior College Students Enrolled in Transfer and in Certain Terminal Programs in 13 Junior Colleges, 1956

Group	No.	Mean	Standard deviation
Transfer	2,938	99	25.73
Terminal	2,973	91	25.85
Technical	1,426	96	26.24
Medical semiprofessional	350	91	25.67
Other semiprofessional	226	88	28.94
General	128	86	28.31
Business	843	85	17.34

Data from the other two studies relate to those who were classified as either transfer or terminal students while in the two-year college. All three studies showed that the aptitude of transfer men and women was greater by several points than that of terminal men and women. The two studies which showed scores for students as they were classified while enrolled in junior college revealed smaller differences between transfer and terminal women than between transfer and terminal men. On the other hand, the difference between women who actually transferred and those who did not was slightly larger than the difference between the men who actually transferred and those who did not. This would suggest that a higher degree of self-selection takes place among women who transfer than among men—that among the women who enroll in a transfer program in the two-year college, only the more able tend to transfer.

Table 2-3 provides additional information obtained from 13 of the cooperating junior colleges on differences between transfer and terminal students. These colleges, ranging in size from the very small to the very large, were situated in five different states. They were able to provide ACE scores of their students enrolled in 1956 in transfer programs and in five categories of terminal programs. Again, the transfer students were shown to be superior to the total terminal group by an 8-point difference although the terminal technical students (in engineering and related fields) had exactly the same mean score as the transfer students.

Table 2-4. Mean ACE Scores of Junior College Terminal and Transfer
Students in 13 California Junior Colleges

Group	Mean	No.
Transfer men	97	2,182
Transfer women	97	968
Terminal men, business	85	252
Terminal women, business	85	648
Terminal men, technical	81	637
Terminal women, technical	87	97
Total students	93	4,784

SOURCE: Data drawn from J. W. McDaniel, chairman, California Junior College Norms Project, California Junior College Association (Los Angeles, California: Educational Testing Service, 1953).

Much the same type of information is shown in Table 2-4, which presents more detailed data from the California study of students in 13 junior colleges. Both transfer men and women were shown to be superior to men and women in the two terminal fields of business and technical subjects.

A further comparison of aptitude scores of transfer and terminal students enrolled in various subject fields was possible through analyses of the data from 8 of the 31 junior colleges which submitted ACE information on their students and which also indicated the curricula in which the students were enrolled in junior college. Table 2-5 shows the mean scores for the transfer and terminal students in specific curricula. The mean scores of students in some of the curricula were higher than those shown in the preceding tables, apparently because of some unknown selective factor operative in the particular group of institutions. To be noted especially is the fact that those curricula which attracted high-ability transfer students also attracted high-ability terminal students and vice versa.

Table 2-5. Ability of Junior College Transfer and Terminal Students among Curricular Fields in Eight Institutions

Major	Transfer students				Terminal students			
	No.	Mean	Sigma	Range	No.	Mean	Sigma	Range
Natural science	22	115.59	22.90	79–169	—	—	—	—
Engineering	69	113.57	24.22	56–164	129	100.74	23.10	37–163
Fine arts	18	106.67	19.55	54–132	30	99.97	23.90	51–148
Medical	29	105.37	18.00	83–145	101	100.00	22.40	52–138
Communication arts	8	107.75	16.10	76–130	19	97.63	29.50	25–142
Liberal arts	99	106.87	26.25	67–154	179	98.25	27.02	37–170
Law	16	105.43	15.70	76–127	—	—	—	—
Education	81	100.91	23.60	46–150	68	94.67	21.00	38–159
Forestry	3	124.03	3.30	118–128	11	90.18	23.20	52–129
Industrial arts	58	99.29	18.21	56–138	411	95.48	21.85	29–159
Unknown	123	100.46	23.00	52–156	286	93.96	23.60	23–172
Business	92	105.09	20.00	52–140	320	91.18	24.79	29–153
Home economics	10	97.50	20.80	67–129	15	89.39	16.00	67–115
Social service	—	—	—	—	14	90.14	22.10	30–131
Physical education	21	95.00	17.30	55–131	29	86.37	19.30	47–130
Nursing	16	101.68	24.80	58–142	24	78.79	27.40	22–157
Agriculture	10	82.80	22.60	48–118	20	85.35	24.30	47–134

Two further comments regarding differences in aptitude between transfer and terminal students are appropriate. First, the similarities as well as the differences between the groups should be emphasized. Differences in mean scores notwithstanding, there is a great overlap in scores made by students in the two groups. For example, further analysis of the scores made by students entering the 31 cooperating colleges showed that close to one-fourth of the ones who became terminal achieved a score of 110 or more. Thus if it is assumed that a score of 110 indicates ability to do acceptable four-year college work, almost 1,000 of the more than 4,000 terminal students in the sample showed themselves capable of becoming good transfer students. This number is to be contrasted with the 744, or 37 per cent, of the total of 1,993 transfer students with a score above 110. Such an overlap does not necessarily suggest that able students who do not transfer should be encouraged to do so—although perhaps many of them should. As further discussed in Chapter 4, many occupations for which terminal students should be educated require high ability.

A second comment further emphasizes the point that junior colleges which enroll superior transfer students also enroll superior terminal students. In fact, in comparing the two groups in the 31 cooperating colleges a rank difference correlation coefficient of .89 was found. This tendency would seem further to confirm the likelihood of overlap in abilities among students in the two groups in any individual college and would further illustrate the differences in student bodies among the two-year colleges.

The various sources of evidence cited above make it clear that as a group junior college freshmen score somewhat less well on measures of academic aptitude than four-year college freshmen. Also, it is obvious that students enrolled in transfer programs score higher than students enrolled in terminal programs.

In considering the differences between students in two-year and four-year institutions, two facts are important. One is the great overlap in aptitude among students in the two types of colleges, and the other is the difference among individual two-year institutions in terms of the students who enroll. The very great overlap in aptitude among students entering the two types of colleges is illustrated in Figure 2 from data obtained by the Center's national sample of 200 institutions.

Some observations should be made with respect to the aptitude distribution of two-year and four-year college students. For example, roughly 6 per cent of the freshmen entering two-year colleges in the Center's study of 200 colleges had a score of 134 or more, which is one standard deviation above the mean of students who entered four-year colleges. Only two undergraduate colleges in the sample had mean scores of more than 134, and they were both private, highly selective institutions in the East. This would suggest that two-year colleges enroll a small number of students who can properly be characterized as the very able and to whom the college has an obligation for the optimum development of talents. On the other side of the scale, 16 per cent of the students entering two-year colleges had a score of 68 or less, which is one standard deviation below the mean of the total group of two-year college entrants. Interestingly enough, it was found that a score of 69 was approximately equal to a score of 100 on the Army Gen-

Fig. 2. Overlap in ACE scores of Freshmen Entering Two-year and Four-year Colleges. Four-year colleges——————— Two-year colleges - - - - - -

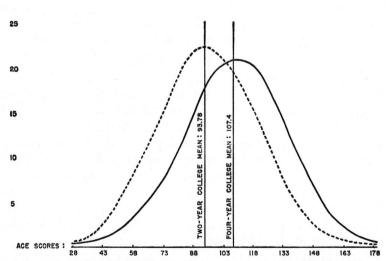

SOURCE: A study completed by the Center for the Study of Higher Education of students entering 200 colleges and universities in 1952.

eral Classification Test, which was considered equivalent to an IQ
of 100. Although it is of some significance that no more than 16
per cent of the students in two-year colleges fell below that level,
even that proportion means that junior colleges have to provide
types of programs and methods of instruction appropriate to a
sizable group of students who have an aptitude below that customarily regarded necessary for a regular baccalaureate degree
program.

On the other hand, roughly 30 per cent of the students entering junior colleges in the study were above the mean of the students
entering four-year colleges. There is, then, in the junior college a
very large segment of students who are well able to carry on college work as rigorous as that offered in other higher institutions.

This same overlap was documented by Harold Seashore in a
comparison of aptitudes, as measured by the CQT test, of students
in two-year and four-year colleges. His findings included:

1. The median score for junior college freshmen is near the 25th
   percentile for senior college freshmen.
2. About 24 per cent of junior college men and 20 per cent
   of junior college women are above the respective medians for
   freshmen in four-year colleges.
3. There are many junior college students whose scores would
   be considered superior in senior colleges, and many low-scor-
   ing college freshmen would also rate low in junior colleges.[4]

Ability of freshmen student bodies in junior colleges of all
types varies greatly, as shown in Figure 3. The interval between
the bottom and the top of the thin vertical lines in the figure
represents the range of scores for each of 54 junior colleges which
fell in the national sample of 200 colleges drawn by the Berkeley
center. The midpoint of the shaded part of the line denotes the
mean ACE score for the respective college and the extremes of
the shaded portion represent the area enclosed by one standard
deviation above and below the mean. The great variation among
the institutions is evident, as is the fact that the mean score
in more than 25 per cent of the junior colleges is higher than that
of the mean in all 200 institutions in the national sample.

[4] Harold Seashore, "Academic Abilities of Junior College Students," *Junior
College Journal,* American Association of Junior Colleges, Washington, October, 1958, p. 75.

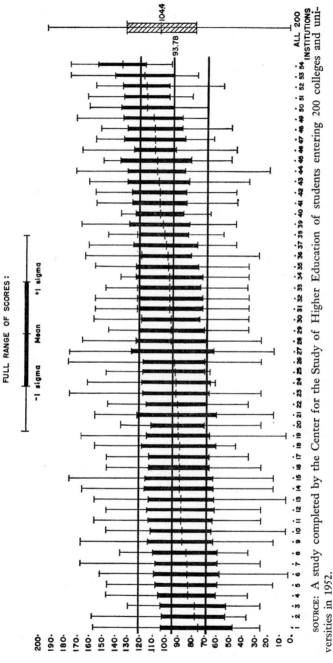

Fig. 3. Distribution of ACE Scores of Students Entering a Random Sample of 54 Two-year Colleges

FULL RANGE OF SCORES:

−1 sigma   Mean   +1 sigma

SOURCE: A study completed by the Center for the Study of Higher Education of students entering 200 colleges and universities in 1952.

39

Both the overlap among students in the two-year and four-year colleges and the differences among individual institutions indicate the incorrectness of the generalization that students in four-year colleges are always superior to students in two-year colleges. Also, it is incorrect to generalize that individual students enrolled in transfer programs are always more able than those enrolled in terminal programs. Furthermore, the categories of transfer and terminal, as applied to students still in junior college, are not firm. Many terminal students later transfer and many more transfer students become terminal. The relation of academic aptitude to the tendency of students to graduate from junior college and to transfer to a four-year college is discussed in Chapter 4.

The ACE means reported in the various tables reveal only a very small aptitude difference between the sexes. The largest difference was a 6-point difference in favor of the men shown by the CQT norms. Mean ACE scores for men and women entering the Minnesota junior colleges in 1952 were identical.[5]

In a follow-up study of junior college students reported in Chapter 4, the women who transferred outperformed the men in several respects. Thus while junior college men and women are nearly equal in ability, with some studies showing slightly higher scores for the men, the women apparently often utilize their aptitude to greater advantage.

SOCIOECONOMIC BACKGROUND

The socioeconomic levels from which junior college students come naturally vary with the type of junior college. For example, it would be expected that the students entering high-tuition private junior colleges would be from higher levels than those entering most public junior colleges. However, even private junior colleges vary greatly in the types of homes from which their students come. A few of these colleges do serve young people from low-income families. On the other hand, the fact that tuition and residence costs in most of them are by necessity relatively high

---

[5] An examination of the component parts of the total scores would probably reveal greater differences between men and women, for example, differences in verbal and quantities scores, which would have implications for counseling.

means that students are drawn mainly from upper-middle-class and upper-class groups. Public junior colleges, being primarily local and inexpensive to attend, draw heavily from the lower half of the socioeconomic distribution, as shown by the various studies discussed below.

According to the study of Minnesota college entrants[6] classified by fathers' occupations ("high" and "low" status), only 29 per cent of the students entering Minnesota junior colleges came from a high (professional and semiprofessional) occupational level. In contrast, about 56 per cent of the students who entered the private colleges in Minnesota were from the high level. Also, 42 per cent of the men and 51 per cent of the women entering the University of Minnesota were from the high group. Somewhat surprising was the fact that the state colleges in Minnesota drew a slightly smaller proportion of students from the high level than the junior colleges. In state colleges, 27 per cent of the men and 21 per cent of the women were from the high group.

Similar results were obtained from an analysis of data procured from six of the public junior colleges which cooperated in the study. These colleges reported the occupations of the parents of almost five thousand students enrolled over a period of three years ending in 1957. Only one-fourth of the group came from the higher level in an arbitrary high-low classification similar to that used in the Minnesota study. The largest group of students (almost a third) came from a skilled-labor background. Only a tenth came from families in the professional category.

In a case study of the San Jose City College, Burton Clark compared the social backgrounds of students from the San Jose community who enrolled in the local junior college with those who entered (1) Stanford University, a nearby high-cost selective private university, (2) the publicly controlled University of California at Berkeley, (3) a local state four-year college somewhat less selective than the state university, and (4) with the general San Jose population.[7] Classifying students by the father's occupation into blue- and white-collar social categories, Clark found that more than three-fourths of the junior college students came from lower

[6] Darley, *op. cit.*, table 4.
[7] Burton R. Clark, *The Open Door College: A Case Study*, McGraw-Hill Book Company, Inc., New York, 1960.

white- and blue-collar homes. The local state college also drew heavily from this group but not quite to the same extent as the junior college. As would be expected, the two universities drew primarily from the upper white-collar group, with Stanford drawing somewhat more heavily from it than the state university. The junior college drew almost an exact representative sample of the city-wide occupational structure. Clark also compared students entering the four colleges by the economic status of the students' home neighborhoods in San Jose and found the same general differences.

Robert Havighurst and Bernice Neugarten, in discussing the social classes represented in various types of higher institutions, estimated that no more than 5 per cent of the upper and upper-middle classes would be represented in the "opportunity college," which, as they described it, is the typical metropolitan junior college.[8] Though the other studies reported here indicate that public junior colleges as a group draw more than 5 per cent from the higher social classes, their main enrollment comes from the middle and lower classes.

The fact that junior college students tend to represent a cross section of a given community has at least two implications. First, it further confirms the role of the junior college as a democratizing agent in higher education. The large proportion of students from the middle and lower social classes in the junior college must mean that they cannot or do not attend other types of higher institutions. A possible exception may be found in the unselective state colleges or teachers colleges in some states. However, since each state college usually serves a region, it is necessary for some students to live away from home. It is therefore easier and less expensive for many students to attend a local junior college than a state college some distance away. If the junior college attracts those from lower groups who otherwise would not enter college, it may be salvaging certain talents for society that otherwise would be lost.

A second implication is that a great burden is placed on the junior college to motivate capable students from lower social groups to continue in college and to perform at an acceptable academic

[8] Robert J. Havighurst and Bernice L. Neugarten, *Society and Education*, Allyn and Bacon, Inc., Englewood Cliffs, N.J., 1957, p. 257.

level. The high correlation between social class and college attendance is generally recognized.[9] In lower-class homes neither parent may have attended college, and the college "yardstick" as a criterion for social or economic success frequently does not exist. True, there are exceptional cases of drive for social mobility. Further, some parents may desire and encourage their children to go to college because they never had such an opportunity. But such exceptional cases do not offset either the ordinary parental lethargy or the economic drive which encourages students from the lower groups to leave college and get jobs. The junior college must often motivate such students or lose them. The service of the junior college to society will depend upon how well the institution can assimilate the entire student body into a social, cultural, and intellectual context in which each student is inspired to grow according to his aptitudes and interests.

AGE RANGE

A limited amount of recent information on the age of junior college students was obtained from 10 of the junior colleges co-

Table 2-6. Age Range of 13,304 Regular Day Students
Enrolled in 10 Junior Colleges

Age	No.	Per cent
16–17	270	2
18	3,256	24
19	2,331	17
20–22	1,314	10
		53
23–25	2,506	19
26–29	1,554	12
30 and over	2,073	16
		47
Total	13,304	100

[9] For a report of a study completed in 1951 at Indiana University on the relation of class structure to social and academic achievement, see Kate Mueller and John H. Mueller, "Class Structure and Academic and Social Success," *Educational and Psychological Measurement*, vol. 13, no. 3, pp. 468–497, Autumn, 1953.

operating in the study. Since more than thirteen thousand students were included and since the institutions covered a wide range in size, type, and location, the data in Table 2-6 may be considered reasonably illustrative of junior colleges in general.

Slightly more than half of the students were in the sixteen to twenty-two category—the typical college age range. About a fifth were in what might be called the "older youth" category of twenty-three to twenty-five. It is significant that about a sixth of the group were thirty years of age or older.

In the last decade two developments have advanced the average age level in most colleges. One was the return of veterans following World War II and the Korean conflict. The other has been the nationwide trend for mature people who have missed all or part of college to enter college later in life. Wise reported that even between 1953 and 1957—long after the influx of World War II veterans—there was a 47 per cent increase in the number of people between twenty-five and thirty-four enrolled in college.[10] The tendency for older youths and adults to pursue college work will mean the continuous presence of many "oldsters" on most campuses. This should be particularly true in local junior colleges where men and women with work and family responsibilities can attend college in their home communities without disrupting their personal lives.

The wide age range of students suggests the necessity on the part of junior colleges for adapting their instructional methods, their social programs, and their student personnel services to meet the needs and interests of the different age groups. The junior college in which half of the student body is twenty years of age or more is obviously accommodating persons who either did not graduate from high school or, what is more likely, for various reasons did not enter college immediately after high school graduation. Such students bring maturity, experience, definiteness of purpose, motivation, and other assets. They may be at a disadvantage as a result of their long absence from study, heavy personal responsibilities, and the like. They are adults and expect to be treated as such. At the same time they may wish to enter into the entire life of the institution and not be set apart from younger students.

[10] Wise, *op. cit.*, p. 7.

EXTENT OF HIGH SCHOOL GRADUATION

Although public junior colleges are usually required by law to admit students of more than eighteen years who are not high school graduates, a sample of nearly fourteen thousand students enrolled in eight public junior colleges—all but one of them in California—showed that only 6 per cent were not high school graduates. The increasing prevalence of high school graduates is likely to mean that, except for a limited number of older men and women whose high school experience was interrupted, the proportion of junior college entrants who are high school graduates will be even greater in the future than it is now.

MARITAL STATUS

An index of the marital status of junior college students is available from six public junior colleges. Of more than eight thousand students enrolled in the six colleges, 23 per cent were married. (Wise found that of college students throughout the country, 22 per cent were married.[11]) The range of married students among the six colleges ran from 11 per cent in a junior college in a rural area to 31 per cent in a suburban college in a metropolitan area. These percentages are probably smaller than they would have been a few years earlier when a large number of married veterans were enrolled, but they are still significant. Furthermore, the trend toward marriage at earlier ages would indicate that junior colleges will continue to be attended by a sizable number of married students. With nearly a fourth of the students married, an institution is faced with possible differences in its social program and student personnel services as compared with an institution in which nearly all students are unmarried.

RATIO OF MEN TO WOMEN

As in all colleges, men students in junior colleges outnumber women students considerably. In the 75 two-year colleges which cooperated in the over-all study of the 1952 entering class, the ratio of men to women was three to one. This unusually high ratio

[11] Wise, *op. cit.*, p. 10.

may be accounted for in part by the fact that several of the institutions were technical institutes and thus drew a heavy proportion of men. A ratio of two men to one woman in junior colleges was found in the study of college entrants in Minnesota in 1952.[12] Enrollment data reported by the U.S. Office of Education show that in 1958 "first-time" opening enrollment of degree-credit students in junior colleges was comprised of approximately 62 per cent men and 28 per cent women.

The ratio of men to women in coeducational colleges varies with the type of college. For example, in the Minnesota study of 1952 entrants, more women than men entered the state four-year colleges and the four-year private colleges, but the reverse was true for the university and the junior colleges. In the study of the students entering the different types of two-year colleges which cooperated in the 1952 study, it was apparent that most of the comprehensive community colleges in the sample enrolled many more men than women.

The ratio of men to women in a given college has a bearing on curriculum emphases as well as on certain phases of the student personnel program. A predominance of men, for example, means special stress on programs in the fields in which men are traditionally interested such as technology, science, engineering, and business administration. It may suggest, further, an approach to conventional academic subjects in a manner that will captivate the interest of men at that age level. Those who counsel students must be cognizant of the occupational, educational, and personal problems of men. Greater stress may need to be placed on finding part-time work opportunities. There is a danger, however, of overstressing the interests of either sex. In a junior college with two or three times more men than women it is possible that the educational interests of women are neglected. This is particularly true in providing special programs for women who may not transfer to higher institutions.

REASONS FOR ATTENDING AND WITHDRAWING FROM JUNIOR COLLEGE

Additional insight into the characteristics of junior college students can be obtained by examining the reasons given by them

[12] Darley, *op. cit.*, table 2.

for entering the junior college, and for withdrawing before the attainment of their educational objective.

In most cooperating institutions data that could be classified into reasons for entering and leaving were not readily available. It was possible, however, to obtain responses from almost three thousand students in four colleges to questions on their primary reason for attending. Two-thirds of these students listed either (1) persuasion by parents, counselors, and friends, (2) location of college (proximity), or (3) lower cost. These same reasons have been reported in numerous unpublished studies. The percentage of students who choose the two-year college—particularly the public junior college—because of its program or its prestige is small in comparison to those who choose it because of parental influence or expediency. In one sense this could be unflattering to the junior college. On the other hand, it could hardly be expected that in the minds of many students this type of college could compete in prestige value with the average four-year college or the university; thus the student in explaining his reason for attending will point to the obvious. Once he is enrolled he may or may not be enthusiastic about the institution, depending on how well the college is able to inspire him to use his opportunity and to make him feel satisfied.

From reports on drop-out studies completed by 20 two-year colleges between 1949 and 1957, it was possible to categorize the reasons students gave for withdrawal. Table 2-7 indicates that full-time employment headed the list of reasons and was followed by others which are characteristic of students of college age.

The reasons for withdrawal given by students suggest that many students are subject to influences which compete with their college program. Jane Matson, in comparing a group of students who withdrew from junior college with a group who did not withdraw but had similar characteristics, observed that there was no significant difference between drop-out and continuing students. Her conclusion was that the student who withdraws from junior college may lack a sense of belonging or identification with the college environment.[13]

[13] Jane E. Matson, "Characteristics of Students Who Withdraw from a Public Junior College," unpublished doctoral dissertation, School of Education, Stanford University, Stanford, June, 1955.

Table 2-7. Reasons Stated for Withdrawing from Junior College Reported by Approximately Ten Thousand Students Enrolled in 20 Two-year Colleges between 1949 and 1957

Reasons stated for withdrawal	No. of students	Per cent
Full-time employment	2,734	28
Personal and health	1,554	16
Moved or transferred	1,084	11
Nonattendance	1,013	10
Academic or faculty action	860	9
To enter armed forces	832	8
Not interested in school or dissatisfied	763	8
Financial	549	6
Marriage	264	3
Educational goals completed	55	1
Total	9,898	100

CHARACTERISTICS OF STUDENTS IN CLASSES FOR ADULTS

Very little has been done in identifying the characteristics of adults who attend junior college part time, usually during evening hours. However, in an unpublished dissertation, Charles Chapman reported a number of findings on more than six thousand students enrolled in the adult programs in six high schools, two junior colleges, and the extension divisions of two senior institutions in Contra Costa County, California.[14]

Among the characteristics he investigated were age, marital status, sex, educational attainment, academic aspirations, occupation, and family income. He found that the junior college adult students were younger than the adults in high school and extension adult education programs. Almost 30 per cent of them were less than twenty-six and only 9.5 per cent more than forty-five years old. More than three-fourths of the junior college group were married. Two-thirds were men. More than a third were high school graduates and more than 10 per cent college graduates. More than a fifth were working for the A.A. degree. A fourth were in occupa-

[14] Charles E. Chapman, "Some Characteristics of the Adult Part-time Students Enrolled in the Public Schools of Contra Costa County during the Fall Term, 1957," unpublished doctoral dissertation, University of California, Berkeley, 1959.

tions of the craftsman and foreman type, a fifth were professional and technical workers, and a seventh homemakers. Many had ambitions to change their occupations through more education. Half of them reported incomes of less than $6,000 and a fifth reported $8,000 or more.

Chapman also studied the scholastic aptitude of some of the groups through scores attained by the administration of a 20-item instrument; this was prepared and standardized by the Educational Testing Service, and the scores were later converted to the ACE. The test was given to a 15 per cent random sample of the evening students in three of the high schools and the two junior colleges. It was also administered to a sample of full-time day junior college students. The mean score (converted to the ACE 1952 edition) of the evening junior college group was 103.5 and that of the evening high school adult group was 91.3. The mean of the evening junior college group was also above the mean of the full-time day college students, whose mean score was 100.2. In fact, the evening junior college group attained a mean score slightly higher than the college-going high school seniors who were originally used as the normative group for the test.

If the Contra Costa situation can be considered reasonably typical of junior college adult groups in general—and the industrial, occupational, and social characteristics of the area would suggest this—it may be assumed that students in junior college programs for adults tend not only to have the basic characteristics requisite for high motivation but also the ability to pursue a program with requirements comparable to the college freshman level.

CONCLUSION

The data in this chapter reaffirm the point made many times in this report that there is no stereotyped student body in the two-year college. The diversity of junior college student bodies in terms of aptitude, socioeconomic background, marital status, sex, and other factors has several important implications. Some of them are:

The diversity of programs in the junior college must provide opportunity for the widely varying levels of ability.

Counseling services are of special importance if students with different abilities and from many different backgrounds are to be assisted in ascertaining occupational and educational goals most appropriate to each of them.

Each college should accumulate a body of facts about its own student body which will serve as a guideline for educational policies and procedures. Much would be gained from cooperative studies by several institutions.

New types of data are needed, particularly on the motivation of students of varying abilities from lower social groups.

Perhaps the most important single point to be made is that each student brings a set of emotional and mental characteristics which in a sense are the raw materials for the college to process. The over-all description of the student body and the measures of central tendencies are important, provided they do not cause the staff to lose sight of individual differences. Without any suggestion that colleges are educational factories, there may be some logic in comparing an educational institution with a manufacturing establishment. Both agencies are engaged in a transformation process. The factory must convert its raw material into a finished product. The finished product may or may not be for ultimate consumer use—it may be only a product for use by another factory in a long series of steps toward eventual consumer utilization. The process of the educational institution has an impact on a student which, hopefully, changes his behavior in socially desirable ways. Instruction in the junior college may mean the end of formal full-time education. For those who transfer, the process is only partly completed, and they, like the finished product of a factory that is used by another factory, go to another institution for further changes. Both the factory and the school have the common problem of determining their methods in accordance with the nature of the raw materials. The task for the school, however, is infinitely more complicated because no two pieces of raw material are alike and because people do not lend themselves to change like inanimate objects. Hence it is all the more important for the school to know what its students are like. Their characteristics should help to determine the nature of the school just as the school seeks to bring about the changes in the students.

CHAPTER 3

An Educational Program with Many Purposes

The diversity of its student body imposes on the two-year college the responsibility of providing an equally diverse educational program. This is difficult because of the extent to which two-year college students differ in their goals and in their preparation for college work. Some plan to transfer to four-year colleges, others do not. Some will enter with educational deficiencies, others will have all the requisites for college. All will live in a complex world in which they will have personal, civic, and occupational responsibilities to discharge and leisure-time activities to perform. The task is further complicated by the fact that many junior colleges are called upon to serve adults and render special community services. To meet all these obligations is a major challenge for the junior college.

That the college recognizes its responsibility for program diversity is evident by the functions which it generally assumes. However, the magnitude of its services has led to such questions as these: To what extent does the two-year college, particularly the community college, fulfill the many functions it assumes? Does it tend to be all things to all people? How does it accomplish its many purposes? What are the characteristics of its various programs and the problems in connection with each?

PROGRAMS FOR TRANSFER AND TERMINAL STUDENTS

The following two chapters deal exclusively with the transfer and terminal functions of the two-year college. Because of the

51

later treatment of the two functions, the discussion of programs for transfer and terminal students in this chapter is limited.

Transfer Programs

Few two-year colleges can avoid the responsibility of offering standard lower-division courses that permit students to transfer with junior standing to a four-year college after two years in a junior college. Even technical institutes, established wholly as terminal institutions, sooner or later are likely to be subjected to student and community pressures to offer transfer courses. Of the 243 institutions which responded to the original check list, almost 91 per cent offered a transfer program. Of the 75 cooperating institutions, 69 offered a transfer program. The 6 that did not were technical institutes, and in several of them a surprising number of students were able to use their technical and general educational courses for transfer purposes.

The fact that technical institute work may on occasion be transferable illustrates the point that the transferability of a course depends on its acceptance for credit by a four-year college, particularly the four-year college of an individual student's choice. However, four-year colleges vary in what they will accept; hence a course may be transferable to one institution but may not be acceptable to all.

The transfer program must satisfy the needs of students who expect to continue their education either in colleges of arts and science or in various professional schools, such as engineering, business, and law schools. In one sense the task of preparing transfer students is becoming more uniform because of the trend away from specialization and toward a base of liberal arts in the lower-division curriculum. Although this trend varies among four-year colleges and to some extent among regions of the country, it reduces the necessity for the two-year college to offer a wide variety of specialized courses and permits it to concentrate more on courses which meet letters and science requirements. To be sure, there are variations even in these requirements, particularly in science and mathematics, for students in different preprofessional fields. Nevertheless, such variations are more easily met than the requirements for more highly specialized courses in the professional fields.

However, planning for the transfer student still presents many problems. For one thing, the differences in requirements among four-year institutions make it difficult for the two-year college, particularly the smaller institution, to offer a sufficient variety of courses to meet the needs of transfer students. Reluctance on the part of some four-year institutions to accept courses in the same field but different from the specific ones which they require often forces the two-year college into a pattern identical with the four-year institution. For example, it is futile for a two-year college to attempt to develop interdisciplinary courses designed to meet general educational needs if the credits from such courses are not transferable to many four-year colleges. The result is that some two-year colleges identify themselves so closely with a four-year institution that they organize and teach most courses in exactly the same manner as in the particular four-year college. When this happens, the junior college forfeits its identity and its opportunity to experiment in the development of a program most appropriate for it.

Problems pertaining to articulation and communication with four-year colleges, to requirements for admission to individual courses, and to grading standards also arise in connection with the transfer curriculum. They all bear on the record made by students who transfer (see Chapter 5).

Terminal Programs

Of the 243 institutions, 86 per cent indicated they provided programs for students not expecting to transfer. The institutions not offering such programs were primarily extension centers of universities or private junior colleges, although a few of the extension centers and a number of private colleges were offering some work for the terminal student.

As indicated in the following chapter, the extent of the terminal program is limited more by student interest than by the willingness of colleges to offer it. Nonetheless, many two-year colleges do have students interested in preparing for some immediate occupational goal.

Theoretically, a terminal program may either be general (general education, liberal arts, and the like), occupational, or a combination of the two. Interviewed administrators reported that few students are interested in a strictly terminal general education curriculum. As as result, most terminal curricula have a strong occupational orientation, although a limited amount of general education is usually included.

The work for which the junior college may offer training depends on two factors. First, it depends on the occupational needs of the community. Despite mobility of workers, junior colleges cannot establish expensive specialized programs unless there are local outlets for the product and local advisers to the program. Exceptions may be made in the preparation of students for more general and less technical fields, such as business. Second, since public agencies should not unnecessarily duplicate efforts, occupational education in the junior college depends on programs offered by other agencies in the same community, such as the vocational courses in the local high school system or in vocational and technical schools maintained by some city school systems. The city of Los Angeles has simplified the problem of jurisdiction after high school by including in the junior college system two of its former vocational schools—one in business and the other in trade and technical education—thus permitting centralized direction and coordination of all vocational efforts beyond the high school. Oakland, California, in establishing its junior college followed a similar procedure. The Los Angeles and Oakland examples may well be considered by other city school systems.

Occupational education at the two-year college level is most often classified as "technical" or "semiprofessional." Although not always used in the same context, these terms denote a level of training less than that required for a profession but greater than it is possible to acquire in the four-year high school period. They connote also a combination of general and specialized education. Examples of curricula which are frequently organized on such a level are electronics, machine technology, petroleum technology, building technology, dental assisting, dental technology, nursing, laboratory technology, engineering technology, drafting, law enforcement, and programs in business, including stenography, retailing, and general business. More rare are such programs as hotel and restaurant management at San Francisco City College and the various programs for the garment industry offered by the Fashion Institute of Technology, a public two-year college in New York City.

However, not all occupational training in two-year colleges is organized on a semiprofessional level. Often it takes on the characteristics of trade training such as is frequently offered by high schools in government-subsidized programs. Examples of these programs are automotive mechanics, body-fender work, machine shop, electric shop, welding, carpentry, and cosmetology. Rare programs in this category include meat processing, gunsmithing, watch repairing, and barbering.

Persons who believe the two-year college should offer training at the trade level point to the fact that even though the number of skilled workers in the United States is decreasing in proportion to other workers many are still needed. Since the American high school now tends to de-emphasize vocational training, the argument is made that the responsibility for educating skilled workers rests with the two-year college. Such practice, it is said, is in harmony with the advancing age level of beginning workers and with the added maturity in young workers which employers desire.

Those who are not acquainted with the two-year college are often surprised to find it offering specialized vocational courses. It is to be remembered, however, that most public two-year colleges have a responsibility to the community that supports them. If skilled workers are needed and if no other agency is training them, the local college is justified in doing so. Furthermore, there are some students whose superiority of manual skills over conceptual skills makes this type of outlet appropriate for them.

On the other hand, the junior college offering highly specialized vocational training programs faces two dangers. One is overspecialization, which, in a swiftly changing technological economy, may result in the preparation of workers with skills for jobs that no longer exist. The other is that the two-year college may be content with this more conventional occupational training program and may lose sight of its newer and more significant role of preparing technicians for an age in which science and automation are becoming increasingly important. Of the two occupational levels, preparing workers for the trades is probably easier. The two-year college can ill afford to follow the line of least resistance.

MEETING THE OBJECTIVES OF GENERAL EDUCATION

More than 10 years ago the President's Commission on Higher Education, in discussing the need for general education, said:

The failure to provide any core of unity in the essential diversity of higher education is a cause for grave concern. A society whose members lack a body of common experience and common knowledge is a society without a fundamental culture; it tends to disintegrate into a mere aggregation of individuals. Some community of values, ideas, and attitudes is essential as a cohesive force in this age of minute division of labor and intense conflict of special interests.

The crucial task of higher education today, therefore, is to provide a unified general education for American youth. Colleges must find the right relationship between specialized training on the one hand, aiming at a thousand different careers, and the transmission of a common cultural heritage toward a common citizenship on the other.[1]

The need for a unifying educational experience is, perhaps, greater in junior colleges than in other higher institutions. The junior college student body is especially heterogeneous in social, cultural and educational background, and in academic ability. Furthermore, many students do not continue their formal education beyond the junior college. Two years is too short a time to provide the necessary perspective, particularly if a considerable part of the student's program is taken up by vocational courses. It is therefore important to discover how purposefully and systematically junior colleges have developed programs of general education.

The Meaning of General Education

Although more agreement on ends rather than means has emerged after decades of debate, there is still no unanimity on the nature of general education. To some writers, and to some faculties, it means a common basic curriculum; to others it means common outcomes of a fundamental educational experience, which, while leading to common ends, may rely on diverse means. To some it means an understanding of the major concepts, principles, and methodologies of major fields of knowledge (as opposed to the content of narrower disciplines). To others, general education is given a behavioral definition, as that education which prepares a

---

[1] *Higher Education for American Democracy: A Report of the President's Commission on Higher Education,* Harper & Brothers, New York, 1948, pp. 48–49.

man to live more fully as a person and more effectively as a citizen. This concept of general education has been given a more explicit definition in an earlier study of general education in California junior colleges reported by Johnson:

> Students in California Public Junior Colleges differ greatly in experiences, needs, capacities, aspirations, and interests. The general education program aims to help each student increase his competence in
> 1. Exercising the privileges and responsibilities of democratic citizenship.
> 2. Developing a set of sound moral and spiritual values by which he guides his life.
> 3. Expressing his thoughts clearly in speaking and writing and in reading and listening with understanding.
> 4. Using the basic mathematical and mechanical skills necessary in everyday life.
> 5. Using methods of critical thinking for the solution of problems and for the discrimination among values.
> 6. Understanding his cultural heritage so that he may gain a perspective of his time and place in the world.
> 7. Understanding his interaction with his biological and physical environment so that he may better adjust to and improve that environment.
> 8. Maintaining good mental and physical health for himself, his family, and his community.
> 9. Developing a balanced personal and social adjustment.
> 10. Sharing in the development of a satisfactory home and family life.
> 11. Achieving a satisfactory vocational adjustment.
> 12. Taking part in some form of satisfying creative activity and in appreciating the creative activities of others.[2]

Johnson comments: "None of the goals listed is a mutually exclusive compartmentalized objective. Instead they constitute a seamless web of human development."[3] Each goal assumes changes in students' behavior, brought about not only by knowledge, but, presumably, also by attitudes and motives. The results of general education are to be evaluated less in terms of what the person *knows*

[2] B. Lamar Johnson, *General Education in Action*, American Council on Education, Washington, 1952, pp. 21–22.

[3] *Ibid.*, p. 22.

than in terms of what he *does*. This is a difficult kind of education; it is safe to say that most institutions, if they have embraced it in theory, have attained it only in modest measure.

Meeting General Education Objectives

Educational institutions, junior colleges included, attempt to meet the objectives of general education either through conventional courses (ordinarily introductory departmental courses) or through courses or curricula devised especially for general education (departmental or interdisciplinary). Meeting general education objectives through conventional courses has ordinarily been associated with the practice of setting "distribution" requirements (as an offset to requirements for concentration or specialization). Distribution requirements have been criticized (1) because the usual elementary departmental courses have been devised as preparation for more advanced courses in the department rather than for their utility for the nonspecialist, and (2) because the effect has been for the student to acquire fragments of knowledge rather than a coherent view of a broad field of scholarship or of a basic, integrated knowledge of man and his world. Thus Johnson has said:

> One of the difficulties in this approach to general education is the too frequent tendency to teach each beginning course in a field as though every student enrolled in it is planning to take post-graduate and professional work in the field. This happens despite the fact that the vast majority of students will take no more than one or two elementary courses in an area despite the fact that these many students need to derive from their few courses those concepts, principles, and understandings which will have the most lasting usefulness.[4]

Courses devised especially for general education have taken various forms. In the beginning most of them were survey courses supposedly covering broad fields of knowledge comprehensively. These were succeeded in many colleges by more selective courses, built around a limited number of principles, ideas, periods, movements, regions, or problems, but treated in an interdisciplinary fashion.

Only a few institutions have introduced courses focused on be-

[4] *Ibid.*, p. 43.

havior, for example, the activities involved in wholesome family life, the selection of a vocation consistent with the student's interests, aptitude, and potential achievements or intelligent participation in civic affairs.

What kind of general education curricula were offered by the junior colleges in this study?

By far the majority—a total of 188, or 77 per cent, of the 243 two-year colleges studied—relied primarily on conventional or departmental courses to meet their responsibilities for general education. Only 74, or 30 per cent, indicated that they had established courses specially designed for general education. (Nineteen colleges reported that both procedures were used.)

If any course is to serve as a significant element in general education, the teacher must consciously turn it in that direction. The course is likely to make its greatest contribution if it becomes the continuing concern, not only of the individual instructor, but also of the entire faculty and the administration. With a few notable exceptions, this pervasive concern was not discernible in the institutions.

The administrators of the colleges that relied for general education on conventional courses were prone to rest their case on the fact that a good introductory departmental course per se makes a substantial contribution to the students' general education. Although it may be granted that such a course makes some contribution, it is hardly the best medium for the purpose.

The institutions that reported the use of specially devised courses were also asked to indicate the fields in which they had been offered. Their answers are shown in Table 3-1. Natural science and social science head the list and more than half of the institutions reported courses in the humanities. In the language arts category, 12 colleges reported English courses. A question could be raised as to whether these courses were really designed especially for general education or whether they were merely conventional English courses. Also, a few colleges reported such subjects as remedial English, remedial reading, and "trade English." While these may be meritorious offerings, they would seem to make a limited contribution to general education at the college level.

The mere availability of courses, conventional or otherwise, is not sufficient indication of the seriousness with which a junior col-

Table 3-1. Fields in Which Courses Especially Designed for General
Education Were Offered in 78 Two-year Colleges

Subjects	No. of colleges	No. of states	Percentage of 78 colleges
Natural science: general courses in physical and biological science and special courses in specific natural-science fields	67	11	86
Social science: general course and special courses in specific fields	62	11	80
Psychology and personal development: applied psychology, orientation to college, family life education, and personal development	52	8	66
Language arts: communication, English, speech, and others	46	10	59
Humanities: general course, Western civilization, philosophy, world literature, great books classes, and others	40	10	51
Fine arts: music and art appreciation, special art courses	19	4	24
Mathematics: special courses	16	5	20
Health education	15	3	19
Homemaking: home economics, consumer economics, personal finance, and others	11	3	14
Preprofessional orientation: introduction to business, engineering orientation, and others	10	5	13
Miscellaneous: courses with "general education" or "general curricula" labels	9	8	11
Occupational orientation: vocational planning, work experience, industrial relations	4	2	5
Agriculture and conservation	4	2	5

lege takes its responsibility for general education. The extent to which students take such courses is a better index. If a college relies on conventional courses, it might be assumed that the group most likely to obtain breadth and perspective would be the students preparing to transfer to senior colleges. Yet the curriculum requirements of many preprofessional programs restrict the students' experience in the various fields of knowledge. It is even more unlikely that specifically prescribed vocational subjects will permit the terminal student to venture far beyond his special curriculum. In fact, an examination of the suggested or required sequence of courses in terminal curricula in the cooperating institutions showed very limited requirements in general studies.

Table 3-2. Specific Courses Required for Graduation in a Sample
of 230 Junior Colleges in 15 States

Subjects	No. of colleges requiring courses	Per cent requiring courses	Per cent requiring 6 semester units or less	Per cent requiring over 6 semester units	Per cent requiring courses but not reporting units
English or communication	197	86	54	28	4
Physical education	138	60	55	0.4	4.6
American institutions	105	46	33	11	2
Social science	85	37	23	10	4
Natural science	85	37	21	13	3
Health education	67	29	28	0	1
Mathematics	56	24	13	2	9
College orientation	40	17	15	0	2
Foreign language	30	13	3	7	3
Religion, ethics	29	13	7	5	1
Humanities	23	10	8	2	0
Psychology	22	10	8	0.4	1.6
Speech	14	6	5	0	1
Fine arts	12	5	4	0.4	0.6
First aid	12	5	3	0	2
Philosophy	9	4	3	1	0
Business*	7	3	1	1	1
Military science	4	2	1	1	0

* Three colleges required business only in their certificated or industrial program; two colleges required accounting of all their students.

Another approach to the utilization of general education courses is an examination of graduation requirements. Table 3-2 summarizes the subjects or fields required for graduation reported by 230 junior colleges. As would be expected, English or communication headed the list, one or the other being required in 86 per cent of the institutions. Physical education, which ranked second in frequency of requirement, and American institutions, which ranked third, reflect the influence of statutory requirements in a number of states where one or both subjects are required. If American institutions and social sciences are combined, the category would rank close to English in frequency of requirement. The percentages of colleges requiring work in fields other than those mentioned, plus natural science (which is required in one-third of the colleges) drop rapidly, reflecting the small spread generally required of students.

Summary of General Education in Junior Colleges

The data summarized above and interviews in the 75 cooperating institutions (all of which were included in the larger sample of 243 institutions) lead inescapably to the conclusion that junior colleges have made relatively little progress in developing well-organized curricula for general education. Among the factors responsible for this was the lack of a compelling conviction that an adequate program of general education requires a conscious and systematic effort. Although many institutions listed general education in their catalogues as one of their major functions, few had formulated the specific objectives of general education in operational terms. Such formulation, however, is the step in curriculum-making that dictates the content and organization of courses and, to a considerable degree, the methods of teaching and learning.

Inadequacies in general education programs of junior colleges have been cited in earlier reports. Reynolds,[5] after examining the permanent record of the graduates of 32 public junior colleges, concluded that junior colleges were falling far short of providing an adequate general education program, particularly in certain fields of general education and more so in certain curricula. Johnson, at the conclusion of the two-year study of general education in California public junior colleges, wrote in his final report:

> As one examines the graduation requirements of California junior colleges with the goals of general education in mind, he is impressed (1) by diversity of practice, (2) by the spotty and limited recognition given some of the general education objectives, and (3) by the apparent failure as yet to make any provision for some of the others. These impressions are further confirmed by an examination of recommended programs listed in junior college catalogues.[6]

[5] James W. Reynolds, "General Education in Public Junior Colleges," *Junior College Journal*, vol. 16, p. 308, March, 1956.

[6] Johnson, *op. cit.*, p. 49.

Thornton cited as a deficiency "the failure on the part of the junior colleges to evaluate the degree of attainment of the goals set for general education."[7]

The present study shows that little more has been accomplished in the past decade.

It should not be assumed, however, that no sound program of general education can be found in junior colleges. Some two-year colleges in this study were making every effort to develop such a program. Furthermore, in an institution that places so high a premium on good teaching as the junior college does, some of the objectives of general education will be met regardless of the lack of institution-wide concern and planning.

No one should be too quick to criticize junior college personnel for not having done more. There are major obstacles that hamper progress. The demands of vocational curricula make severe inroads on time for general education. The insistence on the part of senior colleges that junior college courses submitted for transfer credit be identical with their own is a real deterrent because, in meeting specific transfer requirements, the junior college is unable to set up its own general education program. Another difficulty is that of procuring teachers who understand general education and are committed to it—teachers who have the background for the kind of teaching general education requires.

Whatever the obstacles, progress will be made only if there is understanding, desire, and energy to achieve it. On this point the President's Commission declares:

> The effectiveness of any general education program will depend on the quality and attitudes of those who administer and teach it. Its success will be commensurate with the faculty members' recognition of the importance of such instruction to society and their willingness to assume initiative and responsibility in reorganizing instruction and rearranging the life of the institution to accomplish its objectives.[8]

[7] James W. Thornton, Jr., "General Education," *The Public Junior College*, Fifty-fifth Yearbook of the National Society for the Study of Education, Chicago, 1956, part I, chap. 4, p. 137.

[8] *Higher Education for American Democracy: A Report of the President's Commission on Higher Education*, Harper & Brothers, New York, 1948, vol. I, p. 60.

A PROGRAM FOR STUDENTS WITH EDUCATIONAL DEFICIENCIES

It is often said that the junior college must perform a "salvaging" function. What does the term mean? How are students salvaged? Is it logical for society to expect the junior college to perform this function? What problems does the acceptance of this responsibility pose for an institution?

The term, applied to the junior college, may have several meanings but in this report it will be limited to the following special educational services:

Providing opportunity in junior college for the student to take subjects which he may not have completed in high school and which are required for admission to a senior college or for admission to a sequence of courses in a junior college.

Providing the student who lacks skills necessary for the successful pursuit of certain college subjects an opportunity to improve his skills after entering the junior college. Among them are reading, writing, speaking, and mathematical skills.

Providing for students whose high school grade-point average is not sufficiently high to admit them to a four-year college an opportunity to improve their scholastic record and thus become eligible for admission to such a college.

The problem of deficiencies is not limited to the two-year college. Frequent discussion of the subject in collegiate circles makes it apparent that four-year colleges and universities are also highly cognizant of the problem and that many of them are in the process of developing new admission standards that make it necessary for students to fulfill specific requirements and demonstrate academic competence before they are admitted. The public two-year college, and particularly the junior college, is not, however, in a position to meet its problem in the same way because in most states it must admit all high school graduates and adults who seek admission. Its task, then, becomes one of assisting many students in attaining realistic goals that are closed to them at high school graduation. This responsibility weighs heavily on the junior college, regardless of the student's declared intentions. If he proposes to follow a lower-division program that will gain him entrance to a four-year college, the subject prerequisites of his chosen courses must be completed to the satisfaction of the next institution, and his ability to carry the program leading to transfer must be well ensured. Otherwise, the junior college jeopardizes both its commitment to and its relationships with the student, his parents, and the senior institution to which he may transfer. If the student indicates his desire to enroll in a terminal occupational program, he must be able to complete course sequences and to perform at a level that will make him the caliber of employee that employers have reason to expect of a junior college graduate.

Students with subject deficiencies were found to be admitted to more than 90 per cent of the public junior colleges, sometimes on a provisional basis but usually as regular students. Courses which carried credit toward the A.A. degree and which were comparable with those at the high school level were offered in most of these institutions. Students could proceed with those parts of their chosen curriculum—even a transfer program—for which they were eligible while they were making up deficiencies in the parts for which they were ineligible.

Inquiry into the methods of how junior colleges were assisting students to improve their skills in reading, writing, speaking, and mathematics showed a wide range of practices. All institutions recognized the problem and more than three-fourths of them were attempting to meet it. Two types of programs are commonly referred to as "remedial." One is the course which runs for a full term, that is, a semester or quarter. It may be a course taken instead of a standard college course in the same subject. For example, students who do not qualify for the standard freshman English course may be enrolled in "English X." In some colleges, two levels of the "sub" courses had been established. This type of course may also be designed to improve a specific skill, such as the reading rate and comprehension, and is not regarded as a substitute for another course. A second type of remedial course is in the nature of a workshop or special help class to which students are assigned to improve their skill and supplement their work in a regular course that they are carrying concurrently.

Credit is likely to be given for remedial work completed in a regular class continuing for a quarter or a semester but less likely to be given when students are assigned to supplementary workshops or extraclass sessions. Obviously, credit for remedial work is generally useful only for junior college graduation and is not likely to be transferable.

In about three-fourths of the public junior colleges the results of achievement tests were found to be used for purposes of assigning students to remedial courses. Frequently the results of such tests were combined with other test results, such as the verbal or quantitative scores on aptitude tests, or with demonstration of ability through performance, such as writing a paper. Assignment to regular or remedial classes was then made on the basis of a composite score, including the scores on the achievement tests and the essay. Students assigned temporarily to workshops and other special help groups were most often assigned on the basis of their relatively poor performance in a course in which their lack of a certain skill appeared to be impeding their progress.

A Matter of Policy

Some complex questions arise in connection with the salvage or remedial function of the two-year college. There are persons who dislike both the terms "salvage" and "remedial," and they are not defended here. It is the program for students who enter with deficiencies that is important and not the term that describes it. Persons inside and outside the junior college who disdain this function are placed in the dilemma either of suggesting a selective admission policy for junior colleges or of recommending some other way to achieve the optimum development of each student.

To become selective might make the job of the public junior college easier, but it would raise questions of social policy. There is, for example, a question whether in the foreseeable future any lessening of effort in the salvaging of youthful talent is desirable. A system that encourages and assists students to avoid a premature termination of education has the result that many of them will later fill highly necessary and useful posts at a time when trained manpower may be badly needed. This would suggest that some type of institution should exist giving high school graduates with certain deficiencies an opportunity to remedy them and prove themselves capable of college work.

If it is agreed that talent should be salvaged, the question remains: Which agency should do the salvaging? If four-year colleges become more selective, what agency other than the junior college is there to perform the salvaging function? Some persons place responsibility on the high school to make sure that graduates who plan to enter college are able to meet admission requirements and that they have the necessary skills. It is also argued that so long as junior colleges admit virtually everybody, the high school student is not encouraged to perform at optimum capacity because he knows that his deficiencies can be made up in junior college.

Certainly, the two-year college should not be considered an antidote for any failure on the part of the American high school. As the high school has come to be comprehensive in nature, serving practically all children of all the people, it has, like the two-year college, encountered difficulties in providing appropriate programs and instructional techniques for its diversified student body. Its critics have not always viewed it constructively. Recommendations made in the Conant study of the American high school will undoubtedly result in some acceleration of student performance.[9] Clearly the high school does have the responsibility to see that each student plans well and performs at a level commensurate with his ability. The high school can no more pass on to the junior college the obligation to correct the deficiencies of its graduates than the junior college can expect the four-year college to do for transfer students what should have been done in junior college.

On the other hand, some students inevitably need special help upon entering junior college. Some do not decide on college early enough in high school to meet requirements. Others become motivated too late. Still others have low aptitude and achievement levels. What agency is to assist them? To date the American tradition is on the side of providing some type of opportunity after high school to most students desiring it and of making performance the method of screening. Under these circumstances the junior college must make such opportunity available, or some other type of institution must be created for the purpose.

More than three-fourths of the administrators interviewed expressed the belief that the junior college, particularly the public junior college, has no alternative but to provide ample opportunity for the removal of deficiencies. A broad sampling of opinion on the

---

[9] James B. Conant, *The American High School Today*, McGraw-Hill Book Company, Inc., New York, 1959.

subject was also obtained through an item in the questionnaire on staff attitudes described in Chapter 7. The respondents were asked to rate the importance of high school level courses in the junior college for students whose academic record makes them ineligible to enter directly into the conventional college course. Of the more than three thousand two hundred teachers and administrators responding to the item, only 27 per cent rated such courses as unimportant. Almost 50 per cent said they were important and approximately 25 per cent rated them as very important.

The opinion of the junior college personnel on the role of the junior college in helping students to remove deficiencies is therefore quite clear. It is well that it is, for if such work were considered unimportant or undignified, the program would be virtually negated by the attitude of the staff.

CONSIDERATION OF THE ACADEMICALLY SUPERIOR STUDENT

No less important than the special attention that the two-year college pays to the deficient student is its responsibility to the academically superior student. These two types of students are not mutually exclusive. An able student may not decide on his final occupational and educational goals while in high school and thus may enter the junior college with subject deficiencies to make up. Less rarely will a student with high academic aptitude require special help in developing his communication and mathematical skills to the point where he can carry college work satisfactorily. Even so, the more gifted the student, the more important it is that his ability to read and write be developed to the maximum. Thus, attention may profitably be given to the improvement of the basic skills of the able as well as the less able student.

However, the main point of inquiry concerning the superior student centers on the question of what the two-year college can do to enrich or accelerate his educational program. This question is not limited to the two-year college. In the last few years it has received widespread attention at all educational levels. Its importance at the college level has been well identified by Wolfle[10] and others who have investigated the need for better utilization of specialized

[10] Dael, Wolfle, *America's Resources of Specialized Talent*, Harper & Brothers, New York, 1954.

talent. Certainly the manpower demands of society in general and of the United States in particular are such that the maximum development of the gifted is a responsibility that no collegiate institution can ignore. The relatively large number of junior college students with superior ability makes it impossible for these colleges to escape their responsibility for assisting able students to perform at an optimum level. This responsibility will become even greater with the further development and utilization of two-year colleges throughout the country.

Two ways of serving superior students are open to the junior college. One is to assist them while they are still in high school and the other after they are enrolled in junior college.

Obviously, working with high school students is limited to situations where the junior college and the high school are in the same community or to the relatively few private junior colleges that also operate a high school program. The most common method of assisting able students while they are still in high school is for the local college to admit them part time to college classes. This practice is presumed to enrich the students' educational experience by making it possible for them to participate in a greater variety of offerings and at an advanced level. If credit is awarded for the college courses, the practice also results in an acceleration of a student's progress toward a college degree. A survey of California junior colleges[11] made in late 1958 showed that of the 51 colleges responding, 31 permitted high school students to enroll in junior college courses. Their admission was generally based on recommendation by high school counselors or administrators. The reporting junior colleges did not indicate how they defined "gifted students," nor did they report that the students had difficulty in competing in college classes. Other means of working with able high school students reported by the California colleges included permission to use the college library and to audit college classes.

When high school students are admitted to junior college classes, the question arises as to whether they should receive high school credit, college credit, or both. If the student needs the credit to complete high school graduation requirements, the credit from the college courses may be converted into high school units. If he

[11] Information from an unpublished report made at the meeting of the California Junior College Association, fall, 1958, by H. Lynn Sheller.

does not need the credit for high school purposes, it may stand simply as college credit. Whether or not the student is given credit both toward high school graduation and as college work depends upon the local junior college or any college to which the student may wish to transfer the credit.

If the plan of admitting high school students to junior college classes is to function, the administrations of the high school and of the junior college must both be solidly behind it. They must believe that high-ability students should not be held to the conventional high school structure. Cooperation between the two administrative units is necessary. Good counseling of students is essential. The plan usually does not include large numbers of students, but, for the few whose program can be enriched or safely accelerated, the utilization of a local junior college for that purpose seems both sensible and expedient.

The two-year college has many opportunities and considerable flexibility to serve superior students once they are enrolled in the college as regular college students. In the last few years the colleges appear to have moved from a general recognition that special consideration should be given to "the gifted"—though the term is defined in different ways—to numerous experiments on how to serve them best. The problem has been discussed at most educational conferences in which junior college personnel participated.

Junior colleges provide various special services to regularly enrolled students of high academic aptitude, and many other services are frequently proposed. One is the honors program. There are varying interpretations of what such a program entails, but its most common pattern is to permit superior students to enroll in specially designed supplemental courses in such fields as the humanities, philosophy, science, and mathematics and to make them eligible for special honor upon the successful completion of such courses. This practice holds many possibilities for enriching the program of able students. Whether it can be used to accelerate a student's program depends largely on the acceptance for credit by four-year colleges of honors courses completed in junior college.

The progress of able students is also sometimes accelerated by giving the student advanced standing by the use of examinations. In other cases, examinations are used as a means of waiving course prerequisites, even though students do not receive credit for courses they are permitted to pass over as a result of the qualifying examinations. There may arise the problem of transfer of credit gained by examinations or for courses for which prerequisites were waived. This, like the problem of credit for honors courses, should be met realistically by the two- and four-year colleges as they consider the best way to serve the superior student.

An increasingly prevalent practice in junior colleges is to attempt to serve the able student through homogeneous grouping of students in numerous subject fields. The grouping is based on previous academic achievement or on scores made on a standard academic aptitude test, or both. Junior college administrators and teachers who favor this method claim that only by separating the more able students—particularly the very able—can the most effective instructional methods be employed for them and an appropriate level of academic standards be maintained.

Another apparently effective device is the designation of special counselors for academically superior students. The counselor's task in this case is to work intensively with a small group of high-ability students, encouraging and assisting them in planning their educational programs in ways that result in the maximum challenge and development of each student.

New plans and procedures for assisting the abler students will undoubtedly be devised. Practices will vary in scope and methods. Of first importance is the necessity for junior colleges to recognize their responsibility to the gifted student and through staff participation to determine an institutional policy to serve him. Each faculty member should make use of special assignments and supplemental learning experiences for outstanding students. If academic excellence is to be stressed, public recognition for outstanding scholarship should become a concern of each junior college. Too often recognition is given only to students with successful activity records. However, there are limitations to the amount of special help individual teachers can give superior students. There is obvious need for special attention and assistance to the superior student if the junior college, along with other units in American education, is to meet the social and technological demands of the next decade. More specifically, the junior college should move ahead in facilitating both early admission and advanced standing for superior students. To do this, however, the junior college must have the encouragement and support of four-year colleges so that students will not be penalized when they transfer. By close cooperation the two-year and four-year colleges could expedite either or both of these devices under proper controls to the advantage of many students.

A PROGRAM FOR ADULTS

In its second report The President's Committee on Education beyond the High School[12] commented on the four major educational complexes that have evolved—the traditional system of schools and colleges, an elaborate educational program under the military, a mushrooming system of education operated by private business for its own employees, and *a great variety of programs of continuing education under the broad title of "adult education."* The committee pointed out that one out of every three adults, an estimated fifty million, participates in various adult education programs, some primarily vocational, others primarily recreational or cultural.

The two-year colleges of the nation are now looked upon as important agencies for serving adults. In the 1959 *Junior College Directory*,[13] 306,152 persons were reported in adult education programs in junior colleges in the United States. The directory also listed a total of 94,432 special students, of whom many undoubtedly were adults.

Of the 179 public institutions in the over-all sample, 158, or 88 per cent, offered programs of service to adults and to the community. Of the 64 private institutions responding, 18, or 28 per cent, offered such service. The few public colleges which did not offer adult programs were in small communities that made few demands for such programs or in communities in which some other segment of the public school system had been given the responsibility for adult education. Usually, the other agency was the high school, although in a few instances a separate adult education department of the local school system operated the program. In many communities both the junior college and the high school (or other

---

[12] The President's Committee on Education beyond the High School, *Second Report to the President,* Washington, 1957.

[13] *Junior College Directory*, American Association of Junior Colleges, Washington, 1959.

public school agency) participated in some way in the adult program. Interviews with public junior college administrators in all sections of the country left no doubt that they included the adult education function among their important responsibilities. Some administrators, in places where the function was performed by another agency, expressed sharp concern over the fact that school authorities did not make the junior college the administrative unit for the program.

The Concept of Adult Education

There is a common misconception that adult education is limited to evening programs; that it is comprised of a series of unrelated, noncredit courses developed through speculation or on popular demand; and that the courses pertain primarily to crafts, recreation, or vocational skills. These stereotypes do not fit the majority of junior college adult programs. In the average community the junior college adult program is looked upon favorably by adults, not only because of its prestige as a college program but also because of the resources within the faculty of the college. The college soon becomes a center of attraction for adults. It is often called upon to organize classes for adults in off-campus locations during the day. It generally regards its period of operation as from early morning until late evening. Increasingly, regular day classes are also offered at night, thus enabling a part-time student eventually to complete two years of college work during evening hours. In fact, many adults who wish to do college work earn their A.A. degrees as part-time students. Credit and noncredit classes are scheduled with considerable care, often on the advice of key community groups and advisory committees. In short, adult education in the junior college tends to have many facets and to be woven into the general pattern of a community-centered institution.

Enrollments of Adults in Subject Fields

The types of courses for which persons enroll in an adult education program are an indication of the program's contribution to the welfare of the community. Within the last few years, considerable concern has been expressed in some states—some of it by legislative bodies—over the fact that the public schools were spending tax monies for adult recreational activities under the guise of an educational program. Such activities as dancing, swimming, bridge, ceramics, and lapidary courses were singled out as examples. Although it may be argued that teaching the skills of such activities is a defensible objective, an institution's program is more vulnerable to criticism if such subjects constitute any great share of its offerings.

To permit examination of the types of subjects which junior colleges offer and the proportion of adult students who enroll in each subject, the cooperating institutions were asked to submit the list of class offerings for the fall semester, 1956, together with the number of students enrolled in each class. Adequate lists were received from 37 institutions representing all sizes and types of two-year colleges in most sections of the country. The 37 institutions accounted for almost 100,000 class enrollments in credit and noncredit courses. A system of subject categories was then developed and tabulations of the class enrollments were made.

Table 3-3 shows that enrollments in the business category head the list, with trade-technical and industrial arts subjects a close second. It is significant that a group representing a general education classification, including the fields of language and communi-

Table 3-3. Distribution of Adult Education Enrollments by Subject-matter Categories in 37 Junior Colleges, Fall, 1956

Categories	Enrollments in each category	Percentage of total enrollment
Business	16,951	18
Trade technical, and industrial arts	15,988	17
Language, communication arts, and humanities	14,049	15
Social science	12,209	13
Arts and crafts	7,569	8
Mathematics	7,042	8
Home economics: homemaking, family living	6,416	7
Natural science	4,596	5
Recreational and physical education	3,443	4
Undescribed courses in general education	3,051	3
Agriculture, landscape gardens, etc.	718	1
Police and fire training	620	1
Total	92,632	100

cation arts, social science, fine and applied arts, mathematics, natural science, and liberal arts, accounts for slightly over half of the total adult enrollment. Interestingly, too, if business and trade-technical and industrial arts courses were considered jointly as the vocational phase of the adult program, they would constitute approximately a third of the total enrollment. This proportion corresponds almost exactly to the proportion of enrollments in such subjects in the day program. The fact that in the category for social and physical education only 4 per cent of the total were enrolled shows that there is no justification in criticizing this type of education as being overstressed.

Administering the Adult Program

An institution that undertakes to extend its program over many hours each day and to offer a great variety of subjects to a diverse population creates for itself many responsibilities and problems. The additional administrative load occasioned by curriculum-building, employment of personnel, record-keeping, and supervision is heavy.

In practically all the cooperating colleges a special administrator directed and supervised this phase of the program. Where, then, does this position properly fit in the line organization of the college? In a few instances where the college was a part of a unified school district, the director of the adult program reported directly to the office of the superintendent of schools instead of to an administrative officer at the college. Such an arrangement has the disadvantage of making it impossible for the administrative head of the college to integrate the total community college program. In approximately 90 per cent of the cases the adult administrator reported to the chief administrator of the college. This practice appears logical because many concerns of the adult administrator have to do with over-all policy and general administrative problems. On the other hand, it has a weakness in those institutions in which a designated person, such as a dean of instruction, is responsible for the instructional program for regular full-time students. The entire instructional program of the college for both day and evening classes and for students at all levels and ages logically constitutes an educational unit. This is especially true in institutions which, in addition to organizing special classes for adults, also continue the regular day program through evening hours. Such situations require close relationships between the adult administrator and the administrator in charge of instruction—either by having the former report to the latter or by effecting some close liaison between the two. Unfortunately, many colleges tended to operate two instructional programs independently of each other.

Of the many problems connected with the operation of an adult education program, only three pertinent ones are mentioned here. The first is the problem of how far a college should go in making student personnel services, particularly counseling services, available to its adult clientele. About a third of the cooperating institutions which offered adult programs reported that they made regularly assigned counselors available to students enrolled in the evening program. Generally this meant having a counselor on duty during evening hours whom students could see if they needed help. In many junior colleges the only counseling assistance available to part-time evening students was the over-the-counter advice given by the administrator of the evening program or an office clerk. Counseling services—or their lack—in junior college evening programs should not be taken lightly. If students in increasing numbers are to seek educational services during evening hours, either for college credit or to increase their personal competencies, the college offering the services has some responsibility for helping them make wise educational choices in line with their goals.

A second adult education problem is the ever-present one of how best to interpret community needs as a guide to building a program. It is one thing to offer a program which "meets community needs," but another to help a nebulous body such as a community to interpret its needs. There is always the danger of paying undue attention to the expressed desires and interests of individuals or small groups. Kempfer aptly said:

> Adult education in focusing upon the individual has too often been concerned with *little* needs. If harnessed to total improvement of our communities and our democracy, it will be concerned with *big needs*.[13a] [Italic ours.]

[13a] Homer Kempfer, "Adult Education in the Community College," *Junior College Journal*, vol. 21, pp. 18–25, September, 1950.

The most important responsibility of the adult administrator is to build the best possible program. This responsibility is even greater than that of administering the program.

The institutions visited reported various practices used in determining adult offerings. Few of them relied to any extent on the older procedure of "we will offer any course which a specified number of people request." Instead, it appeared that as a group the adult administrators were taking their job of program-building seriously. They were working with key community groups, such as professional and business agencies, industrial groups, and chambers of commerce. Many of them had organized lay advisory committees. They appeared to be sensitive to the needs of the society and, based on the belief that the times require better-informed people, scheduled courses in the social sciences, humanities, natural sciences, and English—all of which were proving to be popular, as is evident from Table 3-4.

A third problem is that of coordinating the college adult education program with that of other agencies, including other segments of public school systems. In many places the high schools and other agencies were operating adult programs long before a local junior college was established or at least before it started a similar program. As adult programs were established in the junior college, differences of opinion and even conflicts often ensued as to the role of each of the institutions.[14] Visits in certain communities revealed that differences of opinion still existed about a priority in the "right" to offer certain courses. The situation is made more complex by the fact that the junior college enjoys a certain advantage in being a college, and thus ordinarily is able to attract more students for same type of class than the high school. In school districts which maintain both junior colleges and high schools, the governing board must make the final decision as to what agency shall serve in what ways. In colleges maintained by separate junior college districts, by the state, or by private resources, there is an obligation to avoid unnecessary duplication of effort and to work closely with other agencies in the development of a program that best serves the community.

[14] For a discussion of an example of such a conflict, see Burton R. Clark, *Adult Education in Transition (A Study of Institutional Insecurity)*, University of California Press, Berkeley, Calif., 1956.

A PROGRAM OF COMMUNITY SERVICE

The term "community service" has come to denote generally the various *special* services which an educational institution may provide for its community. Examples of such services are workshops, forums, and institutes; research and advisory assistance to community groups; cultural and recreational activities, including community music and theater groups; and widespread use of the college plant for community activities. There is obviously a close relationship between adult education and many of these special services. In fact, adult education may be classified as one type of community service. The formal classroom phase of it is discussed separately in this report only for purposes of simplification.

Comparatively little appears in the literature on special community services. In fact, the only major publication dealing with the junior college which has devoted as much as a chapter to the topic of community services was the yearbook of the National Society for the Study of Education entitled *The Public Junior College*, published in 1956. In it Reynolds classified the range of possible community services discussed in other studies into the following categories: (1) mutual aid for meeting college-community needs, (2) community experience programs (utilizing the community as a laboratory for the college), (3) community study and research problems, (4) public affairs education, (5) specialized community services, (6) community development, (7) community participation and leadership training, (8) use of mass-media communication, (9) public relations programs, (10) community use of school plant, and (11) adult education.[15]

Information from the two-year colleges in the states studied and from the cooperating institutions led to the conclusion that two-year colleges generally were performing a wide variety of community services over and beyond formalized classroom instruction. Of the 243 colleges in the larger sample, 219, or 90 per cent, reported special services of the type that would fall in the categories listed in Table 3-4. The number of colleges reporting

[15] James W. Reynolds, "Community Services," *The Public Junior College*, Fifty-fifth Yearbook of the National Society for the Study of Education, Chicago, 1956, part I, chap. 8, pp. 140–160.

activities or services in these categories is shown in the left column of the table.

Table 3-4. Number of Two-year Institutions (out of a Total of 243 Reporting) Indicating the Performance of Special Community Services, Spring, 1956

No. reporting	Community service categories
145	Widespread use of the college physical plant by community groups
114	Assistance by college in safety and thrift campaigns, fund drives, and the like
107	Organization of special events, such as workshops, institutes, forums, for business, professional, or governmental groups either for the purpose of in-service training of employees or the general improvement of the group
105	Promotion of cultural and recreational activities, such as the development of community musical groups, sponsoring of little theater groups
83	Promotion by the college of community events in which public affairs are discussed
66	Organization projects with other community agencies relating to the improvement of health conditions in the community
65	Use of the college staff and students in making studies of the community (such as occupational surveys, sociological studies)
42	Widespread use of college staff as speakers to community groups
42	Organization of services using college staff or students, or films and lectures from outside, to further the conservation of natural resources
41	Research by college staff and students for business or professional groups in the community
41	Organization of child-care programs for demonstration and instructional purposes

The largest category was that of making the school plant available for community groups. This service may not be comparable in significance to others in the list, but interviewed administrators stated almost unanimously that it makes an important contribution to the community and that it welds the college and the community more closely together.

The other categories are more indicative of the unusual services that make an institution a community college. Their value would depend to some extent on whether they were "one shot" services or performed more or less regularly. Visits to the cooperating colleges made it clear that in many of the institutions these services were not performed frequently.

The extent and effectiveness of such programs depends largely on the amount and type of administrative leadership they receive. More administrative time will be needed in a large community than in a small one. In Pasadena, for example, where the city college is responsible for the adult education and community service program for the entire city, an administrative dean is in charge. He is assisted by a dean in charge of extended day activities and his two assistants—one for special services and the other for services on other campuses. Most colleges are not large enough to require the personnel assigned at Pasadena, but the example indicates the degree of administrative concern and leadership for this phase of the program in one institution. In smaller institutions the leadership for the program was found ordinarily to rest with the person in charge of the adult program. Discussion with persons on the various campuses brought out the fact that the initiative for special programs and services often came from individual teachers and department chairmen in fields such as business, drama, music, art, social science, and natural science. Initiation of such services on the part of the staff should be highly desirable, although there must necessarily be some centralized direction. In some institutions, the logical person to assume responsibility for direction of special services is the person in charge of adult education. However, this person may easily become so immersed in the details of a formal adult program that he may not have time to develop an additional program.

Among the special service programs, the following appeared to be particularly significant in the visited institutions:

Lectures and Forums. The subjects included political problems of international and national scope, family relationships, homemaking, family financial security, human relations, community planning, mental health, and problems of the aged. Among the speakers were some with national reputations, members of the college staff who by experiences, such as foreign travel, were qualified to discuss special subjects, community leaders, and specialists in business or professional affairs.

Conferences, Institutes, and Workshops. Less formal than lectures and forums and characterized more by group participation were activities planned with community groups to deal with special problems. A college in the South reported offering each year a series of one-day "short courses" of the conference and demonstration type on such subjects as irrigation, animal husbandry, crop farming, and maintenance of farm machinery. Many institutions reported special conferences for local merchants, real estate agencies, and insurance groups. One college reported an annual institute for newspaper publishers and reporters. Workshops on leadership training for youth-serving agencies, parent-teacher associations, and similar organizations were held by several institutions. A few colleges had special workshops for teachers.

Utilizing Special College Facilities for Community Service, Particularly for Elementary and High School Students. One college with a planetarium in a new physical science building used it for demonstrating the solar system to outside groups. Several colleges with special collections in natural or social sciences reported on the extent to which younger students were brought by their schools to the college to see the exhibits. A technical institute in the East reported that it made its laboratory for testing the strength of materials available to industries. Another college used its test-scoring equipment for other public agencies in the community.

Assistance by Students and Staff in Projects for Community Betterment. Examples in this category were occupational and industrial surveys of a community completed by the college and reported to the community; use of college personnel for bond drives, parking surveys, and market analyses; and use of the staff as special consultants to groups engaged in special community or industrial problems. Several colleges reported the contributions made by physical science teachers in such projects as testing local water supply and in making other chemical or geological analyses. One institution in the East operates a community guidance center, staffed by college personnel, which provides free counseling services to college students and services to other youths and adults in the community for a moderate fee. (The legal requirements for such a practice were met by incorporating the college student body and making it the agency for providing the services.)

Taking the Initiative in Community Projects Which Are Subsequently Assumed by Other Agencies. A community college in New York State reported its early efforts to establish a clearinghouse for social welfare and educational agencies—an effort which led to the creation of a permanent organization. The same college reported its successful efforts to develop a county library service. Several administrators told of the leadership of their institution in developing local historical and fine arts societies. The development of a community choral or instrumental music group which later was taken over by a community-wide agency seemed to be a common experience.

Special mention should be made of two other examples of community service. One is the open-circuit television program in operation in the Chicago City Junior College. While primarily for the purpose of offering credit and noncredit courses, the extensiveness of the day and evening programs makes it a significant means of disseminating information and of stimulating thought in those who wish to tune in for only parts of the program of particular interest to them.

The other example is an activity known as the Community Educational Project at San Bernardino Valley College in California. This project, initiated in 1951, states as its goal "the creation of a situation, through education, in which local people, working together, can solve the problems they face in common." Those responsible for the project say that they consider these problems to be "not only such immediate pressing physical problems as water, the need for growing and diversified industry and sound planning, but also such intangible but nonetheless equally vital problems as developing an understanding of the American heritage, the free enterprise system, sound human relations practices, world affairs, and a deepening sensitivity to good design and beauty in everyday living." Original financial support for the project was granted to San Bernardino Valley College by the Fund for Adult Education. Present financial support comes in part from Valley College district funds and in part from national organizations, such as the National Association of Educational Broadcasters. The project has been experimenting with the development of a new communication system through which people can learn about community problems, discuss them, and come in touch both with each other and the institutions, agencies, and groups responsible for action in the different areas of community life. Through radio and television programs, problems of community living are discussed. These discussions are then supplemented by small groups of citizens organized into groups meeting in homes and in other places.

Consultation services are made available to local organizations interested in more effective educational methods. Study materials are also prepared for the use of interested groups.

These examples of community services illustrate an additional means by which a two-year college can become a community college. In fact, it is hardly conceivable that an institution could long remain in a community and not feel the obligation and the challenge to perform such services. On the other hand, the services require time, energy, and often money. Furthermore, constantly changing patterns of community life change the types of services desired. For example, a number of institutions which once had conducted outstanding lecture and forum services reported that attendance had now fallen so low that they are being curtailed or eliminated. Television and other forms of recreation were suspected as reasons for this declining interest. Two-year colleges can undoubtedly perform even greater community services by more extensive use of local television.

DEVELOPMENT AND ADMINISTRATION OF THE INSTRUCTIONAL PROGRAM

The development of a curriculum in a two-year college rests on the same basic principles as those used in any educational enterprise. However, the multipurpose nature of the junior college and its close association with the local community result in certain unique problems—problems concerning such matters as interpreting needs; providing for diversity of program, often in a relatively small institution; and articulation with other educational agencies.

Curriculum development in the two-year college is a process that should be guided and evaluated by an expressed institutional philosophy of education and a set of goals stated in terms of outcomes for students. It should be based on the expressed and interpreted needs of students, the community, and the larger society. It is continuous in terms of construction, revision, and evaluation. It involves the teaching staff—directly through periodic consideration by the entire staff and indirectly through appropriate committees. It also requires centralized direction and administration.

Institutional Philosophy and Objectives

It should not be assumed that all colleges should proceed in the same way in serving their students. In addition to a consideration of the kinds of students a college enrolls, the program of a college should depend on the expressed educational philosophy and objectives of the institution. For, unless staff members are in agreement on basic educational principles and on what they hope to accomplish for the students, they are not likely to plan, teach, and evaluate with purposeful direction and unity. In one sense, a statement of a basic philosophy and a written set of objectives are to an institution what a road map is to the tourist or a flight plan to the pilot—they chart the direction. Today all regional accrediting associations include among their evaluative criteria a reference to the desirability of such an expression on the part of an institution applying for accreditation.

Through examination of published statements, interviews with staffs, and the inclusion of a question in the faculty-attitude questionnaire,[16] an attempt was made to determine how far the 75 cooperating colleges had gone in formulating and expressing their educational philosophy. The results were disappointing because, although a number of colleges had published excellent statements, most of them had not. There seemed to be confusion over what might be regarded as general functions of the college and what may be thought of as objectives stated in terms of desired outcomes for students. General functions of an institution are broad—they set forth the major purposes for which the institution was established. For example, if a community expects its junior college to provide a transfer program, the implementation of a transfer curriculum becomes one of the college's functions. Likewise, if the college is expected to serve students not intending to transfer, the offering of various terminal programs becomes one of its functions. But regardless of whether students are in transfer or terminal programs, the college may be expected to help them achieve certain understandings, attitudes, and skills which affect their personal, civic, and vocational well-being. If the college considers the specific changes and developments it hopes to effect in students as individuals, the objectives become narrower and

[16] Described in Chap. 7.

more behavioral. For example, if the staff decides that one of its important tasks is to improve the ability of students to communicate well with others, verbalized goals of the college will be to help each student increase his competence in expressing his thoughts clearly in speaking and writing and in reading and listening with understanding. Such specific behavioral objectives may increase the competence of students in many areas such as health, family life, creative activities, citizenship, understanding the complex physical environment—all in addition to the competence necessary for the student's chosen vocational field. The objectives may be even further specified as to the areas of knowledge and understanding, the types of attitudes and appreciations, and the specific skills and abilities necessary in achieving the objectives. These more detailed and specific desired outcomes for students are different from the mere over-all purposes of the college stated in broad general terms.

The catalogues and other publications of 70 cooperating institutions (counting the Wisconsin and Pennsylvania extension centers as one each) were examined, and an attempt made to categorize the references to institutional philosophy and stated goals. In 28 instances the college indicated its objectives by a one- or two-sentence statement which set forth a limited number of goals, such as responsible citizenship, critical thinking, self-realization, and development of good character. The publications of 15 institutions listed objectives more completely, some of which were supplemented by short philosophical statements on how the institution regarded its role in education. In 8 colleges institutional objectives were not mentioned in the publications examined. In the publications of 19 institutions the objectives were primarily in terms of the functions to be performed or types of students to be served. In a few colleges fairly detailed objectives, interwoven with references to educational philosophy, had been agreed upon by the staff and put in writing but had not been included in the printed documents of the institution either because of the length of the statements or the fear that the wording of them "would sound too much like educational jargon."

It would be unfair to imply that the faculty and administration in two-year colleges are entirely unguided by a philosophy of education even though not all their publications make the point clear. Any staff working together over a period of time tends to crystallize its thinking concerning its mission. Furthermore, many administrators interviewed testified that much time was spent in faculty groups discussing the nature and purposes of the junior college. Visits with small faculty groups and occasionally with entire faculties left the impression that teachers were seriously dedicated to the junior college and to the students they serve.

That the majority of the faculty members consider their college to have a basic philosophy and a set of objectives was revealed by their response to an item in the faculty-attitude questionnaire. Of the more than 3,200 respondents to a question on whether a statement of philosophy existed, 88 per cent answered yes, 3 per cent no, and 8 per cent did not know. Asked whether they believed that the educational orientation of most faculty members was in accord with the statement, those to whom this question applied answered as follows: yes—80 per cent; no—9 per cent; don't know—11 per cent. These responses suggest that the cooperating institutions have given more consideration to their basic philosophy than the report in the preceding paragraphs might indicate. It may be that many of the respondents were prone to consider a statement of general functions as the equivalent of a statement of objectives. Also, it may be that in a college where philosophy and objectives are discussed frequently in staff meetings even though they are not put in writing, the teachers conclude that the staff has agreed on its goals.

The existence of a written statement of educational goals— even if prepared and agreed upon by the staff—obviously does not ensure a good educational program. But agreement on goals, whether written or not, is a first step toward adequacy of program and instruction.

Organizational and Administrative Techniques

Obviously, the organizational pattern required for curriculum-making and administration will depend on the size and nature of the institution. The small private college concentrating primarily on a transfer program has a less comprehensive problem than the larger public junior college which, in addition to its program for the transfer student, offers extensive terminal and adult education programs. Because of the variation in size and type of the cooperating institutions, it is impossible to report standard practices. However, as a result of the institutional visits and a study of the administrative plans found in operation, the following generalizations are possible:

Without exception an administrative officer devoted a major part of his time to the curriculum. In 20 out of the 75 institutions, this person was the chief administrative officer of the college. In 45 of the colleges the responsibility was delegated to a person with the title of "dean" (meaning academic dean) or to a person with the title of "dean of instruction" or "director of instruction." In the remaining 10 institutions the responsibility was delegated to administrators with various titles, including "vice president," "registrar," and "coordinator of instruction." In some instances the person in charge of curriculum also had other administrative or teaching responsibilities. Larger institutions used several full-time or part-time administrative assistants for curriculum-planning and supervisory purposes.

Most colleges had some type of departmental organization—usually including a fairly wide scope of subjects, such as business or social science. The authority and released time given to department or division chairmen ranged from supervisory powers and duties with as much as 50 per cent release from teaching time to no released time, with duties limited primarily to assistance in constructing class schedules, communication with teachers, and the like.

An atmosphere of democratic participation in curriculum-building prevailed in the institutions. Some type of faculty curriculum committee existed in practically all colleges visited. Department chairmen and the appropriate administrative officer sometimes constituted the committee, but in most colleges the faculty was also represented. The committee was either a purely advisory body or made decisions regarded as recommendations to the administration or the governing board. Most administrators felt curriculum committees exercised a good control over undue proliferation of courses.

Very little was reported on over-all evaluation of the curriculum, which is not surprising in view of the limited number of institutional studies reported in Chapter 6. The failure of most two-year colleges to evaluate constantly their total program is a serious default. Their failure may be no greater than that of four-year institutions, but it is nonetheless a factor that should be the concern of administration and staff of two-year institutions.

Its variety of students, its close relationship to the local public schools as well as the four-year colleges, and its multiplicity of functions place the junior college in a unique situation and create for its staff a heavy responsibility to plan and implement the most appropriate instructional program. Precedent and practices in other types of institutions are poor guides for a program in a two-year college. Only by considering the local institutional factors can the curriculum-planning be done adequately. This requires faculty-administration cooperation, a great amount of time and effort, and continuous administrative direction. Of all responsibilities that fall on the two-year college, this is the most grave.

The two-year college is indeed performing many functions. Some colleges are truly all things to all people. Some functions are performed better than others, and institutions vary greatly in the extent and nature of their services. This variation is true even among institutions of the same type. The variation among colleges and the deficiencies noted in this chapter indicate some of the problems in providing an appropriate instructional program. Despite the progress made by these colleges as a group in developing a comprehensive program after high school, the need for improving the program and for making good on a number of common claims should concern all connected with the two-year college movement.

CHAPTER 4

The Transfer
and Terminal Functions

To what extent does the junior college serve both as a transfer and as a terminal institution? No question about this institution is asked more frequently and no question is more important in an investigation of the junior college's role in higher education.

That the junior college is generally expected to serve a dual purpose is well established in the literature. Junior college champions have attributed much of its significance—indeed much of its uniqueness—to the fact that, unlike most four-year colleges, it intentionally serves the two-year student as well as the student who expects to attain a baccalaureate degree. Many state study commissions and national agencies have in fact recommended the further development of the junior college on the basis that it does perform both functions.

One of the purposes of this study was to inquire into the relative emphases on the two functions and on the problems which junior colleges face in the discharge of a dual responsibility.

PERCENTAGE OF STUDENTS TRANSFERRING

The most revealing evidence on the actual role of the two-year college is information indicating whether the majority of students entering it terminate their formal education there or transfer to senior colleges. Such information is difficult to obtain. In 1940 Eells arrived at certain data indicating that 75 per cent of the freshmen entering a group of junior colleges in 1937 did not continue their formal education beyond the sophomore year.[1] The data were compiled by a comparison of gross freshmen and sophomore enrollments as reported in the 1939 *Junior College Directory* and by a report from almost four hundred colleges in the 1940 edition of *American Junior Colleges* on the number of 1939 junior college graduates who transferred to a higher institution in the fall immediately after graduation. No information was available on whether the reporting institutions obtained information on the transferring graduates by making a follow-up study or by estimating on the basis of transcripts issued. Also, no allowance was made for the gap which often exists between the time a student leaves junior college and the time he enters a four-year college. A limited number of other smaller studies completed in individual states during the early 1930s showed that the number of students who went beyond junior college ranged from 15 to 20 per cent.

A Study of the 1952 Entering Class in 63 Cooperating Two-year Colleges

Since the number and percentage of students who transfer from two-year colleges could be ascertained best by studying a group of entering students, the cooperating institutions were invited to participate in such a study. Sixty-three[2] institutions accepted the invitation and submitted data in accordance with a uniform research plan designed by the director of the study. The fall, 1952, groups of regular entering day students were selected so that four academic years would elapse before June, 1956, the minimum cut-off date for the study. The institutions enrolled 17,627 beginning regular students in September, 1952. A control card was set up for each student on which was recorded aptitude test data, date of withdrawal (and reason therefor) from junior college, date of graduation, and like matters. Notations were made of all transcripts issued to four-year colleges. By a follow-up to each four-

[1] Walter C. Eells, *Present Status of Terminal Education*, American Association of Junior Colleges, Terminal Education Monograph 2, Washington, 1941, pp. 60–62.

[2] The extension centers in Pennsylvania and Wisconsin were each reported as one, although the six centers in Pennsylvania and the eight in Wisconsin were included.

year college to which a transcript was sent it was possible to find out if the student entered a senior college, whether and when he received his baccalaureate degree, and other pertinent facts about his attendance. It was then possible to determine the percentage of entering students who transferred, the percentage of graduates who transferred, the types of four-year colleges and universities to which students transferred, and facts about the persistence of the transfer students in the institutions to which they transferred.

The median percentage and percentage range of the students entering all two-year colleges in the study who transferred, of the students entering who graduated (from the two-year college), and

Table 4-1. Median and Range of Percentages of Students Entering Two-year Colleges, Fall, 1952—Who Transferred, Entering Who Graduated, and Graduating Who Transferred
(N: Colleges = 63; Students = 17,627)

	Per cent entering students who transferred			Per cent entering students who graduated*			Per cent graduating who transferred*		
	Public	Private	Total	Public	Private	Total	Public	Private	Total
Median	33	42	33	32	57	35	56	58	56
High	67	69	69	73	81	81	87	91	91
Low	10	15	10	11	27	11	10	20	10

*The Pennsylvania and Wisconsin state university centers do not formally graduate students, hence are excluded from columns relating to the records of graduates.

of the graduates who transferred are shown in Table 4-1. Table 4-2 shows a distribution of the colleges by intervals of percentages reported for each of the categories studied. Table 4-3 contains comparable information to Table 4-2 except that it is limited to students in the cooperating public colleges and it shows data for men and women separately. Table 4-4 shows the median and range of percentages of men and women entering all the colleges who transferred and who graduated, together with the percentage of graduates who transferred.

Some caution must be exercised in drawing conclusions from the data contained in the four tables. First, the entering students of only one fall term were studied. Greater reliability undoubtedly would have been achieved by examining the record of additional entering classes, but the time and monetary restrictions of a longitudinal study inevitably limited the sampling. Second, the cut-off date had to be set at a point only four academic years following the date of entrance. Greater validity would have been gained by ex-

Table 4-2. Distribution of Two-year Colleges Reporting Percentages of Students Entering, Fall, 1952—Who Transferred, Who Graduated, and Graduates Who Transferred

(*N*: Colleges = 63; Students = 17,627)

Percentage intervals	No. of 2-year colleges reporting percentages								
	Entering students who transferred			Entering students who graduated*			Graduates who transferred*		
	Public	Private	Total	Public	Private	Total	Public	Private	Total
99–90	—	—	—	—	—	—	—	1	1
89–80	—	—	—	—	1	1	2	—	2
79–70	—	—	—	1	1	2	5	2	7
69–60	3	4	7	4	3	7	14	2	16
59–50	4	—	4	2	2	4	12	2	14
49–40	8	2	10	8	—	8	12	1	13
39–30	17	1	18	14	3	17	1	2	3
29–20	12	3	15	14	1	15	—	1	1
19–10	8	1	9	7	—	7	4	—	4
9–0	—	—	—	—	—	—	—	—	—
Total	52	11	63	50	11	61	50	11	61

* The Pennsylvania and Wisconsin state university centers do not formally graduate students, hence are excluded from columns relating to the record of graduates.

tending the cut-off date. Third, each institution had to make its own interpretation of what constituted a regular entering student and was free to exclude students enrolling for a minimum number of hours for a special course.

To the extent that these limitations permit, the data as summarized in Tables 4-1 to 4-4 indicate that for most students the two-year college was a terminal institution. More specifically, it was found that:

Of the 17,627 regular students who entered some type of two-year college in 1952, only one in every three (33 per cent) had by June, 1956, transferred to a four-year institution.

There were differences between the transfer rates of private and public institutions. In the private institutions 42 per cent transferred, compared with 33 per cent in the public institutions.

Table 4-3. Distribution of Public Two-year Colleges Reporting Percentages
of Men and Women Entering, Fall, 1952—Who Transferred,
Who Graduated, and Graduating Who Transferred
(*N*: Colleges = 63; Students = 17,627)

| Percentage intervals | No. of 2-year colleges reporting percentages | | | | | |
| | Entering students who transferred | | Entering students who graduated* | | Graduates who transferred* | |
	Men	Women	Men	Women	Men	Women
99–90	—	—	—	—	1	1
89–80	1	—	—	1	4	4
79–70	1	—	1	2	9	3
69–60	2	1	3	4	8	6
59–50	4	4	3	3	15	12
49–40	12	5	7	8	9	8
39–30	17	15	15	11	—	6
29–20	8	13	16	12	1	4
19–10	7	9	5	8	3	3
9–0	—	5	—	1	—	3
Total	52	52	50	50	50	50

* The Pennsylvania and Wisconsin state university centers do not formally graduate students, hence are excluded from columns relating to the record of graduates.

As would be expected, the percentage of junior college graduates who transferred was higher than the percentage of entering students who transferred. The median percentage of graduates who transferred was 56 as compared with 33 per cent of the entering students.

There was a great range among institutions, both public and private, in terms of the percentage of students transferring, thus indicating the diverse nature of the institutions and their student populations. The range was somewhat greater in public colleges than in private ones. Among the public colleges the range of entering students who transferred was from 10 to 67 per cent, in the private institutions from 15 to 69 per cent. For graduates transferring the range in the public institutions was from 10 to 82 per cent, for private colleges from 20 to 91 per cent.

Although not reflected in the tables, there were interesting differences in the transfer rate among institutions according to type of control.

The median percentage of students transferring from local and state junior colleges was almost exactly 33 per cent. This figure

Table 4-4. Median and Range of Percentages of Men and Women Entering
Two-year Colleges, Fall, 1952—Who Transferred, Entering
Who Graduated, and Graduating Who Transferred
(N: Colleges = 63; Students = 17,627)

	Per cent entering students who transferred		Per cent entering students who graduated*		Per cent graduating who transferred*	
	Men	Women	Men	Women	Men	Women
Median	36	30	32	33	58	50
High	81	67	74	80	100	100
Low	10	1	11	8	10	1

*The Pennsylvania and Wisconsin state university centers do not formally graduate students, hence are excluded from columns relating to the record of graduates.

was in contrast to 63 per cent of students entering extension centers who transferred. The academically oriented institutions transferred a median of 62 per cent of their students, the comprehensive junior colleges 33 per cent, and the technically oriented schools 16 per cent. These data are not surprising because the extension centers and academic junior colleges are geared to prepare their students to attend senior institutions. The terminal nature of the technical institutions is evidenced by the fact that they had the highest proportion of graduates (65 per cent of their entering students) and yet the lowest proportion of transfer students. The dual nature of the comprehensive junior college is manifested by the large but less-than-majority number of students it sends to senior college.

Of the students entering, 36 per cent of the men transferred as contrasted to 30 per cent of the women. About the same percentages of men and women were graduated from the junior colleges, but 58 per cent of the men graduates transferred as contrasted to 50 per cent of the women graduates.

Another matter with which the study was concerned is the tendency of students entering two-year colleges to be graduated from them. In this respect it was not possible for the summary to include data from the Pennsylvania and Wisconsin extension centers, because neither university formally graduates students from the centers by awarding them a two-year degree. The University of Wisconsin reported that approximately 24 per cent of the students entering the centers remain for two years. Since the university also reported that 51 per cent of the center students transfer, it is apparent that a large percentage of the students transfer before two years—presumably at the end of one year. Pennsylvania reported that between 20 and 30 per cent of the students in its centers complete two years and then transfer to the main campus. Many of the specialized courses are not taught in the centers, and students registered in some curricula may remain in the centers only one year. In other curricula, such as engineering, they may stay only one year and a half. For all other public two-year colleges the median percentage of entrants who fulfilled graduation requirements was 32 as compared with 58 per cent in private institutions. Again, the wide range among institutions should be noted.

The fact that only a third of those entering public two-year colleges and slightly fewer than three-fifths of those entering private junior colleges were graduated provokes questions concerning the holding power of both types of junior colleges. Two-year college personnel have several explanations of the situation. One is that many entering students have definite short-term personal or vocational goals which are satisfied in less than the two-year period. Also, some students transfer to senior colleges before completing the two-year period. A sizable number of students complete two years in the junior college but do not choose to satisfy the graduation requirements.

The foregoing data on the percentage of students graduating from the two-year college do not permit a precise comparison with those reported by Iffert, but from his study of retention and withdrawal of college students it is interesting to note the extent to which students in four-year institutions were found to attend only two years or less.[3] In the public institutions in the Iffert study 46.6 per cent and in the private institutions 36.6 per cent did not go beyond two years. Clearly, the factor of drop-outs exists in all types of collegiate institutions. The four-year public college also becomes a terminal institution for almost half of its students by the end of the first two years. Considering the difference in function in the two types of colleges, it is incorrect to assume that attrition is more serious in the two-year than in the four-year institution.

TYPES OF FOUR-YEAR COLLEGES TO WHICH STUDENTS TRANSFERRED

Table 4-5 shows that by far the majority of transfers from both public and private two-year colleges matriculated in public four-year colleges or public universities. The public four-year college and the public university each enrolled approximately a third

Table 4-5. Types of Higher Institutions to Which 5,356* Students Entering Two-year Colleges in September, 1952, Subsequently Transferred

Transferred from	Transferred to							
	4-year public college		4-year private college		Public university		Private university	
	No.	Per cent	No.	Per cent	No.	Per cent	No.	Per cent
Public 2-year institutions	1,576	33	607	13	1,882	40	639	14
Private 2-year institutions	141	22	120	18	256	39	135	21
Total	1,717	32	727	14	2,138	40	774	14

* This figure does not correspond with the total number of students known to have transferred because the types of institutions to which all students transferred were not reported.

of the transfers. Students from private junior colleges had a slightly greater tendency to transfer to private four-year colleges than did the students from the public two-year colleges, but even they were much more inclined to go to public than to private institutions.

[3] Robert E. Iffert, *Retention and Withdrawal of College Students,* U.S. Department of Health, Education, and Welfare Bulletin 1, 1958, p. 16.

The reason why transfer students enroll in greater numbers in public senior institutions than in private institutions is probably economic. If many students attend junior college because they cannot afford to go elsewhere, they would most likely decide to complete their undergraduate work in a public institution where costs are usually less than in private colleges. Even the students who attend private junior colleges may feel the need for economy in their last two years of college. With them, however, the decision may be more on the basis of desiring a large public institution in contrast to the smaller, more intimate type in which they have spent two years.

STUDENT ASPIRATIONS AT THE POINT OF ENTERING TWO-YEAR COLLEGES

The student's distribution among curricula depends in large measure on their intention to transfer. Officials in each of the institutions visited were asked about the tendencies of students to indicate their expectations. Administrators in technical institutes reported that most students entering declare their intention of preparing for a job and of going directly into employment upon leaving the institute. Despite this declaration, some students transfer. The few junior colleges in the study which regard themselves as wholly preparatory institutions naturally enroll only those students who plan to transfer, although not all do. With few exceptions, the large number of institutions which claim to offer a comprehensive program serving both terminal and transfer students reported that between two-thirds and three-fourths of the entering students indicate that they expect to transfer. This, it seemed, was true regardless of the number and type of terminal offerings in the institution.

In most two-year colleges at least two-thirds of the entering students say they will transfer yet the study of those who entered in 1952 revealed that only one-third of them did transfer. This fact poses some interesting questions. It could be asked whether this discrepancy is good or bad. It may be that the junior college plays an important role in causing students to become realistic about their goals and in screening those who should not continue in college beyond two years. On the other hand, it may be that the junior college fails to encourage many able students to continue with a baccalaureate program and thus is derelict in this responsibility.

The data outlined above have serious implications for the student personnel program in two-year colleges. Only to the extent that everything possible is done to help each student determine the goals and program most appropriate for him will the junior college perform the unusual distributing function expected of it. This cannot be accomplished without intensive personal contacts between qualified counselors and students, and a college that is short-suited on counselor time is undoubtedly short-suiting its students. (See Chapter 6.)

THE RELATION OF ACADEMIC APTITUDE TO STUDENT OUTCOMES

Important as it is to know the percentage of entering students who graduate and who transfer from junior college, it is equally important to reflect on the factors which have a bearing on such outcomes. Obviously, there are many possible determinants that singly and collectively may account for what happens to students after admission to junior college. Though academic aptitude is not necessarily the most important factor, it is desirable to observe its relation to graduation rates, transfer tendency, and the extent to which baccalaureate degrees are eventually attained.

Information on the relation of the aptitude of beginning students to their history after entering was obtained, by an analysis made in the Center of information recorded on the individual control cards used by 31 of the two-year colleges. These accounted for more than six thousand students who entered the colleges in September, 1952. The 31 colleges were distributed among 12 states and were representative of many sizes and types of institutions. Data were used only from those colleges whose control cards included ACE total scores or scores from other tests which could be equated with ACE. All scores were converted to an equivalent of the 1949 edition of ACE.

The results of the study are summarized below to answer several basic questions. The facts are presented solely as representative of the *particular institutions in the sample* and only for the purpose of showing relationships between ability and outcomes. No judgments are implied in this section on such matters as (1) the ability level of students who should be admitted to the junior college or (2) who should be accepted for transfer.

What is the relation of academic aptitude to the probability of graduation from junior college? A comparison of the mean scores of entering students who graduated with those who did not indicates that ability, as measured by an aptitude instrument, is important in predicting probability of graduation. Table 4-6 (columns 6 and 7) shows that mean scores of the graduates were higher by 9 points than those of the nongraduates.

Similar results were obtained by a study[4] in Minnesota of al-

Table 4-6. Mean ACE Scores of Junior College Transfer and Terminal Students by Graduate and Nongraduate Groups

	Transfer			Terminal			Total	
	Graduate	Non-graduate	Total	Graduate	Non-graduate	Total	Graduate	Non-graduate
Mean	103	99	101.67	95.15	87.59	90.47	99.54	90.40
Standard deviation	26.20	20.91	24.43	26.74	29.57	25.67	24.60	25.70
Range	18–176	15–184	15–184	14–193	10–172	10–193	14–193	10–184
Number	1,154	839	1,993	1,204	3,002	4,206	2,358	3,841

most 650 students who entered the 10 junior colleges in that state in September, 1952. In this study the graduates were compared with the students who withdrew. As measured by both rank in high school class and scores made on the ACE, the ability of the students who graduated was higher than that of those who withdrew, although there was great overlap between the two groups. The graduates attained a mean ACE score of 109, 4 points above the mean score of 102 attained by the withdrawals; the high school percentile rank of the graduates was 64, 6 points above the percentile rank of 52 attained by the transfer students who withdrew.

Comparisons of differences in ability between graduates and nongraduates may not be as significant for junior colleges as for four-year colleges because some students entering the junior college do not intend to graduate. As was indicated in the preceding

[4] John G. Darley, "Factors Associated with College Careers in Minnesota," unpublished manuscript, Center for the Study of Higher Education, Berkeley, 1959, table 4.

section, students may attain their educational objective without graduating. They may transfer, even with as many as 60 units of credit, and still not meet junior college graduation requirements, or they may go into employment. On the other hand, the substantial differences in the mean scores of the two groups would suggest that it is the less able student who tends to drop out of junior college. Thus, the over-all data on abilities are important aids in program planning, counseling, projecting enrollment, and a host of other institutional concerns.

What is the relation of academic aptitude to the tendency of junior college students to transfer? Of the students who entered the 31 colleges, approximately 2,000 transferred to senior colleges and the remainder of more than 4,200 terminated their formal education with the junior college. Table 4-6 shows that the mean score of the students who transferred was more than 11 points higher than of those who did not transfer. The data in Table 4-6 are also arranged to show the number and the mean scores of both the transfer and terminal groups according to whether they were graduated from the junior college. Of the students who transferred, 1,154 were graduates. The mean ACE score for this group was 103. A total of 839 students transferred without being graduated and the mean score of this group was 99.

By far the greatest proportion of students who did not transfer were nongraduates, and their mean score (87.59) was lower by nearly 8 points than the mean score (95.15) of students who graduated but did not transfer. The differences between these two groups may indicate that the lower-ability students simply dropped out of school, whereas the higher-ability students who graduated were those who followed a two-year program leading to a specific occupational outlet.

The differences in ability between the students who transferred and the ones who did not may not be surprising, but they hold implications for counselors, teachers, and administrators. In a sense, they can serve as a general predictor of likelihood of transfer. Note must also be taken of the great overlap in ability of the two groups as indicated by the range of scores and by the high standard deviations. Thus, while it may be safe to generalize that it is the students of higher ability who tend to transfer, it is the individual student who must be considered in the counseling and programing process.

What is the apparent relation of aptitude to attainment of a baccalaureate degree? Information bearing on this question is found in Table 4-7. Of the 1,993 students who transferred from junior college to senior college regardless of whether they were graduated from junior college, 748 had obtained the bachelor's degree by June, 1956, the cut-off date of the study; 493 were still in residence in the four-year college; and 700 had dropped out. As might be expected, the aptitude level of those who completed the requirements for the degree in the normal time was higher than the aptitude level of those who had not attained the degree.

Table 4-7. Ability of Junior College Transfer Students by ACE Means According to Different Levels of Achievement

	Students who graduated	Students still in residence	Students who dropped out
Mean	108	100	99
Standard deviation	19.60	24.50	22.86
Range	44–177	23–169	15–168
Number	748*	493	700

* Minus 52 nurses, making total N = 1,993.

Mean scores were also obtained according to the major subject fields of 748 transfers who completed requirements for a bachelor's degree in the four-year period (Table 4-8). Engineering majors headed the list and exceeded the lowest group (agriculture) by 29 points. Other than engineering, the groups with scores higher than the mean of 108 for the entire group were those in the liberal arts category. The large number of students with majors in business and education and the fact that both groups had the same mean score of 103 should be noted. An analysis of variance showed the differences in means for the various subject groups to be significant well beyond the 1 per cent level.

To what types of four-year institutions do junior college students of different aptitude levels transfer? As noted earlier in this chapter, about a third of the students in the 1952 class who transferred went to public four-year colleges and 40 per cent went to public universities. With the procurement of aptitude data it was possible to determine what differences existed among the students who transferred to various types of four-year institutions. Table 4-9 shows that the students from the 31 colleges, like those in all the colleges in the study, transferred predominantly to public four-year colleges and universities. The mean scores of the students who transferred to four-year colleges, public or private, were about the same—96 and 98. Likewise, there was little difference in the aptitude of those who entered public universities and those who entered private universities. However, the transfers entering universities of either type had mean scores several points in excess of those who entered four-year colleges.

Table 4-8. Mean Scores of Transfer Students Who Earned Bachelors' Degrees According to Various Majors
(*N's* from 31 junior colleges)

Major	Mean	No.	Sigma
Engineering	122	60	23.50
Communication arts	119	11	19.60
Liberal arts	117	110	24.40
Natural science	113	38	17.20
Social science	111	53	25.40
Fine arts	110	27	16.40
General	106	13	24.00
Home economics	106	19	23.70
Business	103	127	22.60
Education	103	184	21.00
Industrial arts	103	10	26.90
Miscellaneous	101	16	18.60
Medical	101	12	24.40
Social service	101	7	22.50
Physical education	97	38	20.70
Agriculture	94	23	24.35
Total	108	748	19.60

There is a positive relationship between student aptitude and achievement. The colleges which had the greatest proportion of more able students according to ACE scores tended also to have the greatest percentage of students graduating, transferring, and obtaining baccalaureate degrees. (A coefficient of concordance of .581 was obtained, significant beyond the 1 per cent level.) The highest single relationship existed between the ability of the stu-

Table 4-9. ACE Means of Junior College Transfers to Four-year Public
and Private Colleges and Universities
(N = 1,988)

	4-year college		University	
	Public	Private	Public	Private
Mean	96	98	108	106
Standard deviation	24.52	24.80	24.85	22.11
Range	18–169	15–169	41–184	42–168
Number	779	267	677	265

dents and the extent to which they graduated from junior college. (A rank difference correlation coefficient of .619 was obtained.)

There were exceptions to this high correlation which could generally be explained. For example, one college with a high mean score for its freshmen rated low in terms of the percentage of students who transferred, mostly because it was a technical institute and its students did not plan to seek the baccalaureate degree.

ENROLLMENTS IN TERMINAL AND TRANSFER PROGRAMS

A good index of the emphasis that an institution places on specific functions is the types of programs offered and the extent to which students distribute themselves among curricula. Responses from the 243 institutions that completed the original check list indicated that a total of 79 different specialized terminal programs was offered, many of them by only a few colleges. Since such a list was too unwieldy to report in one table, only programs offered in six or more colleges were selected for presentation in Table 4-10, which also shows the number of states in which each program was offered and the approximate total enrollment in each field. Some institutions reported that they offered certain programs but omitted enrollment data, making it necessary to account for them separately in column 4 and to regard the enrollment data in column 3 as approximate.

The field of business decidedly heads the list, both in terms of the institutions offering terminal programs and enrollments. A total of 163 colleges reported business programs as compared with

Table 4-10. Approximate Enrollments in Curricula Designated as Terminal
in Two-year Institutions in 15 States, 1955–56

Curricula	States represented	Colleges offering curricula	Approximate enrollments reported	Institutions reporting curricula but not enrollments
Business	14	163	25,684	19
Agriculture	9	66	2,322	11
Engineering aide	11	64	7,202	10
Homemaking	10	63	1,724	7
Auto, diesel mechanics	8	61	2,334	10
Nursing	9	54	1,438	9
Electronics	9	50	2,508	6
Radio, TV	10	45	1,112	14
Secretarial	11	42	925	8
Machine shop	6	43	904	8
Laboratory technician	10	42	744	9
Commercial art	8	37	1,151	5
Electrical shop	6	31	728	8
Welding	6	28	522	8
Photography	4	24	407	2
Graphic arts	6	24	404	4
Drafting, design	6	23	771	7
Dental assisting	6	23	975	4
Aviation	4	20	1,029	3
Air conditioning, refrigeration	6	20	701	3
Building trades	6	18	499	4
Peace officer training	3	17	1,002	4
Printing	2	16	408	3
Merchandising	8	15	491	1
Sheet metal	3	15	88	6
Elementary education	7	15	479	4
Cosmetology	2	14	573	3
Recreational leadership	5	14	88	6
Carpentry	3	14	151	2
General education	10	14	3,121	3
Mill and cabinet	4	11	162	1
Clothing, tailoring	4	9	590	—
Medical secretary	6	9	200	1
Music	5	8	49	2
Architecture	3	7	128	1
Fine arts	5	7	58	4
Woodwork	4	7	40	4
Restaurant, hotel management	2	6	439	—
Petroleum	3	6	165	2
Nursery education	3	6	85	4
Journalism	2	6	30	2

66 colleges offering agriculture, which ranked second in frequency of offering (but sixth in enrollments). Business enrollments approximate total enrollments in all other fields. If the enrollments that relate to the engineering field were added (such as electronics and drafting), they would easily rank second in frequency, both in number of offerings and enrollments. Special attention is called to the curriculum "engineering aide," reported by 64 colleges in 11 states, with an enrollment of more than seven thousand students. Notice is also called to the category "general education," which is a term for a general curriculum offered in certain institutions for students who have no specific vocational goals yet do not indicate the, intension of transferring. Elementary education was listed as a terminal program by 15 institutions in 7 states. Although work at the two-year college level in education is not generally considered to be terminal, the program is so classified by these institutions because in some states persons with two years in such a curriculum may be certificated to teach.

A more restricted and precise analysis of enrollments in terminal programs and a comparison of how this number compares with those in transfer programs were made of students in 70 of the cooperating institutions for the fall term, 1956. As indicated in Chapter 3, it is difficult to categorize students or to describe them as pursuing a transfer or a terminal program. Although some junior colleges label the subjects they consider to be transferable, the final decision as to their transferability depends on the institution which must finally evaluate the credits. Also, students may be enrolled in hybrid programs—taking some subjects that will transfer and others that may not. Students' vocational objectives are constantly shifting, which means that even if they are classified in one curriculum one semester, they may be in a different program the following semester. Students enrolled in certain structured, definitely labeled, vocational programs in the trades can be considered terminal; but the higher on the semiprofessional scale or the more general the program is, the greater is the difficulty in determining the category.

With these difficulties in mind, the cooperating institutions were asked to analyze the number of students in the total transfer program and those in *each* of the terminal programs for September, 1956, and to do so on one of two bases: (1) those institutions in which the classification of curricula was considered sufficiently rigid

Table 4-11. Enrollments or Declared Majors of Students According to Transfer and Terminal Programs in 70 Two-year Institutions, Fall, 1956

	Total enrollments			Transfer-program enrollments			Transfer programs, per cent of total enrollments			Terminal-program enrollments			Terminal programs, per cent of total enrollments		
	Public	Private	Total	Public	Private	Total	Public	Private	Total	Public	Private	Total	Public	Private	Total
California	28,326	335	28,661	19,058	335	19,393	67	100	68	9,268	—	9,268	33	—	32
Georgia	792	—	792	576	—	576	73	—	73	216	—	216	27	—	27
Illinois	4,243	491	4,734	2,743	434	3,177	64	88	67	1,500	57	1,557	36	12	33
Iowa	717	642	1,359	690	506	1,196	96	79	88	27	136	163	4	21	12
Massachusetts	242	1,229	1,471	186	981	1,167	77	80	79	56	248	304	23	20	21
Minnesota	570	288	858	356	288	644	62	100	75	214	—	214	38	—	25
Mississippi	2,222	—	2,222	1,587	—	1,587	71	—	71	635	—	635	29	—	29
New York	5,050	162	5,212	284	71	355	6	44	7	4,766	91	4,857	94	56	93
North Carolina	970	1,303	2,273	753	1,205	1,958	78	92	86	217	98	315	22	8	14
Ohio	—	298	298	—	—	—	—	—	—	—	298	298	—	100	—
Oklahoma	1,503	—	1,503	1,354	—	1,354	90	—	90	149	—	149	10	—	10
Oregon	1,017	—	1,017	—	—	—	—	—	—	1,017	—	1,017	100	—	100
Pennsylvania	886	600	1,486	470	471	941	53	79	63	416	129	545	47	21	37
Texas	6,214	115	6,329	5,231	115	5,346	84	100	84	983	—	983	16	—	16
Wisconsin	1,524	—	1,524	1,524	—	1,524	100	—	100	—	—	—	—	—	—
Total	54,276	5,463	59,739	34,812	4,406	39,218	64	81	66	19,464	1,057	20,521	36	19	34

to determine enrollments by specific curricula were asked to report accordingly, and (2) those institutions which did not or could not make such a definite breakdown were asked to report the number of students who, at the time, had declared their educational goals to be either transfer or terminal and were pursuing a program accordingly.

The resulting information from 70 institutions reported in Table 4-11, classified according to states and types of control, indicates the relatively small percentage of students who were pursuing terminal programs. Of the students enrolled in these colleges for the semester indicated, one-third were pursuing terminal programs and two-thirds were enrolled in the transfer program. The transfer enrollments were higher in private colleges than in public institutions, the percentage of transfer and terminal enrollments in private colleges being 81 and 19, as compared with 64 and 36 in the public institutions. The heavy emphasis indicated in certain states was occasioned by the types of institutions in the sample. In both Ohio and Oregon, for example, the only cooperating colleges were technical institutes. In Wisconsin, the only participants were extension centers, and they offered only preparatory work. In New York, one of the cooperating colleges was a state technical and agricultural institute, and two of the other three public institutions were community colleges specializing primarily in technical curricula. But even in the individual technical institutes studied, from 10 to 33 per cent of those entering and from 10 to 43 per cent of the graduates transferred.

The great range among the private institutions could normally be expected because one such college was a technical institute and several others offered only a transfer program. However, the range was also great among the several private institutions of the same general type, that is, women's colleges, men's colleges, and coeducational institutions.

An analysis of students enrolled in specific terminal programs in the 70 cooperating institutions showed a slightly different rank order of enrollments by fields than was true of the larger sample of all responding schools in the 15 states. The largest single group in the 70 institutions was a category that included all the various technological subjects running from semiprofessional to skilled-trade instruction. The second largest category was in business training.

The other categories, in order of size, were (1) students classified as terminal in general or miscellaneous programs, (2) other semi-professions, and (3) medical semiprofessions, including laboratory technicians, vocational nurses, and medical and dental assistants.

Although not requested to submit a breakdown of student majors in transfer curricula, 21 cooperating institutions nevertheless volunteered such information. Since these colleges constituted a fairly complete range in size and geographical distribution, and since

Table 4-12. Transfer Enrollments by Curricula in 21 Junior Colleges, Fall, 1956

Curriculum or major field	Enrollments	Per cent
Engineering	2,005	21
Liberal arts	1,476	16
Education	1,423	15
Business	1,395	15
Medical, premedical, medical technician	767	8
General, miscellaneous	484	5
Natural science	418	4
Fine arts	271	3
Agriculture and forestry	198	3
Social science	201	2
Law	197	2
Communication arts, drama, TV, etc.	141	2
Physical education	120	1
Home economics	109	1
Industrial arts	69	1
Criminology	54	1
Total	9,328	100

together they reported more than nine thousand transfer students, the distribution of majors according to curriculum reported by them is probably reasonably representative. According to Table 4-12, the largest group of preprofessional students—one-fifth of the total—was in engineering. The liberal arts group ranked second, and students preparing for education third. The fact that engineering and education majors were high on the list is indicative of the contribution made by the two-year college to fields in which acute shortages have been the subject of much national discussion.

OTHER STUDIES RELATING TO THE TERMINAL FUNCTION

Two studies of national scope recently completed by other agencies bear on the role of the two-year institution in preparing students for employment and supplement the data in the preceding pages. The first study was conducted under the auspices of the American Society for Engineering Education. This study grew out of the society's concern for the work of and required training for the engineering technician. In the definition of terms developed for the design of the study, "technical institute type of education" was defined as follows:

> The term refers to the intermediate strata of technological curricula which are of from 1 to 3 years duration (full-time) beyond the high-school level. Curricula are technological in nature, and they differ in both content and purpose from those of the vocational school on the one hand, and from those of the engineering college on the other hand.
>
> Such curricula emphasize the understanding of basic principles of mathematics and science, rather than the acquisition of manual skills. High-school graduation is required for admission, and mathematics through algebra and geometry usually are prerequisite.
>
> The programs of instruction are similar in nature to, but briefer and more completely technical in content than, professional curriculums. The major purpose is to prepare individuals for various technical positions or specialized areas of activity encompassed within the broad field of engineering enterprise.[5]

The plan of the study called for a contact with institutions of higher learning offering less than four-year programs designed for the preparation of engineering technicians. In addition to surveying the field by questionnaires, representatives of industry and education visited a number of institutions and sought to determine the ways in which they prepare technicians and also the demands of local industry with respect to technicians. One of many items of information emanating from the study referred to the number and types of technical engineering programs offered and enrollments in them. In the final report of this study, the following statement is

[5] *The National Survey of Technical Institute Education, 1956–57*, pamphlet issued by the American Society for Engineering Education.

made concerning the role of the junior college in preparing technicians:

> The junior and community college in the pattern of education beyond the high school also holds considerable potential for technical-institute education. It must be emphasized however, that this potential is in large measure distinctly in the future, and that its effective development depends upon some effective reorientation of traditional concept and philosophy. With some notable exceptions, Survey findings reveal that most of the approximately 650 junior and community colleges of the U.S. are dedicated to, or at least preoccupied with, preparatory programs designed for college transfer and these preponderantly in the field of "liberal arts" or "general" subject matter. From this academic extremity, many of these schools jump to the opposite extremity of vocational and shop courses featuring the development of manual skills. Most such schools have left untouched the intervening area of curricula designed to develop occupational proficiency in the engineering and related technologies. In some instances there have been casual and ineffective attempts to serve this area through modifying general curricula or shop courses through the injection of some scattered courses in science and/or mathematics.
>
> However, analysis of Survey data reveals some 46 institutions in the junior-community college category to be doing significant work in the area of technical-institute education. Of these, one has curricula accredited by ECPD, and the remainder probably could qualify if they were interested and authorized. Even so, and making further allowances for the fact that technical-institute education is not necessarily a logical or productive enterprise for every junior or community college, the future potential of this class of institution is considerable and of especial significance in view of the "tidal wave" of students expected at the college level during the next decade.[6]

The second study bearing on the topic of occupational programs was made by Armsby, Eells, and Martorana of the U.S. Office of Education in 1957.[7] The purpose of this study was to de-

[6] G. Ross Henninger, director, National Survey of Technical Institute Education, American Society for Engineering Education, *The Technical Institute in America*, McGraw-Hill Book Company, Inc., New York, 1959.

[7] Henry W. Armsby et al., "Organized Occupational Curriculums: Enrollments and Graduates, 1956," *Higher Education*, vol. 14, no. 4, Washington, December, 1957.

termine enrollments and 1956 graduates in programs of the type commonly considered terminal and defined by the authors as having *all* the following four criteria:

High school graduation (or equivalent, including maturity) is required for admission to the curriculum.

The curriculum is designed to prepare students for *immediate employment* in an occupation or cluster of occupations, rather than for further advanced study leading to a bachelor's or higher degree.

Completion of the curriculum requires *at least one but less than four years* of full-time (or equivalent) attendance. A "year" means an academic year of approximately nine months.

The curriculum leads to a certificate, diploma, associate degree, or other *formal award*, signifying that the student has completed an *organized* curriculum in an occupational area.

Questionnaires were sent to 1,886 higher institutions. Returns were received from more than 94 per cent of the four-year institutions and almost 90 per cent of the two-year institutions, which would have included most if not all two-year institutions in the Berkeley study. A total of 348 of the four-year colleges and 312 of the two-year colleges reported data on organized occupational curricula. On the basis of these returns the following summaries were made:

Of the institutions responding to the inquiry, more than two-thirds of the two-year colleges reported that they offered terminal programs.

Of the almost 96,000 full-time enrollments in such programs in all institutions, approximately half were in two-year institutions.

Of the more than 144,000 total enrollments (full-time and part-time), approximately 40 per cent were in engineering-related curricula and 60 per cent in curricula not related to engineering.

Although differences in sample and lack of specific data make it impossible to compare in detail the findings of the U.S. Office of Education study with those of the study herein reported, it would appear that the results are similar. About the same percentage of the two-year institutions in each study reported that they offered terminal programs. The approximately forty-eight thousand full-time enrollments in occupational programs in two-year institutions reported in the U.S. Office of Education study can hardly represent more than one-third of the total full-time enrollment in the 312 two-year colleges that submitted the data, and it will be recalled that one-third of the students in the cooperating colleges were enrolled in terminal curricula. The proportion of students enrolled in engineering-related programs was high in both studies.

OBSERVATIONS AND CONCLUSIONS

It is obvious from the data presented that the two-year college in America is focused more on the transfer than the terminal function. If, then, the institution is adjudged unique solely on the basis of its special services to students who do not transfer, it fails to measure up. It is paradoxical that, in the institutions studied, about two-thirds of the students prepared to transfer yet, from a given entering class, only one-third of them actually went beyond the junior college. Conversely, only a third of the students were enrolled in courses which ostensibly prepared them for employment, yet two-thirds of them went into some type of life activity without further college experience.

Although the relationship between students transferring and the courses they pursue in junior college may be significant, the over-all proportions must not be applied to individual institutions or to different types of institutions. There were differences among the several types of colleges in the sample as indicated by the high and low points in the range of percentages in Tables 4-1 and 4-4 as well as the distributions of percentages in Tables 4-2 and 4-3.

But even after noting the exceptions, the evidence indicating the relatively light emphasis by the two-year college on the terminal function calls for some analysis of the situation and some reevaluation either of the curricula offered or of the claims made for the two-year college.

In making such an analysis the central question is not whether students should transfer from the two-year college. In fact, there is no bench mark in American higher education that provides a standard of how many people should attend college for two years or less or for more than two years. The junior college may well perform a maximum service if only a third of its students transfer.

A more fundamental question is what the junior college should do for the students who *do not* transfer. On this point the matter is not simplified by a value judgment that the two-year college falls short of its obligation by not offering more work of an occupational nature, however true that may be in certain instances. Rather, the inquiry leads to a consideration of (1) values placed by students and parents on types of college education and (2) the type of education that has the greatest value for the terminal student.

Administrators, counselors, and teachers in most of the two-year colleges visited agreed that no matter how hard an institution endeavors to effect a terminal occupational program, it is difficult to interest students in the program except in highly specialized institutions. One reason for this difficulty is the prestige values that pertain to "regular" college work. Students and parents tend to place high social values on education leading to a baccalaureate degree, even if they know that attaining such a degree is unlikely. One might even presume that such an attitude would cause students not in terminal vocational programs to look down on those who are, but happily this did not appear to be true in the institutions visited. The principal explanation for small enrollments in terminal offerings seems not to be a disdain for occupational training but simply a cultural factor that causes students to covet the reputation of being a preparatory student. Undoubtedly, too, many cling to the transfer program even when they know they may need soon to go to work because they think that some day they may be able to pursue a degree—as well they may. Unfortunately, too, many students were not informed in high school about terminal programs and the occupations to which they lead, and thus have not had the occasion to become interested in such programs when they entered the junior college.

Many problems concerning a terminal program—some of which result in the attitudes mentioned in the preceding paragraphs —arise from an honest disagreement over what should constitute such a program. Administrators and faculty in the two-year colleges differ from one institution to another on this question. Staff members in certain junior colleges expressed the belief that the regular lower-division program prepares students for employment as well or better than do specialized vocational curricula. For example, the staff of a private junior college (with many characteristics of a community college) in a highly industrialized city in Massachusetts reported that local industry supported its view that the standard engineering curriculum constitutes the best means of preparing engineering technicians who go to work at the end of two years. Officials said that industry placed great stress on fundamentals and was willing to teach the specifics required after the worker was employed. The opposite was reported by staff members in other institutions who said that employers are more interested in highly specialized skills than in general background. A compromise opinion was more often expressed—an opinion that the occupational program in the two-year college must be a combination of skills, theory, and some general education (the amount and kind recommended varying greatly among the colleges), organized on what is often referred to as a "semiprofessional" or "technical institute" level.

It is evident that employers do not agree on what constitutes the best preparation for a job. There is often little unanimity on this subject among industries or companies or even among personnel at various managerial levels in the same company. Advisory committees are helpful to a junior college in planning an occupational program, but care must be taken to have a cross section of employers on a committee if all points of view are to be represented.

There has been much discussion in recent years about the training of technicians, particularly in two-year colleges. Again, the colleges have not always been sure—nor are they yet—as to what a technician is or of what his training should consist. The Engineering Council for Professional Development has prepared definitions and many studies (including the one just completed for the American Society for Engineering Education) have further identified the need for such definitions. All this is of assistance to the colleges. Another task to be performed, however, is that of convincing promising high school graduates that it may be wise for them to prepare as technicians. Industry will have to carry its share in publicizing the need and future for technicians if the idea is to take hold.

A major difficulty in planning technical-vocational programs in the future may be related to some of the reasons for the decline of vocational education at the secondary level. Rapidly increasing mechanization and automation demand much more than mechanical skills. Further, they make it impossible for an educational institution of any kind to duplicate the costly and highly intricate machines and techniques of a rapidly changing industry. Without doubt vocational-technical education of the future must provide for broad backgrounds in applied mathematics and science, the art of communication, and an understanding of people. It must also promote cooperative ventures with industry which can make its irreplaceable facilities the laboratory of the school.

A good example of an apparently effective cooperative program currently exists in the Erie County Technical Institute at Buffalo, New York. There cooperative programs have been established in the following curricula: building technology, electrical technology, industrial chemistry, industrial technology, mechanical technology, and metallurgical technology. Students are assigned to cooperative programs under a uniform pattern. They work in pairs so that two students fill one job for an entire year. This is accomplished by having the first- and second-year classes divided into two groups or sections. Students in section 1 attend school for the first two quarters or 24 weeks. They then spend 12 weeks in a cooperative job. At the end of their 12 weeks they return to the institute and the students in section 2 go into industry for 12 weeks, taking up the positions previously held by the students in section 1. Thus at the end of the first year each section will have had three quarters in school and one quarter in industry.

At the beginning of the second year, section 1 again spends 12 weeks in the cooperative jobs while section 2 is in school. When section 1 returns to school, section 2 goes into industry. During the remainder of the senior year both sections are in the institute.

Cooperative contacts are made by department heads who are responsible for student guidance and placement. They determine the student's suitability for a specific position on the basis of his institute record, the results of aptitude tests, and the reports received from the student's classroom and laboratory instructors. The department head makes a study of the various job requirements. He analyzes the job to determine its needs and training possibilities, and on the basis of all the information available tries to match the student's abilities with the job requirements.

During the cooperative employment period the department head, through assignments and reports, guides the student's observation of plant procedure and assists him in relating his practical experience to his technical studies. He secures reports from the cooperative employer relative to the student's ability and character. Reports indicating unsatisfactory progress on the part of the student are followed up by the department head and remedial measures are recommended. Officials of the institute reported that institute and industry are highly satisfied with the program.

A highly developed formal cooperative program is also in operation at Ohio Mechanics Institute in Cincinnati. Somewhat less ambitious programs exist in a few other institutions. In general, however, the two-year colleges in the study were making relatively little use of work experience except in an informal way.

Junior colleges have many internal problems with respect to developing terminal programs. Many interviewed were willing to admit that the institutions themselves are partly to blame for the lack of emphasis on terminal work. The unwillingness of some staff members to accept the comprehensive function of the junior college and not merely give lip service to it, the prestige values attached to the more conventional college program, and the extra effort and finances required to implement an occupational program—all to some extent explain this situation. The result is that programs of this kind often are not undertaken, are poorly planned, and poorly explained to the public and the students. Reference will be made in Chapter 6 to the role of counseling in connection with the success of a terminal program. Suffice it to say here that although counseling is by no means the only critical item, a terminal program can hardly be expected to function without a good guidance program.

The small junior college in a semirural area has special problems in developing a terminal program. It cannot spread its students too thinly among too many programs, nor does it have many specific local training needs. The changing agricultural economy and manpower needs, together with the tendency to move away from the small community, leave the rural junior college without the firm terminal mission of its sister institutions in the city.

The claim made by the junior college—that it is unique because of the extent to which it offers special programs for terminal students—is exaggerated, but the extent to which some junior colleges have established popular terminal programs indicates that a need for them exists and can be met. Those in the two-year colleges should recognize the comparatively light emphasis of the institutions as a whole on the terminal function and the heavy emphasis on the transfer programs. If by its own practices this institution is not really unique in serving a terminal function, no attempt should be made to convince the public that it is different from the four-year college in this respect. Likewise, those who are not connected with the junior college but look at it in theoretical terms should examine its record more closely; they should not be too quick to condemn the two-year college for not emphasizing the terminal function but rather should consider the societal and cultural values that account in part for the situation.

The distribution of enrollment in the public two-year colleges in the State of New York is worthy of note. As described in Chapter 8, there is a heavy emphasis on technical education in the two-year college in that state. In all 19 of the state's public two-year colleges, including the 6 state-supported agricultural and technical institutes that were in operation in the fall semester, 1958, more than 90 per cent of the 14,023 students were in technical terminal programs. Enrollments of terminal students reported by the office of the executive dean of Community Colleges of the State University of New York were classified according to technologies. The six classifications and enrollments in each were: agriculture, 820; ornamental horticulture, 210; industry, 5,433; service (including business), 4,307; health, 1,274; fashion design, 604.

The high enrollment of terminal students in New York's two-year colleges may be construed as evidence that the best way to interest students in occupational training is to establish separate terminal institutions. However, the two-year college cannot be evaluated *solely* on the percentage of the students who enroll in terminal programs. Any community must determine whether there are equal opportunities for both transfer and terminal students. Even in New York the two-year colleges most recently established are of the comprehensive type, and recent legislation permits locally controlled technical institutes, with state approval, to become comprehensive institutions.

In the final analysis it would seem that if training for mid-level occupations is to be even more important in the future than it has been in the past, the two-year college, and particularly the community college, should continue to be a logical agency to do the training. If it does not meet this responsibility, the alternative may be another type of institution which will meet it. This would seem unnecessary and unfortunate.

CHAPTER 5

Performance and Retention
of Transfer Students

Although only half of the students who expect to transfer do so, the importance of the two-year college as a preparatory institution cannot be minimized. Furthermore, its role in higher education cannot be described without investigating the performance of its students who transfer to four-year colleges.

Many persons find it difficult to believe that the junior college can effectively prepare students for advanced college work—that an institution with few of the characteristics of four-year colleges and universities and with a highly diversified student body can sufficiently stress academic excellence. The record of the junior college in this regard must stand on its own.

If the two-year college does an acceptable job as a transfer institution, it may increasingly be looked to as a means of accommodating a large number of freshmen and sophomore students. If the transfer students do not do well, then either their shortcomings in the next institution and the apparent reasons for their poor performance must be investigated and corrective steps taken, or the junior college should not be looked to so extensively as a transfer institution.

Numerous studies on the performance of transfer students in particular institutions have been made. Bird reported on a number of them and arrived at general conclusions favorable to the junior college transfer.[1] A doctoral study completed by Nall in 1958 at the University of Colorado on the performance of junior college transfers to the University of Colorado arrived at results less favorable to transfer students.[2] Certain colleges and universities make it their practice to study the problem annually and to report results to the junior colleges from which their transfers come. For example, the Office of Relations with Schools at the University of California has periodically made summary studies of how transfers compare with native students. The practice of conducting such studies appears to be gaining momentum with the result that a considerable body of information on the subject is becoming available.

Because no study of transfers had been completed under a uniform design in widely scattered four-year colleges and universities, several such institutions, known to enroll each year a number of junior college transfers, were invited to participate in a longitudinal study using a design from the Berkeley research center. Sixteen institutions agreed to cooperate and submitted data for this report. The plan consisted of a study of two groups of students who were classified as juniors in the fall term, 1953—those who had taken all their lower-division work in the institutions and were classified as native students, and those who had transferred from junior college with junior standing. The objective was to compare the basic groups on scholarly performance (as expressed by a median grade-point average), persistence, and graduation by the end of two years following junior classification.

Certain institutions were able to supply information beyond the minimum requirement in the uniform design. In three instances it was possible to make comparisons between men and women. Three institutions analyzed retention, performance, and graduation by schools or colleges within the university. Four institutions also submitted information on those who had transferred from other four-year institutions. Certain minor variations from the general

---

[1] Grace V. Bird, "Preparation for Advanced Study," in *The Public Junior College,* Fifty-fifth Yearbook of the National Society for the Study of Education, Chicago, 1956, chap. 5.

[2] Alfred W. Nall, "The Academic Success of Junior College Transfers to the Junior Level at the University of Colorado," unpublished doctoral dissertation, University of Colorado, Boulder, 1958.

design proved to be necessary. Most institutions calculated grade-point averages on a 3-point scale with an A yielding 3 points, and so on, but a few used a 4-point scale with an A having a value of 4 points. One institution calculated the cumulative median value for each term. In two colleges it was necessary to use a different combination of years for which data were more readily available. Condensed statistical reports for each of the institutions are found in the appendices.

Additional information on the record of transfer students was obtained from the 61 junior colleges which cooperated in the study of their 1952 entering class. Each of them was asked to secure data on the persistence and graduation of its students who transferred to four-year colleges.

FINDINGS FROM THE FOUR-YEAR COLLEGES AND UNIVERSITIES

The information compiled for the four-year institutions is reported by states.[3]

California

In California, studies were completed for two state colleges, two major campuses of the state university, and a large private university.

Fresno State College (Appendix A). The junior college transfers performed academically only slightly less well than the native students, generally by 0.2 of a grade point until the last half of the senior year when the margin was reduced to 0.1. The grade-point average of the native students in the fall semester of their junior year was 1.63, that of the transfers 1.40. In the second semester the corresponding averages were 1.71 and 1.33. The decline in the record of the transfer students during the second semester after transfer was unusual and could be explained only by intensive case studies. In the first semester of the senior year the native students again earned a 1.71 grade-point average, and the transfers increased theirs to 1.50. By the last semester of the senior year the grade-point average of the native students had risen to 1.81, that of the transfers to 1.71. The retention rate for the two groups was not markedly different in the junior year, but in the

[3] For details on the study in each institution see appropriate appendix.

senior year the percentage of transfers persisting was less by 12 points than the percentage of native students persisting.

The transfer group performed considerably less well in terms of degrees received. At the end of the fourth semester after junior classification, 77 per cent of the native group, as compared with 39 per cent of the transfers, received degrees. However, a higher percentage of the transfers received degrees after the normal time, reducing somewhat the differences in the percentages of the two groups.

San Jose State College (Appendix B). The transfers to San Jose State College compared favorably with native students. The difference was only 0.13 of a cumulative grade point in the first quarter after junior classification and less than 0.05 in each subsequent term until the last when the grade-point averages were essentially the same.

As to retention, the groups were similar for the first year, but the rate of attrition in the second year was greater for the transfer than for the native group. The number of transfers entering the last quarter of the senior year amounted to only 69 per cent of the original group as compared with 84 per cent of the native group.

An interesting story is told in Table B-1 of the report on San Jose. Of the total native group, approximately 72 per cent received degrees at the end of the normal two-year span as compared with approximately 52 per cent of the transfers. In both groups the percentage of women receiving degrees "on time" was higher than for the men. However, in both groups more men than women received degrees after the senior year, so that the percentage of nongraduates was not materially different for men and women.

University of California—Berkeley and Los Angeles (Appendix C). The results of the study at the University of California were not unlike those of previous studies completed by the university's Office of Relations with Schools. However, the study was more comprehensive than preceding studies because it sought data on retention and performance in the individual schools and colleges in the university.

In interpreting the data from the university, it is necessary to note the two categories of junior college transfers: (1) the "eligible" students, that is, those who were eligible for admission to the University of California at the time of high school graduation, and (2) the "ineligible" students who did not meet university entrance requirements at high school graduation. The two categories are compared separately with native students, thus making three groups in all.

Five tables in Appendix C describe the relative performance of transfer and native students on the two campuses. Table C-1 presents an over-all view of the persistence of all groups through the normal semester of graduation and into the following semester. Table C-2 shows the median grade-point averages, together with the units attempted and the percentage persisting, of the three groups through each of the four semesters of the junior and senior years. It also shows the number of nongraduates persisting consecutively beyond the fourth semester of the senior year. Table C-3 compares the percentages of each group receiving degrees in specified periods. Table C-4 summarizes the persistence and performance record of the three groups in selected colleges in the university. Table C-5 supplements Table C-4 by indicating the record of baccalaureate degrees earned by each of the groups in the selected colleges in the university.

The following generalizations were possible from the study:

The differences on the Berkeley campus between the records of the native students and junior college transfers eligible for the university at the time of high school graduation were very slight—in academic load, academic performance, degrees earned, and even in persistence, the two groups were about the same. Persistence to degrees was also high at the Medical Center after transfer there.

The record on the Berkeley campus of the junior college transfers ineligible for the university at the time of high school graduation was less good in achievement and degrees earned and far less good in persistence than either of the other groups. However, the 56 per cent of the junior college ineligible group who did persist performed well, and nearly 90 per cent of this 56 per cent succeeded in earning degrees.

The differences on the Los Angeles campus between the records of the native students and both groups of transfers favored the native student. Here the academic record of the junior college eligible group lay somewhere between that of the native student and the junior college ineligible group. Withdrawal was about 35 per cent among the transfers and 17 per cent among the native students.

Generalizations for the total groups did not apply uniformly to the records made in individual schools and colleges at either Berkeley or Los Angeles although the records of the native students and junior college eligibles at Berkeley remained very close, with sometimes the native students and sometimes the junior college eligibles surpassing the other group. In applied arts and engineering at Los Angeles the junior college eligibles and native students performed alike.

In connection with the last point it is important to note the record of the junior college eligible group in two of the professional schools on the Berkeley campus. In both business administration and engineering the eligible transfers earned lower grade-point averages than the natives only in the first semester after transfer. In each of the three succeeding semesters they slightly surpassed the native group. On the other hand, their rate of attrition was greater than that of the natives.

The data in all tables indicate that a large percentage of native students and of both transfer groups continue in letters and science or in a professional school beyond the fourth semester following junior classification before receiving a degree. In other words, the attainment of a bachelor's degree often requires more than four years of study.

University of Southern California (Appendix D). In this institution the junior college transfers compared very favorably with the native group both in terms of persistence and of academic performance. Only in the second semester after transfer was there as much as a 0.1 difference.

The principal difference in the two groups was in the percentage of students who received degrees—67 per cent of the native students as compared with 48 per cent of the transfers. However, the number of students who had not received degrees at the end of the fourth semester but had continued in professional schools was considerably larger for the transfer group than for the native students, which may indicate that the record of degrees earned by the transfers would eventually compare more favorably with that of the natives, though not equal it.

Georgia

University of Georgia (Appendix E). The records made by the transfers from Georgia junior colleges in the state university system, from other junior colleges in Georgia, and from junior colleges outside the state were almost identical with those of the native students with respect to performance, persistence, and degrees received. Only the transfers from Georgia junior colleges outside the university system fell below the others in the earning of degrees in the normal period. Students transferring to the university from the junior colleges in the state system and from outside the state even slightly surpassed the natives in the percentage receiving degrees in the normal period.

Illinois

University of Illinois (Appendix F). In this institution the native students were superior to the transfer students by 0.44 of a grade point in the first semester of junior classification, in the second semester by 0.19, and for each of the two semesters of the senior year by only 0.14. The grade-point average of all transfers dropped in the first semester after transfer, then rose steadily. In fact, the grade-point average for the women transfer students was higher in their senior year than in junior college. The men, however, never quite equaled the level they had attained in junior college. During the fourth semester, the transfer women surpassed the native women in grade points earned.

The native students persisted to a higher degree than the transfer group. However, the rate of persistence for transfer women more nearly approximated the rate for native women, the retention for transfer women being much greater than for transfer men. In the second year particularly, the retention rate for transfer men was markedly inferior to that for native men.

The native group also exceeded the transfer group in obtaining degrees in the normal period. The comparison was (except for women) even less favorable to the transfers when an additional year was added, since by the end of three years after transfer a higher percentage of native students than transfer students had obtained degrees.

The records made by the two groups in the various colleges or areas of enrollment within the university are reported in Table F-2 of Appendix F. They show differences between natives and transfers by sex, although the small number of cases in some subject fields somewhat limits the validity of the general conclusions. In many instances the grade-point averages of the two groups were very similar with the natives sometimes slightly exceeding the transfer group and sometimes falling behind. The following points are evident:

Native women did consistently better according to median grade-point averages than transfer men and women in the College of Commerce. In the College of Education the transfer men had a consistently higher grade-point median than native men. However, the opposite was true for women except during the 1954 spring semester when the median grade point for transfer women was slightly higher than for native women.

Native men enrolled in engineering did consistently better than transfer men, and no women were enrolled in either group. In agriculture, the transfer men had a higher grade-point median than native men for three of the four semesters. In fine arts, native boys were better than transfer men. Native men enrolled in journalism were superior to transfer men the first semester after transfer, but thereafter transfer men had a higher median grade point than native men.

In the College of Liberal Arts and Sciences, all native students surpassed all transfer students except during the fourth semester when the median grade point for transfer women was higher than that for native women. In physical education native women were superior to transfer women for the two semesters for which comparative data were available.

Iowa (Appendix G)

A study was made of about seventeen hundred transfers from different types of institutions, including junior colleges, to the three public institutions of higher education in Iowa. The period covered was from June, 1953, to March, 1955. No comparisons between the records of transfer and native students were made in this case. Table G-1 of Appendix G shows the records made by the composite group of transfers to the three institutions.

With the exception of students transferring from other senior colleges, there was generally a slight differential between the grades students earned before transfer and those they earned after transfer. On the whole, this differential was greatest for junior college students but, except for transfers from public junior colleges to Iowa State College, it was less than 0.5.

The mean average grades after transfer of junior college students compared favorably with the transfers from other types of colleges except at the state university. There the mean average grade of the transfers from other colleges was higher than that of the group from public junior colleges.

There were only negligible differences among the transfer groups in all three institutions in terms of the percentage of the transfers who earned baccalaureate degrees. The attrition was the same for junior college transfers as for the transfers from other colleges.

Kansas (Appendix H)

The five public higher institutions in Kansas participating in the study included the University of Kansas, the Kansas State College, the Fort Hays Kansas State College, and the teachers colleges at Pittsburg and Emporia.

At Fort Hays the transfers were superior to the native students on every count except in the percentage receiving degrees at the end of the two-year period, where they were slightly below the native group. However, the small number of transfer students (11 as compared with 150 natives) may not constitute a sufficient basis for generalization.

In the teachers college at Pittsburg, where the junior college transfer sample was greater (68 transfer and 111 native students), both groups earned the same median grade-point average for the first semester of the junior year, the natives slightly surpassed the transfers in the next two semesters, and in the last semester the transfers surpassed the natives by 0.11 grade points. A slightly higher proportion of transfers than natives received degrees in the normal period.

The study at Emporia also showed only slight variations between the two groups, with almost the same retention rate and with the transfer students academically outperforming the natives for two semesters. A slightly higher proportion of the native group received degrees at the end of the fourth semester.

In both teachers colleges the percentage of students receiving degrees in the normal period of four semesters was small for transfer and native students alike, 46 per cent being the highest figure reported for Emporia's native students.

At the University of Kansas the transfers did less well than the natives in academic achievement although both groups showed consistent improvement through each of the four semesters. The largest differential in grade-point average was in the first semester of junior classification when the natives outdid the transfers by 0.46. The difference was reduced in each of the three remaining semesters and was only 0.28 for the fourth term. The native students also were more persistent; a much higher per cent of them received degrees at the end of the two-year period.

The sample in the Kansas State College included 30 native and 30 transfer students matched by sex and curriculum. After the first semester of junior classification the transfer students from four colleges surpassed the native students in grades earned, retention, and the percentage receiving degrees at the end of the senior year.

Michigan

University of Michigan (Appendix I). A limited study of University of Michigan students conducted in a somewhat different manner permitted some comparison of academic performance of junior college transfers with the record made by *all* juniors for the school years 1953–54 and 1954–55. In each of those years the grade-point average for the year for *all* juniors was 2.7. The junior college transfer group alone for 1953–54 attained a grade-point average of 2.4 for the first semester and 2.6 for the second semester, which compares favorably with that for all juniors. The transfer group attained a grade-point average of 2.8 for each of the semesters of the senior year; there were no comparable data on native seniors. The retention of the transfer group was unusually high (84 per cent). Fifty-nine per cent of the transfers graduated at the end of four semesters, and by the end of eight semesters almost

80 per cent of the original group of transfers had graduated. No data were submitted on retention and graduation rates for native students.

Michigan State University (Appendix J). The study of students at Michigan State University sampled 124 junior college transfers and 1,336 native juniors. By the end of the two-year period after transfer, 68 per cent of the natives and 53 per cent of the transfers received degrees. The natives surpassed the transfers in academic performance by 0.3 grade points in the first term after transfer, but by the end of the senior year the transfer group was doing somewhat better than the natives. The question could be raised whether the differences in the size of the sample for the groups justify any general conclusion that transfer students eventually outperform native students.

Mississippi

University of Mississippi (Appendix K). From the University of Mississippi it was possible to obtain information on the records made by transfers from other four-year institutions as well as on those made by junior college transfers and native students.

All three groups performed equally well academically in the first semester of junior classification, although the junior college transfers did somewhat less well than in junior college. In the second semester the native students and the junior college transfers performed alike, and their median grade-point average was somewhat higher than the transfers from four-year institutions. In the last two semesters, however, the junior college transfers did slightly less well than either of the other groups. This difference in the senior year was particularly true of the men. Without exception, the women in all three groups surpassed the men throughout in earned grade-point averages.

The persistence rate for all groups was comparatively high. However, both transfer groups, and particularly the junior college transfers, had a much heavier attrition rate the second year. Although junior college women transfers did better work than junior college men transfers, they tended to drop out of college more than men and to a much greater degree than women in the other two groups. The junior college transfers did not receive nearly as many degrees as the other groups by the end of the second year; 60 per cent received degrees, as compared with 75 per cent for the native students and 71 per cent for the transfers from four-year colleges.

Data on retention and performance of the three groups in the various departments and colleges in the university are shown in Table J-2 of Appendix J. It may be noted that the junior college transfers excelled in commerce. They did much less well in engineering, although the small number makes generalization questionable. Their grade-point average compared favorably with that of students in other departments, with junior college transfer women doing better than men. Persistence records of junior college transfers were low in all departments, especially for women.

The relatively good record of persistency and performance of junior college transfers in the first year after transfer and the decline in the second year seemed particularly noteworthy. University officials saw the reason for this in the fact that junior college transfer students often are obliged to enroll in lower-division courses to meet university requirements. This, the officials believe, causes the junior year to be easier than it might otherwise be. Difficulties are thus more likely to be experienced in the second year with resulting increased drop-out rates and a lower level of performance.

Texas

University of Texas (Appendix L). Junior college transfers did not perform quite as well as native students. There was a difference of 0.3 in the first semester, which was reduced to approximately 0.2 for the remaining three semesters. However, in the rate of persistence, particularly in the senior year, differences in the two groups were considerable; 95 per cent of the native students remained through the senior year as compared with only 72 per cent of the transfers. Further, 86 per cent of the native students obtained degrees, compared with only 66 per cent of the transfer group.

RECAPITULATION

The variations in the nature of the studies in the different institutions and the great differences among the institutions with regard to the size of the groups studied did not make it feasible to combine all the data. However, the following Tables 5-1 and 5-2 present summaries of data that seemed sufficiently comparable to give an over-all view of the findings.[4]

In general, the data show that for the years studied the transfer students did somewhat less well than the native students in the first term after transfer. However, in most institutions by the end of the senior year they closely approached, and in a few instances slightly excelled, the native students. When there were differentials, they tended to be not more than 0.3 grade points and often less. However, in most institutions, the retention rate for the transfer students during the junior and senior years was markedly lower than for the native students. Likewise, the percentage of transfers receiving degrees at the end of the second year after transfer (the "normal" time required to earn the baccalaureate degree) was generally much lower than for the native students. On the other hand, many institutions reported a greater number of transfer students who completed work for their degrees later, thus indicating that it often takes these students longer to satisfy degree requirements. As reported in the summary for some of the institutions, there were variations in all three factors of performance, retention, and degrees earned according to the schools or colleges in the universities. However, the variation in the pattern in the limited number of schools and colleges in the universities studied does not permit a generalization on this point. There were also differences according to sex; for example, transfer women tended to surpass transfer men in performance.

FINDINGS FROM THE TWO-YEAR COLLEGES

Supplementary information on transfer students was obtained in the study of the class entering junior colleges in 1952. Many of

[4] To make the grade-point averages in the two tables more comparable, the grade-point averages of the institutions that had used a 4- or 5-point scale were reduced one point. (It is recognized that such an arbitrary reduction in points might produce slightly different results than would be obtained if the grade-point averages were figured originally on a 3-point scale. However, the method used is thought to be acceptable for general rough comparisons.) Median grade points earned by native and transfer students are shown only for the first semester (or quarter) after junior classification and for the last term in the senior year. The percentage of students receiving degrees beyond the normal two-year period was available from some institutions but not from others.

Table 5-1. Comparison of Grade-Point Averages between Native and
Transfer Students in Certain Four-year Colleges and Universities
$(N = 10,940)$

Institutions	No. of students classified as juniors, fall, 1953		Median grade-point average, fall, 1953		Median grade-point average, spring, 1955	
	Native	Transfers	Native	Transfers	Native	Transfers
Fresno State College	171	116	1.63	1.40	1.81	1.71
Kansas State Teachers College (Emporia)	173	30	1.77	2.00	1.67	1.97
Kansas State Teachers College (Fort Hays)	150	11	1.80	1.82	2.03	2.02
Kansas State College (Manhattan)*	30	30	1.57	1.28	1.77	1.94
Kansas State Teachers College (Pittsburg)	111	68	1.60	1.89	1.60	2.00
Michigan State University	1,336	124	1.53	1.23	1.60	1.75
San Jose State College	288	233	1.68	1.60	1.72	1.71
University of California (Berkeley)	924	397	1.63	1.15	1.78	1.73
Eligible		(184)		1.45		1.84
Ineligible		(213)		1.07		1.60
University of California (Los Angeles)	593	429	1.68	1.21	1.88	1.63
Eligible		(141)		1.43		1.75
Ineligible		(288)		1.10		1.57
University of Southern California	495	321	1.43	1.27	1.57	1.55
University of Georgia†	321	127	1.82	1.80	2.50	2.44
University of Illinois‡	1,040	168	1.64	1.19	1.83	1.68
University of Kansas	455	81	1.72	1.26	1.87	1.59
University of Michigan	1,556	129	1.70	1.40	1.70	1.80
University of Mississippi	200	88	1.33	1.33	1.76	1.65
University of Texas	546	197	1.50	1.20	1.67	1.50
Total	8,391	2,549				

* Data are a sampling of native and transfer students matched by sex and curricula.
† Class of 1956.
‡ Class of 1954.

Table 5-2. Comparison of Retention and Degrees Received between Native and Transfer Students in Certain Four-year Colleges and Universities
$(N = 10,940)$

Institution	No. of students classified as juniors, fall, 1953		Per cent of students persisting through spring, 1955		Per cent of students receiving degrees, spring, 1955	
	Native	Transfers	Native	Transfers	Native	Transfers
Fresno State College	171	116	86	74	84	54
Kansas State Teachers College (Emporia)	173	30	60	60	45	43
Kansas State Teachers College (Fort Hays)	150	11	64	60	58	54
Kansas State College (Manhattan)*	30	30	79	80	37	53
Kansas State Teachers College (Pittsburg)	111	68	70	63	40	44
Michigan State University	1,336	124	71	78	67	53
San Jose State College	288	233	84	69	72	52
University of California (Berkeley)	924	397	83	66	57	46
Eligible		(184)		77		57
Ineligible		(213)		56		35
University of California (Los Angeles)	593	429	80	66	49	27
Eligible		(141)		67		28
Ineligible		(288)		65		26
University of Southern California	495	321	80	73	67	48
University of Georgia†	321	127	84	83	75	74
University of Illinois‡	1,040	168	86	60	61	41
University of Kansas	455	81	92	82	65	41
University of Michigan	1,558	129		84		60
University of Mississippi	200	88	81	64	75	60
University of Texas	546	197	95	72	86	66
Total	8,391	2,549				

* Data are a sampling of native and transfer students matched by sex and curricula.
† Class of 1956.
‡ Class of 1954.

the data from this study were reported in Chapter 3 in describing the extent to which the junior college is a preparatory or terminal institution. In addition to finding out which students transferred, information was sought on the length of time transfer students remained in the four-year college, and whether they received the baccalaureate degree by June, 1956, the end of four academic years following entrance to junior college.

Table 5-3. Number of Colleges Reporting Percentages of Two-year College Students Who Either Withdrew or Graduated from Four-year College

Percentage intervals	Colleges reporting per cent of transfers in residence less than one year			Colleges reporting per cent of transfers in residence only one year			Colleges reporting transfers who graduated		
	Public	Private	Total	Public	Private	Total	Public	Private	Total
99–90	0	0	0	0	0	0	1	0	1
89–80	0	0	0	0	0	0	0	0	0
79–70	0	0	0	0	0	0	1	2	3
69–60	0	0	0	0	0	0	2	3	5
59–50	0	0	0	0	0	0	6	1	7
49–40	0	0	0	0	0	0	13	2	15
39–30	2	0	2	2	1	3	10	1	11
29–20	8	0	8	7	1	8	10	1	11
19–10	29	5	34	21	5	26	5	0	5
9–0	11	6	17	20	4	24	3	0	3
Total	50	11	61	50	11	61	51	11	62

Tables 5-3 and 5-4 present the basic data on these points. Table 5-3 shows the distribution of two-year colleges reporting percentages of students who either dropped out or attained the baccalaureate degree after transferring to four-year colleges. Going to the third line from the bottom, the table should be read as follows: between 10 and 19 per cent of the transfer students from 34 junior colleges were in residence in a four-year college for less than one year; 26 junior colleges had between 10 and 19 per cent of their transfer students remain in residence in a four-year college for only one year, and so on. Table 5-4 shows the median percentage of transfer students, together with the range, who were in residence in the four-year institution for the indicated periods of time, or who attained the baccalaureate degree. The median percentage of students remaining less than a year in the senior institutions was 13. About the same number were in residence for only a year. Eight per cent were dropped by the senior college because of academic difficulties.

Of all students transferring, 40 per cent received the baccalaureate degree by the end of four years after the time they entered the junior college. Students from private colleges had a much greater tendency to graduate in the normal period.

Table 5-4. Median and Range of Percentages of Two-year College Students Who Dropped Out or Attained Baccalaureate Degrees After Transferring to Four-year Institutions

	Per cent in residence less than one year			Per cent in residence only one year			Per cent graduated		
	Public	Private	Total	Public	Private	Total	Public	Private	Total
Median	14	9	13	12	13	12	37	61	40
High	33	18	33	36	33	36	90	80	90
Low	2	0	0	0	4	0	0	28	0

Although not shown in the tables, there were marked differences between men and women in persistence and attainment of degrees. Men tended to remain in college longer than women, but a somewhat higher percentage of the women who transferred received their degrees within the four-year period after entering junior college.

THE OVER-ALL PROBLEM

The information presented on the foregoing pages has encouraging and discouraging aspects for the cause of the junior college. That transfer students earn grades quite comparable to those of native students undoubtedly reflects a high quality of teaching in the junior college. The comparatively good record of transfers in most institutions may also be due to the natural selection that takes place during the two junior college years. The extent to which many junior colleges gear their transfer curricula and their teaching methods to the needs of students who propose to enter certain colleges and universities is undoubtedly an additional contributor to the success of the transfer group.

In all but one of the studies reported in this chapter the transfer and native students were not matched according to ability, previous academic achievement, and other factors. Although such matching would have yielded more precise data which would have permitted more accurate comparisons, it was not considered feasible in view of the large number of cooperating institutions. If groups were matched, they would probably perform similarly. Indeed, in the study of the small matched sample at Kansas State College, the transfers did better on all measures than the native students. Martorana and Williams[5] earlier made a study at the State College of Washington by equating a group of native and transfer students on several factors including sex, academic aptitude, and high school performance. Their conclusion was that when such students are considered in groups, there is no significant difference in their performance.

On the other hand, the study completed by Nall[6] at the University of Colorado which used the matched-pair method did reveal some differences between transfers from Colorado junior colleges and native students. In the College of Arts and Sciences the difference in scholarship amounted to 0.49 in favor of the native students in both the first and second semesters of the upper division. In the first semester of the senior year the mean difference was reduced to 0.16 and at the point of graduation it was 0.10. Nall reported that the differences in the senior year were not reliable at the 1 per cent level of significance and that they could be attributable to chance. Nall also found that a considerably higher percentage of the junior college transfer students in the College of Arts and Sciences fell below a C average than native students. The same pattern of differences in favor of the native students was found to hold in the School of Business. But though native students showed the superior scholarship in the College of Arts and Sciences and in the School of Business, the reverse was true between the matched pairs in the College of Engineering. Beginning at the third

[5] S. V. Martorana and L. L. Williams, "Academic Success of Junior College Transfers at the State College of Washington," *Junior College Journal*, vol. 24, March, 1954, pp. 402–415.

[6] Nall, *op. cit.*, p. 141 ff.

semester of upper division and thereafter, the transfer students in engineering maintained a higher grade-point average than did the native students and correspondingly fewer of the transfers fell below a C average than did the natives.

The identification of the number of transfers earning grades below a C average, which has also been found in studies at other institutions, including the University of California and the University of Michigan, indicates a need for more intensive studies and analyses of the performance of transfers.

Although the transfer students in most institutions earned grade-point averages comparable to native students, their record in retention and in attainment of baccalaureate degrees is poor. Individual four-year colleges have reported that attrition is not always due to poor scholarship. The data from several institutions in this study show that attrition tended to be greater *following* an increase in the grade-point average for the group. This, of course, suggests that there are other reasons why transfer students (as well as natives) drop out of college. The lower socioeconomic background of many junior college students may mean that motivational and financial factors contribute to their high attrition. The student who attends junior college because it is near his home and less expensive to him may upon transfer find it difficult to meet the higher costs that often obtain in a four-year college. The transfers who in metropolitan areas attempt to commute long distances to a four-year institution may lack money, time, and encouragement to offset the exigencies of college attendance under such circumstances. In some of the institutions participating in the study, the attrition of women was greater than of men, probably because women get married and discontinue their college careers, often in order to go to work so that the husbands may complete college. It may be, too, that social maladjustment following transfer causes some students to drop out. It is believed that junior colleges do not do enough in preparing students for nonacademic life in the four-year college. Even more serious is the fact that most four-year colleges, and particularly the large universities, do little to orient and assimilate transfer students. Nothing comparable to the program for entering freshmen exists. No thorough study has been made of the reasons for attrition among junior college transfers; it should be a worthwhile project.

Aside from nonacademic considerations which undoubtedly influence the length of time students remain in college, there are more objective factors which influence persistence, attainment of degrees, and even scholarly performance. Some of these factors might be called inevitable. For example, since small junior colleges are unable to offer a great variety of courses, some transfer students may not have had certain lower-division courses which are prerequisites for their chosen major fields. These students will need longer to complete baccalaureate degree requirements. Also inevitable is the fact that since students generally have many choices of four-year institutions to which to transfer, they do not always know well in advance the one which they will enter. For the student to meet the specific requirements of one institution does not necessarily mean that he meets the requirements of others. If the student's choice changes, he may have additional work to take and hence be delayed in his progress to his baccalaureate degree.

Other difficulties encountered by transfer students are the fault of either the two-year "sending" colleges or the four-year "receiving" institutions. The two-year college that carelessly counsels students about course requirements in other institutions and about the most desirable pattern to follow in the junior college makes an error that is difficult to correct. Likewise, the junior college that, either through counseling or required admission standards for key transfer courses or both, fails to cause students to become realistic about their ability to pursue a baccalaureate degree program fails in one of its important obligations. The same is true of the junior college that does not insist on rigorous grading standards and study habits on the part of the students who plan to transfer. No service is rendered a student by allowing him to obtain a false impression of his ability to compete with others in a four-year college. Variation among junior colleges in such practices may account to a great extent for the differences in performance of transfer students from the different junior colleges.

Then there are the faults of the four-year college. A common obstacle created by them is their frequent inflexibility in lower-division requirements. For them relentlessly to insist that the junior colleges offer identical or equivalent courses covering the same content and taught in the same manner as in the four-year college simply means that smaller junior colleges cannot satisfy requirements to several four-year institutions. Furthermore, insistence on equivalent courses per se overlooks a basic question of whether a specific subject matter and a given approach to it is more valuable than other related content in the same general discipline and training in intellectual processes in general.

Without doubt one of the great needs in many states is closer coordination between two- and four-year colleges. In the states studied, relationships between the two types of institutions appeared generally cordial. Joint participation in professional meetings and even in specially called meetings to consider problems of relationships are becoming common. However, to work out complex problems of articulation, always with the best interest of the students in mind, requires *continuous* individual and collective effort and cannot be left to high-level conferences once or twice a year. To provide the impetus for and the coordination of this effort, some form of liaison machinery, either structured or informal, seems essential. The exact nature of the plan must be worked out in each state, but it should provide some method whereby teachers and administrators in both types of institution have an opportunity to share in the solution of problems.

The system of articulation committees in California constitutes a good example of working machinery for effecting coordination among the various levels of education. The Association of Secondary School Administrators, the California Junior College Association, and the Division of State Colleges of the state department of education have committees on coordination working with other schools. The University of California, in turn, through its Office of Admissions and Relations with Schools, has three committees—one for relations with high schools, one for junior colleges, and one for coordination with state colleges. Each committee works with the appropriate committees of the other agencies. The joint committees meet semiannually for two consecutive days with a carefully prepared agenda. In the Junior College Conference Committee all topics affecting junior college–university relationships are discussed freely and openly, and there is an agreement that the university will make no final decision on matters affecting the junior colleges without previous consultation with the conference committee.

Effective articulation depends on research pertaining to the transfer student so that both two-year and four-year institutions can be guided by facts. To date, too much has been left to chance. With the current emphasis on the junior college as the institution which presumably will care for an increasing share of the nation's college freshmen and sophomores, representatives from all types of four-year colleges and from all types of junior colleges must use all means of enabling the greatest possible number of transfer students to have a satisfying and successful experience in the next institution.

CHAPTER 6

Student Personnel Services in Two-year Institutions

Most social institutions serve society in multiple ways, and an educational institution is no exception. Some of the many goals of a school or college are achieved through the curriculum, others through more individual and specialized services. The instructional program of an institution and its personnel services are both means of serving and educating the student. A college may have a plant, a faculty, and a curriculum; but unless there is an orderly way of admitting students, some method of assisting them to appraise themselves and to plan their educational and vocational programs accordingly, some means of assuring enriching experiences through campus social interactions, and some attempt to center attention on the individual rather than on the group, the college is an impersonal shell in which students are not conditioned for optimum learning.

This comprehensive concept of education was stated by Williamson and others when they wrote:

> The realization of this objective—the full maturing of each student—cannot be attained without interest in and integrated efforts toward the development of each and every facet of his personality and potentialities. His deepening understanding of his world is not sacrificed to his emotional maturing. His physical well-being does not become a limited end in itself. His maturing sense of values, social and spiritual, is not sacrificed to his under-

standing of the world of man and nature. His need for developing a sound philosophy of life to serve as the norm for his actions now and in adult life is not neglected in the college's emphasis on his need for intellectual and professional competence. Rather are all known aspects of the personality of each student viewed by the educator and personnel worker as an integrated whole— as a human personality living, working, and growing in a democratic society of other human personalities.[1]

No claim of the junior college is discussed more often than its student personnel program, particularly the counseling and guidance phase of the program. Previous chapters in this report have dealt with the role of the junior college in guiding students with varied abilities and backgrounds toward appropriate educational and vocational goals. This it must do in many ways, one of which is through its student personnel program. While this is a responsibility of any institution of higher education, the multiplicity of purposes and the heterogeneity of the student body which characterize the junior college place a special and difficult responsibility on it. The task would be easier if American philosophy condoned the arbitrary channeling of students into educational programs according to some a priori basis instead of according to the student's free choice. The principle of choice, however, has been well established. Many persons in positions of leadership have enunciated it, but none more effectively than Conant in his *Education in a Divided World:*

> It has been well said that really effective counseling is the keystone of the arch of a widespread educational system dedicated to the principle of equality of opportunity. A democracy, unlike a totalitarian state, cannot force its youth into what the authorities consider the appropriate groove of advanced education. In this republic of free men, no official can decree what line of study must be pursued. Though public opinion might well be aware of the fact that the number of doctors should be greatly increased, yet the state is powerless (and should be) to order the most promising youths with a scientific talent into the study of medicine. There is even a strong popular feeling of resentment

[1] E. G. Williamson et al., "The Student Personnel Point of View," *Student Personnel Work,* American Council on Education Studies, ser. 6. vol. 13, no. 13, Washington, September, 1949, p. 2.

against any tendency of educational authorities to limit the number of boys and girls who study any given subject. Any idea of telling them what they must study of a specialized nature would be thrown out of court by the American public without a hearing.[2]

While such points of view give emphasis to the counseling phase of a personnel program, there are other important aspects of the program in the typical two-year college. One is the student activity program. Since most students in public two-year colleges live at home, they stand to miss the social interactions of the typical campus life of a residential college. It therefore becomes incumbent on the junior college to provide opportunity for student participation in out-of-class activities.

The quantity and quality of personnel services in two-year colleges are not always considered commensurate with the need for them. As a spokesman for the Student Personnel Committee of the American Association of Junior Colleges, Humphreys in 1952 expressed concern over some apparent deficiencies in student personnel programs in junior colleges.[3] He concluded that (1) relatively few junior colleges have student personnel programs adequate to meet the needs of their students, (2) student personnel work is not recognized in sufficient degree (in the institutions) as one of the major functions, (3) testing and counseling of students is not satisfactorily developed or pursued, (4) professionally qualified personnel workers are not used in sufficient numbers, (5) adequate in-service training for staff members doing personnel work is lacking, and (6) the chief administrator of the institution or his assistant tends to carry too much responsibility in student personnel programs. Among the items listed by Humphreys as contributing to this situation were the lack of acceptance of the personnel point of view, insufficient finance, lack of qualified personnel, lack of physical facilities, and insufficient time to implement and carry out a program.

Because of the important place of student personnel services in two-year colleges, this study investigated such services. Informa-

[2] James B. Conant, *Education in a Divided World*, Harvard University Press, Cambridge, Mass., 1948, pp. 204–205.

[3] J. Anthony Humphreys, "Toward Improved Programs of Student Personnel Services," *Junior College Journal*, vol. 52, March, 1952, pp. 382–392.

tion was obtained from two sources. First, a check list was mailed to all two-year institutions in the 15 states under study; this included questions on personnel practices, such as the use of psychological tests and the practice of making institutional studies which yield information about students and their outcomes. A total of 243 institutions responded to this check list. The second source was an examination of the student personnel program in the 75 two-year colleges which cooperated intensively in the study. This examination was made at the time of the visit to the institutions through interviews with officers of the colleges and, usually, through a detailed questionnaire completed by the colleges in advance of the visit.

Information was thus gathered on the breadth of student personnel services, the manner in which they are organized and directed, the specific efforts made to make professional counseling time available, and the extent to which facts about students and their outcomes are compiled. In addition, it was possible to obtain a limited number of data concerning the cost of student personnel programs.

THE BREADTH OF STUDENT PERSONNEL SERVICES

With so many different services included in a program, an institution may do a creditable job in performing one or two services yet neglect other equally important functions.

Despite some variation in terminology, there has come to exist a fairly well-accepted list of services comprising a student personnel program in colleges and universities. One of the most recent of such lists is the following prepared by the Committee on Student Personnel Work of the American Council on Education:[4] selection for admission; registration and records; counseling; health service; housing and food service; student activities; financial aid; placement; discipline; special clinics for remedial reading, study habits, speech and hearing; special services such as student orientation, veterans' advisory services, foreign-student program, marriage counseling, religious activities, and counseling.

[4] Daniel D. Feder et al., "The Administration of Student Personnel Programs in American Colleges and Universities," *Student Personnel Work*, American Council on Education Studies, ser. 6, vol. 22, no. 19, Washington, February, 1958, p. 1.

In interviews and questionnaires the following services were reported as part of the personnel program in more than 90 per cent of the two-year colleges: counseling and orientation; promotion and supervision of student activities; maintenance and supervision of student records; placement of students in jobs. Between 75 and 90 per cent of the institutions reported the following services: advisory assistance to student government and finance; administration of financial aid to students; responsibility for assemblies and convocations; advisory service for student publications; discipline; follow-up studies of drop-outs and graduates. Far less frequent in the organized program were such services as the administration of a health program, research studies on student characteristics, coordination of intercollegiate athletics, and supervision of student housing or the student bookstore.

The fact that some of the services were not reported in greater frequency does not necessarily mean that they were not performed in some institutions, because a particular service may not be regarded as part of an "organized personnel program" in a given institution but may be performed in other ways. In a few colleges the maintenance and supervision of student records was not administratively classified as a personnel service yet obviously records were kept. Likewise, most colleges in which men were enrolled engaged in some type of intercollegiate athletic program, yet in only about half of the institutions was the coordination of this program regarded as a phase of student personnel work. Only 59 per cent of the colleges listed the administration of a health program as a phase of personnel. It was discovered that many of the colleges indeed did not maintain a health program. Several of the low percentages did in fact reflect a dearth of services in particular phases of the program.

Certain services enumerated by the Committee of the American Council on Education were not reported by two-year colleges. For example, most public junior colleges do not have selective admission practices. Special clinics are in most two-year colleges regarded as a phase of the instructional program rather than a part of student personnel service. In general, the scope of services checked by two-year college representatives indicate that the breadth of the student personnel program in two-year colleges compares favorably with the recommendations of the Committee of the American Council on Education.

Administrators in the cooperating colleges on all levels of administration commented on the necessity of an adequate counseling program. Most of them indicated that their concept of personnel services was considerably broader than mere counseling, although they did not completely agree on all the services that should be performed. If personnel services in two-year colleges could be evaluated solely on the basis of their breadth and the administrative attitude toward them, the picture would be bright.

ORGANIZATION AND ADMINISTRATION OF STUDENT PERSONNEL SERVICES

If an institution is to perform multiple student services which should be interrelated, they must be coordinated. In fact, the services should not only be coordinated with each other but also with the instructional program. This suggests the necessity for a policy and a coherent plan of organizing and administering the services. Such a plan may be highly centralized with a designated person responsible for the direction of all services and for the supervision of other persons who perform services. On the other hand, the plan may be decentralized, with responsibilities divided among many persons with no coordination other than that by the chief administrator of the institution. With either plan, and particularly the latter, committee machinery may be set up to assist in policy formulation and in coordination.

There is no one best way to organize and coordinate a college personnel program. In *Student Personnel Work in College*, Wrenn states that the principle of coordination applies less to structure than to function. He illustrates how a dean of students may have *line* relationships with certain persons working directly under him but *staff* relationships with many of his colleagues in the same institution who are also engaged in some type of personnel work. For example, the dean of students is not directly responsible for the classroom teacher who is expected to do a certain amount of counseling; yet the dean may be expected to coordinate and assist the counseling function, regardless of who does it. Wrenn states:

> Student personnel administration is therefore a matter of both the execution of certain functions and the coordination of others. . . . Institutions are at the present operating with varying

degrees of effectiveness as far as line-and-staff relationships are concerned, but it must be recognized that differing conditions on individual campuses justify marked departures from any one ideal organizational plan. A college or university can develop its most effective program only by giving careful attention first to the establishment of policies by an agency representing faculty, students, and administration; secondly by administrative provision for the most effective execution and coordination of the various personnel services on the campus.[5]

The manner in which the total student personnel program is organized and coordinated varies greatly in two-year colleges. In about half of the 73 cooperating institutions some type of centralized plan was in operation. Sixteen (22 per cent) had a special administrator of the entire personnel program, usually with the title of either "dean of student personnel" or "dean of students." With few exceptions this person devoted full time to the personnel function and had considerable training in student personnel work.

Twenty-four (33 per cent) of the colleges had as coordinator an assistant general administrator, usually the academic dean or vice president of the college. The tendency in these institutions was for the person second in charge of the college to assume responsibility for both the instructional and the student personnel functions. Other staff members responsible for either directing or performing individual personnel services customarily reported to this second administrator. Noted in a few institutions was the fact that some functionaries, such as the registrar, the deans of men and women, the health officers, or the housing officer, reported directly to the chief administrator.

Thirty-three (45 per cent) of the two-year colleges reported that the only person responsible for personnel services was the chief administrator of the institution.[6] In other words, the responsibility for direction and coordination of this phase of the college program was not delegated. With a few exceptions in small junior colleges where the chief administrator himself did all the counseling, super-

[5] C. Gilbert Wrenn, *Student Personnel Work in College*, The Ronald Press Company, New York, 1951.

[6] "Chief administrator" is defined as the one in charge of the institution. In city or unified school systems where there is both a superintendent of the system and an administrator of the junior college (president, dean, director, etc.), the latter is interpreted as being the chief administrator of the college.

vised student activities, and performed all the other services of a personnel nature, there was a division of responsibility for directing and performing the various services. For example, one person was in charge of counseling, another in charge of student activities and so on, and their work was coordinated only to the extent that they all reported to the chief administrator. To this extent the program could be said to be decentralized.

The plan of administration or coordination is related to the size of the institution. The frequency with which the three described plans were found in two-year colleges of different size ranges is summarized in Table 6-1.

Table 6-1. Administrative Officers Who Coordinate All Student Personnel Services in 73 Two-year Institutions, 1956–57

Enrollment categories	No. of institutions	Chief administrator of institution	Assistant administrator of institution	Special director of student personnel
Under 200	8	4	4	—
200–500	29	20	8	1
500–1,000	19	6	8	5
1,000–1,500	8	2	2	4
1,500–2,500	4	—	—	4
Over 2,500	5	1	2	2
Total	73	33	24	16

In the smaller institutions usually either the chief administrator or an assistant administrator with multiple responsibilities directed the personnel program. In 24 out of 37 institutions with fewer than five hundred students the program was directed by the chief administrator. In 12 institutions the assistant administrator was responsible, and in only 1 college of this size was there a full-time director of personnel services. As institutions reached an enrollment of more than five hundred, there was a greater tendency to appoint a special administrator of personnel services.

Closely related to over-all coordination of the personnel program is the extent to which various members of the college staff are involved in the program. Regardless of who coordinated the program in the cooperating colleges, there was a tendency to designate staff members as responsible for specific student services and to give them appropriate titles. The extent of this tendency is shown in Table 6-2, which indicates by title the staff members (other than the chief coordinator of personnel) who were reported to have personnel responsibilities, and the frequency of such assignments according to size of institution.

Titles in the table were used either in the institution's catalogue or were well known on the campus. Many persons had multiple

Table 6-2. Titles of Staff Members Assigned Responsibility for Specific Phases of the Student Personnel Program in 73 Two-year Institutions, 1956–57 *

Enrollment categories	No. of insti- tutions	Dean of students†	Director of guidance	Director of student activities	Registrar	Dean of men	Dean of women	Place- ment officer
Under 200	8	—	—	—	2	1	2	—
200–500	29	7	11	2	12	2	6	1
500–1,000	19	2	7	3	12	5	7	3
1,000–1,500	8	1	4	4	8	3	4	3
1,500–2,500	4	—	3	1	4	2	2	2
Over 2,500	5	1	3	5	4	1	1	5
Total	73	11	28	15	42	14	22	14

* OMITTED FROM SUMMARY: (1) Physicians and nurses; (2) housing counselors and supervisors; (3) veterans' counselors; (4) department chairmen; (5) infrequently used titles and combinations of titles.

† As differentiated from over-all dean of student personnel.

titles, e.g., "dean of guidance and admissions," "dean of women and registrar," "director of activities and dean of men." For those, the position was recorded under the column which was said to be the most descriptive of the person's chief responsibility. The persons assigned specific responsibilities were not always expected to devote full time to them, and in many instances those persons were faculty members released from part of their teaching duties to carry on some phase of the student services.

Clearly an institution's enrollment affects the manner in which the student personnel program is organized and the extent to which officials are appointed to assist in the program. Not only may there be less need for a special administrator in the small institution but the possible ratio of administrative time to the size of the institution may make it difficult for an additional person to be appointed to assist with the coordination of personnel services.

But regardless of the effect of institutional size on policy, the question may be raised as to whether there can be effective coordination of the many student services by an administrator who is also busy with the details of all phases of the college program. This question would seem particularly apropos where the chief administrator of the institution is the director of the personnel program. The question is not whether the person *can* coordinate all the services but whether he *will* coordinate them in view of the heavy demands on his time, even in a small institution.

COUNSELING IN TWO-YEAR INSTITUTIONS

The cooperating institutions tended to classify all formal advisement services as a part of the counseling program. This was true regardless of the complexity of the student's problem or of the advisement method (individual interviews or groups). Some activities fit the category of counseling per se better than others. There is, for example, a difference between mere program advising and helping a student to appraise his ability in a given occupation. After commenting on the various interpretations of the term "counseling" and the extent to which it is misused, Wrenn defined it as follows: "Counseling is a personal and dynamic relationship between two people who approach a mutually defined problem with mutual consideration for each other to the end that the younger, or less mature, or more troubled of the two is aided to a self-determined resolution of his problem."[7]

Wrenn makes the point that there are different levels of counseling. He refers at one extreme to the professionally trained counselor who may counsel students with complex problems and also assist the faculty with their normal counseling responsibilities. This "fourth level" group is contrasted with a "third level" of faculty who are interested and competent in counseling and used for that purpose. Lastly, he identifies "first and second levels,"

[7] Wrenn, *op. cit.*, p. 59.

which he calls "nominal" counseling, and which involve faculty assistance of counselors in the general advisement of students. Most classroom teachers normally do some counseling of students in their own classes, primarily on the problems of instruction, but conceivably also on other matters that arise in conversation. However, the discussion of counseling here pertains to a more structured situation.

All levels of counseling exist in practice, but some colleges have a higher proportion of Wrenn's fourth level type than others. There is a great variation in the counseling efforts put forth at all levels.

Preadmission Counseling

Counseling efforts may be expended on students before their arrival on campus as well as after arrival. Most two-year colleges, public and private, give incoming students information about the college and its program. Representatives from the college visit contributing high schools to advise students in groups and individually. Since most public junior colleges admit a student without selection, it might be assumed that the college would not require objective information about him other than a high school transcript. However, many of the junior colleges procure additional summarized data from the high schools, and aptitude test results and such items as a completed personal history form are often made available for use in preregistration counseling. Since the public junior college generally has a close working relationship with the local high schools and since it is close to the homes of students, the collection of such data becomes relatively easy.

Two-year colleges increasingly require each entering freshman to report to the college during the summer for an interview with a staff member regarding his college plans in general and the selection of his fall program. The extent and intensity of this initial counseling session vary greatly among the colleges. In approximately half of the colleges in which summer counseling is done, each student is given an adequate opportunity to discuss the range of his vocational and educational problems with a counselor who is aided by test results and other pertinent information to help the student plan his college program. In some institutions such interviews are much less thorough.

Postadmission Counseling

Attention was paid to three aspects of plans for postadmission counseling: (1) the general plan used by the institutions in making counseling time available to students, (2) the personnel used in the counseling process, and (3) practices with respect to the use of test data for counseling purposes. One of two basic plans, sometimes modified, prevailed in the cooperating institutions. One plan used the general teaching staff for the counseling and advising. The other plan used primarily professionally trained counselors or the general administrative staff of the college. The extent to which each plan was used among institutions of various sizes is shown in Table 6-3.

Table 6-3. Staff Members Primarily Responsible for Counseling Students in 73 Two-year Institutions, 1956–57

Enrollment categories	No. of institutions	Counseling primarily by administrators	Counseling primarily by professional counselors	Counseling primarily by faculty	
				Released time	Nonreleased time
Under 200	8	1	—	—	7
200–500	29	6	6	2	14
500–1,000	19	—	2	3	15
1,000–1,500	8	—	4	1	3
1,500–2,500	4	—	1	2	1
Over 2,500	5	—	4	1	—
Total	73	7	17	9	40

When the counseling was done by the teaching staff the students were assigned among the faculty members so that each student had a specified teacher to whom he was expected to go for advisement. Assignments of students to teachers were made either arbitrarily or according to the student's proposed specialization. In several of the technical institutes the chairmen of the different departments of instruction were responsible for counseling the students in the department or for dividing the students among the teachers in the department. Significantly, in most colleges where teachers did the counseling, they did so in addition to their normal teaching load. In only 9 out of a total of 49 colleges using this plan were teachers relieved of part of their teaching load. In one large institution in the Middle West a sizable number of faculty members were released for counseling. In this institution, however, the faculty member who counsels is not arbitrarily assigned a specific group of students to be counseled, but instead sets aside a specified number of hours per week to meeting students by appointment in the college counseling center.

Seventeen colleges reported that most of the counseling was performed by a limited number of designated counselors who had been professionally trained in student personnel work. As is evident from Table 6-3, the use of designated counselors was generally limited to larger institutions. Seven colleges reported that the general administrative staff did all the counseling. Usually, this practice was found in colleges with fewer than five hundred students.

The two general plans are not uniform among the institutions. Each college appeared to vary the basic plan in accordance with its own needs and its staff and also according to its conception of counseling. Naturally, no plan that provides for counseling by a particular group of staff members precludes other members of the staff from advising students informally as the occasion arises.

The role of the person who coordinates the counseling program is important. Whether this person was a general administrator of the college, a dean of student personnel, or a person having a title such as "director of guidance" with responsibilities limited to the guidance phases of the personnel program, generally he was expected to give leadership to the entire counseling program and also to perform some counseling. In varying degrees he served as a resource person and as a referral agent to whom other counselors could send students with special problems. In any institution in which students are generally counseled by faculty members not professionally trained, there should be some specialists who can assist students with problems more complex than those with which the staff member is able to cope. Of the 49 colleges with faculty counseling, 40 reported that such a referral person was available. While this is encouraging, the persons designated as referral agents were often, unfortunately, either general administrators with many other demands on their time or guidance specialists in a college so large that with their other duties, often including teaching, they could not effectively counsel many students. This fact is especially pertinent since students who need to be referred to a specialist usually have difficult problems which require considerable counseling time.

Group Counseling. Aside from varying types of freshman-week activities used for college orientation purposes, the most common type of structured group guidance program was a regularly scheduled orientation course that continued for varying lengths of time. Such a course existed in 70 per cent of the cooperating institutions. In slightly more than a third of the cooperating colleges the course ran for only a part of the first semester. In another third of the institutions the course ran for one semester and carried up to three units of credit. In some institutions it was required of most freshman students, in others it was elective. No intensive analysis was made of the contents of the course, but interviews brought out that in addition to the usual phases of orientation to college and how to study, it included units pertaining to the study of occupations, educational requirements for vocational preparation, and the meaning of test scores. In three instances the course in beginning psychology was expanded to include the desired orientation features. In one college a course in communication required of all freshmen was organized so as to include many orientation topics.

Use of Standardized Tests. The original check list included a series of questions on the tests administered to measure scholastic aptitude, special aptitudes, achievement, interests, and personality characteristics. Usable replies were received from 222 institutions (counting the extension centers in Pennsylvania and Wisconsin separately). All but 10 institutions reported the administration of some type of *scholastic* aptitude test. Most of them used the American Council on Education Psychological Examination (ACE). A few used either the Otis or Thurstone's Primary Mental Abilities Tests. The Pennsylvania extension centers used the Pennsylvania State Aptitude Tests, and most of the New York community colleges used the New York State Scholastic Aptitude Test.

Many institutions used tests to determine aptitudes and abilities other than academic, with clerical and mechanical tests being the most frequent. In addition, 162 colleges (73 per cent of the total reporting) indicated use of *achievement* tests. Most of them sought to determine achievement in English and reading, although several institutions reported the use of batteries to determine general educational development, and several included measures in science and mathematics.

More than 70 per cent of the colleges reported the use of some type of *interest* inventory, the Kuder Preference Inventory being used with greatest frequency. Only 66 (30 per cent) of the institutions reported the use of personality scales.

Although academic aptitude tests were likely to be administered either before or close to the time of admission, unfortunately most institutions did not use the results in a *preregistration* interview with the student. Occasionally, the linguistic score on these tests was found to be a factor at the time of registration in placing students in an English course, and the quantitative score a factor in registration for courses in such subjects as engineering. In practically all colleges, however, academic aptitude test results were used to some extent in counseling and advising students after their registration. Colleges which used special aptitude tests, interest inventories, and personality scales tended to administer such measures only to specific students about whom more information was considered necessary for adequate counseling. When achievement tests were used, the results were usually available at the time of registration so that students could be placed in appropriate courses in such subjects as English, mathematics, and languages. This did not necessarily mean ability grouping except for the students who were placed in special remedial classes.

Some colleges seemed to test for testing's sake; masses of test data were available in files or even in summarized form, but apparently seldom used. Other colleges made test information about most students available to counselors and teachers, and necessary professional assistance was given teachers in the interpretation of test data.

PERSONNEL RESEARCH ACTIVITIES

An important aspect of the personnel program is the research done with respect to the characteristics of entering students, the length of time they remain, what they do after they leave the junior college, and the evaluation made of the factors relating to their performance.

Information of this kind would seem essential to a college,

for guidance purposes and for curriculum making. Information on ability, achievement, interests, and personality may be obtained from test data referred to previously. But the social and economic characteristics of the group are also important, as are some motivational factors which may be measured by home background, family pattern of college attendance, parental attitudes, and the degree of under- or overachievement. It is also essential to have information about students who transfer to other institutions such as how well they have performed in senior college and the relationship between their performance after transfer and their experience in the junior college. The same would be true of students who have entered directly into employment. Opinions obtained from students while still in the two-year college about various phases of the college program, including the personnel program, can be helpful for appraisal purposes.

But despite the value of such data, only a small amount of it is compiled. Out of 225 institutions, only 38 per cent reported that they had ever made a study of the number of entering students who later transferred to a four-year college. Only 40 per cent stated that they had made a study of the number of graduates who had transferred. Sixty per cent had studied why students drop out of junior college during the first semester of attendance. Twenty-seven per cent reported over-all studies of drop-outs to determine why students leave and what they do after leaving. With the exception of one subject, a greater percentage of the public colleges than the private schools had made institutional studies. The exception was that 11 per cent more private colleges reported studies of the number of their entering students who later transferred to four-year colleges.

The 75 cooperating institutions were also asked to indicate their practices with regard to studies about students, but in only two of several major problem areas did more than half of the colleges report that such studies were made. One of the problems most frequently investigated was that of the relationship of psychological test scores to grades made in junior college—64 per cent of the institutions said they had conducted such studies. About a fourth of the colleges regularly polled their current students for opinions on the extent to which they believed the college met their needs and expectations.

On the basis of such evidence it must be concluded that so far as the colleges in the sample are indicative, most two-year colleges conduct very little research of the kind that would facilitate institutional planning and an improvement of student personnel services.

STUDENT ACTIVITIES IN THE TWO-YEAR COLLEGE

Practices with regard to such activities were informally discussed with administrators of the cooperating institutions, but no compilation was made of the nature and kind of activities. Each visited college had a fairly broad program of out-of-class activities. As Table 6-2 indicates, 15 colleges had designated a staff member as "director of student activities." But regardless of whether there was a person who carried this title, there was always someone responsible for the activity program. Table 6-2 also indicates that 11 colleges had a person with the title "dean of students" who gave direction to student activities. In other colleges either the dean of men or the dean of women was responsible. Even though one staff member had over-all coordinating and supervisory responsibilities, other faculty members generally participated as advisers for particular campus organizations and clubs. Administrators regarded the social programs of the various campus organizations and occasional social activities sponsored by the administration as sufficient to give students an opportunity for participation. There was, however, almost universal concern about how much a college should push or control an activity program and how thoroughly it should be supervised. The problem becomes one of a desirable balance between supervision by the college and initiative by the students. This is also a problem in four-year colleges, but three factors make it even more difficult in the two-year college: (1) the limited span of college years in the same institution, (2) the consequent absence of the more mature students in the upper division, and (3) the tendency of students living at home to retain their identity with their family and established peer circles rather than with new associates.

A second closely related problem, mentioned by administrators of junior colleges in rural areas, is caused by the long distances which many students live from the college. These students are frequently transported to and from college by bus. Under such circumstances it is difficult for students to take an active part in school functions.

Whatever the problems encountered by two-year colleges in the administration of the extraclass program, the opportunities for joint staff and student participation in the making and execution of policies are probably greater in this phase of the college program than in any other. Thus, a responsibility falls on these colleges to demonstrate a working relationship which will prove that the faculty and administration and students *can* work together in a way that develops student independence and maturity. Arbuckle voiced this opinion when he said:

> Training for independence and responsibility is surely lacking in any institution that has little or nothing in the way of a developing program that encourages student leadership and student participation in many of the affairs of the institution. . . .
>
> A group of students *can* be responsible for its actions, just as an individual *can* be responsible for his actions.
>
> It is probably pointless to discuss ways and means of selecting and training students for democratic leadership in an institution that does not have a democratic faculty, and whose basic policy toward students would appear to be one of distrust. . . . Faculty members must indicate their belief in the capacity of the students for responsibility by their actions in their daily work with students.[8]

THE COST OF STUDENT PERSONNEL PROGRAMS

Standardized budgetary practices usually make it possible to compute the cost of a given item in per cent of the total cost of operation. But it is much more difficult to measure and compare costs of personnel services. One reason for this difficulty is the great variation in the extent and nature of such services among institutions and in the way the services are organized and budgeted. For example, it is difficult to compare costs between an institution which assigns counseling to teachers and charges the entire cost to instruction, and an institution which either employs full-time counselors or releases teachers from part of their teaching assignment for counseling.

[8] Dugald Arbuckle, *Studet Personnel Services in Higher Education*, McGraw-Hill Book Company, Inc., New York, 1953, pp. 258–59.

However, a limited study of expenditures was undertaken in some cooperating institutions. Since expenditures can be meaningful only in those institutions which in one way or another budget directly for all personnel services, the study had to be restricted to the comparatively few colleges which follow this practice and, among them, to those willing to submit the necessary data. A further limitation was that the study included salary costs only and did not include expenditures for supplies and similar items.

Fourteen junior colleges and technical institutes of varying size and complexity submitted the following usable information:

Total salaries for the professional and clerical staff for student personnel services, 1956–57, including extra salaries for summer, 1956, paid for precounseling of students and for overtime salaries during the school year paid for service to students in the *regular* college program. (Salaries for services to evening part-time students and adults were excluded.) The figures included the prorata share of the salary of staff members who devoted a designated part of their time to student personnel work, including teachers who were released from part of their teaching load for counseling or administrators who divided their time between student personnel and other duties.

Budget amounts for 1956–57 for all professional and clerical salaries in the institution. (Budget items for the extended day and summer school programs were excluded.)

The objective was to determine the percentage that the salaries for student personnel services was of the total budget for educational and clerical salaries for the same year.

Table 6-4 indicates the percentages as determined for the institutions.

The first nine colleges were in California, where the tendency to operate centralized student personnel programs is greater than in most other states and where the scope of services is greater than in some sections of the country. Among these nine institutions a relatively small variation was found in the percentage of student personnel expenditures. This is to be expected because all nine operate on a centralized basis, maintain approximately the same range of services, and are in the size category of more than a thousand students.

The data presented are at best only an indication of what a personnel program may cost. Administrators and governing boards of two-year colleges must realize that professional student personnel services and clerical assistance for them require a substantial budget. Too frequently the philosophy prevails that staff

Table 6-4. Percentage of Expenditures for Salaries of Staff Members Assigned to Student Personnel Services Compared to Total Institutional Budget for Educational and Clerical Services in 14 Junior Colleges, 1956–57

Institution	Percentage of educational and clerical salaries*	Percentage of professional salaries*
A	18	16
B	16	13
C	15	13
D†	15	13
E	14	11
F	13	11
G	13	11
H	13	11
I	12	11
J	10	9
K	10	5
L	8	9
M	7	5
N	3	4

* Campus budgets only. Does not include central office figures in unified or high school districts or districts with multiple college units. Includes salaries of all professionally trained staff members, including teachers and administrators.

† A limited amount of student programing also done by faculty on nonreleased time.

members can render the services on top of a full teaching or administrative load and that extra expenditures for such services can be reduced to a minimum.

CONCLUSIONS

This investigation of student personnel services in two-year colleges was necessarily limited to an over-all view of practices. It was not possible to evaluate the effectiveness of the practices in terms of their impact on students. Thus the only evaluation that can be made is in terms of how extensive the services are, how widely they are performed by staff members who have the preparation and time to perform them adequately, and how they are organized and directed.

In reviewing the total student personnel program in two-year institutions one is confronted with a certain amount of seeming contradiction. There can be little doubt that many of the deficiencies outlined earlier by Humphreys are still present. On the other hand, the increasing emphasis on the necessity for adequate personnel services in two-year colleges generally and the efforts to render them found in most of the cooperating two-year colleges lead one to believe that some advances have been made.

The student personnel services reviewed in the study are difficult to appraise because their range among the institutions is very great, both in breadth and in emphasis. In none of the cooperating institutions were services entirely absent.

Instead of generalizations, the following lists of strengths and weaknesses are offered in an attempt to summarize the program in the states and institutions sampled.

Elements of Strength

1. Administrators recognize the responsibility of a two-year college for an effective student personnel program.

Administrators and others interviewed in the colleges discussed the peculiar responsibility which falls on the junior college to provide an adequate range of personnel services. In practically every college publication—college catalogue, student handbook, faculty manual, promotional brochures—appeared extensive statements on counseling and student activities in the college. This declared responsibility constitutes a foundation on which a program could be built. Without such acceptance by those who must implement a program, little could be expected.

2. Some type and level of counseling program exists in each college.

The term "counseling" is used broadly in the same sense in which it is used in the institutions. In some colleges, this may mean merely academic advising; in others it may include many levels of counseling. There is always some provision whereby students are either *expected* to confer periodically with some member of the college staff for advisement or are informed that they *may* do so should they feel the need for assistance. The range of counseling services among institutions is great but there is no institution without some plan for student-staff relationships for counseling purposes. In numerous institutions the scope of the counseling merits enthusiastic approval.

3. Most colleges have a well-developed student activity program.

The program is generally well planned with the assistance of students, and coordinated and supervised by members of the college staff.

4. A good system of academic records is maintained in all colleges.

Usually the records are centralized and easily accessible to staff members who may use them in counseling. In many institutions individual folders are maintained for each student in which materials pertinent for counseling purposes are accumulated.

Elements of Weakness

1. Many institutions lack policy formulation, planning, and professional direction of the program.

In 57 out of the 73 cooperating colleges the only leader giving centralized direction to the entire personnel program was either the chief administrator or an assistant general administrator such as the academic dean. While this does not in itself necessarily mean inadequate direction, the person with chief administrative responsibilites simply does not have time to give personal attention and leadership to the several staff members involved with personnel services. Besides, the administrator does not necessarily have adequate professional training in student personnel work. Exceptions were found— indeed, some of the chief administrators had once been counselors or deans of student personnel services. However, the average chief administrator can hardly include more than one or two graduate courses in student personnel work in his preparation for general administrative duties.

As noted in Table 6-3, the separate phases of the program— counseling, supervising of student activities, and the like—are sometimes placed in the hands of individual staff members who report to the chief administrator. Though this practice may be desirable because it provides professional direction of specific services, it still has the dangers of a decentralized system in which top administration must coordinate many details and many people.

2. The counseling program in many institutions is inadequate.

A narrow view is often taken on what constitutes counseling. In many colleges the view prevailed that when a student could be assisted in arranging a program of classes which met his personal desires and also met requirements of transfer to a senior college, the major task of counseling had been fulfilled. Important as this service is, it does not include the more important task of helping the student to make certain of his occupational preference by various rational means; to make a wise choice of the next higher institution, if there is to be one; to analyze his achievement record in relation to his aptitude; and to solve some of the personal problems which may be affecting his academic or social adjustment. These are only some of the other aspects of counseling for which *competent* assistance should be available.

This raises the question of what kinds of staff may be needed to render such counseling help, and here another deficiency comes to light. Many colleges lack a sufficient number of counselors with professional preparation in the guidance field. There are arguments in favor of faculty participation in counseling; in fact, it is assumed that students often will seek out faculty members for help whether the teachers are assigned as counselors or not. The question remains, however, whether most teachers, by background and preparation, are able to deal with some of the more complex student problems. Assuming they are not, there should be a sufficient number of professionally trained staff members in each college to perform high-level counseling services and to assist the teachers in the counseling for which they are assigned.

Even if one assumes that teachers are competent to perform most of the counseling, two additional circumstances militate against their doing a satisfactory job.

Teachers are generally expected to serve as counselors over and beyond their normal teaching load. Since in the average junior college this load is between 15 and 20 hours per week, exclusive of time for preparation and other general college responsibilities, the teacher will hardly be able or inclined to find time to confer adequately with students. Under these circumstances, counseling becomes a chance proposition in which both student and teacher follow the line of least resistance. The teacher-adviser system appeared to be more accepted in some of the private junior colleges, perhaps because of a generally smaller student-faculty ratio in the private college.

Another deterrent to good counseling by the faculty results from the lack of adequate in-service training programs. In only half of the colleges where counseling responsibilities were assigned to teachers was a continuous in-service training program in operation. Yet the swiftly changing American occupational structure, the shifting of educational patterns available to young people, the continuous development of new devices to help in the counseling process, all indicate the indispensability of in-service training. Many of those interviewed discussed the desirability of an in-service program for teacher-counselors but reported that little was done in their own college. The lack of such programs is cause for concern about the quality of counseling performed by a diverse group of teachers, many of whom have no particular background for the job and limited motivation.

3. Little research is conducted which enables the two-year colleges to obtain facts about their students.

A function of the personnel program is to gather and disseminate information about students. Few two-year institutions conducted institutional studies on students. When the many possibilities of studies were discussed with the administrators, the usual apologetic response was, "This is something we would like to do but haven't had time to do." Such a dilemma is understandable in light of the relatively small budgets which have been made available for student services and the pressure of time to meet the urgent day-by-day demands of students. Nonetheless, if staff and faculty are to use empirical data in assisting and counseling students, if academic and personal problems are to be diagnosed, and if the institutions are to revise curricula and grading standards, regular studies of many subjects need to be made. It is just as obvious, however, that such studies will not be made unless money is made available for the employment of sufficient help to make them.

4. Two-year colleges make only limited effort to evaluate the personnel program.

Objective evaluation of a student personnel program is difficult. Student opinionaires and follow-up studies of drop-outs and graduates help in revealing strengths and weaknesses about the program as seen by those who respond, but even these do not measure the intangible results. One frequently expressed criterion of a good program is the extent to which students are enrolled in terminal curricula—the hypothesis being that the more effective the personnel program, the more likely it is that a substantial number of students will be in curricula leading to employment rather than in those leading to transfer to a four-year college. As discussed in Chapter 4, there are numerous problems in terminal education, not all of which are affected by the student personnel program. Nevertheless, observations in the community colleges in the sample lend support to the opinion that there is some relationship between the nature of the program and enrollments in terminal offerings.

Froehlich,[9] Arbuckle,[10] and Feder[11] et al. have recommended various categories and criteria for the evaluation of personnel programs by raising questions about the component parts and the expectancies of the program. Shibler[12] points to the necessity for continuous evaluation as well as a review of personnel services in the form of an annual report. Chief administrators of two-year colleges clearly have an obligation to bring about a periodically conducted, cooperative review of student personnel services in which all staff members, together with representative students, evaluate the quantitative and qualitative aspects of the program.

Some Suggestions to Institutions

Considering the strengths and weaknesses of student personnel programs, a few suggestions are offered for staff members and others responsible for these programs in two-year institutions:

1. The student personnel program should spring from the basic philosophy and objectives of the institution. Reference was made

[9] Clifford R. Froehlich, *Evaluating Guidance Procedures: A Review of Literature,* U.S. Office of Education, 1949, p. 2.

[10] Arbuckle, *op. cit.,* p. 18 ff.

[11] Feder, *op. cit.,* chap. 4.

[12] Herman L. Shibler, "Organization of Personnel Services," *Personnel Services in Education,* Fifty-eighth Yearbook of the National Society for the Study of Higher Education, Chicago, 1959, chap. 7.

in Chapter 4 to the desirability of staff agreement on an institutional philosophy and a set of educational objectives. Such philosophy and objectives inevitably hold implications for everything the institution does to serve the student, and it is logical that it should be the basis for determining the quality and kinds of personnel services.

2. Each institution, regardless of size, should consciously structure a *plan* for its student personnel program. The formulation of the plan should call for the participation of administrators and teachers. Student opinion should be solicited and considered. While the governing board may not be concerned with the details of the plan, it may appropriately (and often necessarily) be asked to approve it. The most essential element in the plan is the manner in which the services are to be coordinated, because otherwise gaps will inevitably appear in the services. No matter how small the college, some staff member—even if on a part-time basis—should be made responsible for the direction of the program. An organization chart should show the responsibility of each staff member and the method of coordination.

A planned and adequate program will entail costs. This factor should be made clear to the governing board when the plan is submitted for consideration.

3. The program demands the services of a professionally trained staff. Even in the smallest institutions a staff member with experience and training in guidance should be in charge of all testing and counseling. This person may be engaged full time or part time, depending on the size of the institution. In larger institutions several professionally trained counselors are needed for counseling. The person delegated to direct and coordinate the entire personnel program should have professional preparation in that field. Whether the major part of the counseling is to be done by teachers or by professionally trained counselors should be decided by the institution, with the recognition that professional direction is essential.

4. If the plan makes the faculty responsible for counseling, it is recommended that:

a. Time be allowed for members of the teaching staff who participate extensively in the counseling program.

b. Physical facilities and the housing of student records be such that counseling can be done in private offices and that records are easily accessible.

c. There be a continuing, well-structured, in-service training program for teacher-counselors under the leadership of a professionally trained counselor or outside clinical services.

d. Provision be made for easy referral of difficult cases to a professionally trained counselor.

5. The institution should include in its student personnel program a carefully designed research program to obtain information about students and their progress. This should include follow-up studies of various types.

6. The administration of the college should strive to interpret the objectives and services of the personnel program to students, staff, and community. Those who teach and those who perform personnel services should all understand the program and the reasons for it.

7. There should be a plan for close coordination between those who perform personnel services and those who teach, so that the curriculum and the instructional program are strengthened by information and ideas from those who work closely with students outside the classroom. Student personnel services cannot operate in a vacuum.

8. There should be continuous evaluation of the total program.

Needed Research. Should the counseling in two-year colleges be performed by members of the teaching staff or by professional counselors? The question, bearing on divergent practices referred to many times in this chapter, has stimulated much debate but comparatively little objective evaluation. Those who vote for professional counselors often criticize the adviser system by saying that it tends to "make everybody's business nobody's business." They claim that it is easier for professional counselors or for a limited number of special teachers assigned as counselors to keep up to date and to participate in an in-service training program. They say that assigning students to advisers on the basis of subject areas is unrealistic because so many students change their vocational goals in junior college. On the other hand, those who believe that the faculty should be used in some type of adviser system contend that (1) faculty members are acquainted with the educational requirements in their fields and thus are able better to advise interested students, (2) the process makes for closer student-faculty relationships, (3) misunderstandings between teachers and counselors are avoided, and (4) counseling responsibilities tend to make teachers better teachers. The nature and scope of this study did not permit any evaluation of the two plans. Those interviewed usually defended the plan in their institution, and presented some justifiable points for their rationale.

It seems appropriate, therefore, that some experimental studies be made to determine which of the two methods—or modifications thereof—is the more desirable and also to determine how best to utilize professionally prepared staff to assist counseling teachers. Such studies, if made and coordinated under controlled conditions in a number of institutions, should be extremely helpful in guiding decisions on planning optimum programs.

More adequate personnel services will be needed in the future. The junior college will undoubtedly play an increasingly important role in providing opportunities for high school graduates to explore their capacities and interests and in distributing these students later among many avenues of endeavor, including the four-year colleges; therefore the whole personnel program, and its counseling phase in particular, becomes especially significant. In fact, without good counseling the potentially important role of the two-year college in higher education could well be in jeopardy.

To some extent the situation is paradoxical because the need for additional personnel and counseling services will come at the very time when enrollment increases will require the greatest expenditures possible for facilities and teaching staff. This situation could mean that those who administer the two-year college will be pressured into reducing proportionately the funds available for personnel services. Somehow, in some way, a high-level personnel program must be maintained.

CHAPTER 7

Faculty Attitudes on the Role of the Two-year College*

Earlier chapters discussed the degree to which the two-year college is discharging the functions that society seems to have assigned it. The information presented led to the conclusion that although this institution has become a dynamic segment of education after high school, performing many of its functions well, in other ways it falls short of its expectations and claims. As both its strengths and weaknesses are noted, it is important to inquire into the possible relation between them and the characteristics and attitudes of the staff. To what extent is the success of the two-year college in providing multiple educational opportunities for students with varying capacities and interests dependent on teachers and administrators in sympathy with the purposes of the college? Likewise, to what extent are deficiencies such as the lack of emphasis on the terminal function, the minimal concern about general education, and the inadequacies in student personnel services attributable to the attitudes of the staff?

Teachers and administrators in any type of college inevitably influence, by their attitudes, the nature and quality of program. They are the primary agents of curriculum development, instruction, services to students, and community relationships. They, and the students, make the institution what it is.

---

* Herbert Maccoby, associate research sociologist, Center for the Study of Higher Education, cooperated in the collection and summary of data for this chapter.

It is often said that the junior college staff is highly dedicated. The presumption is that people teach in a junior college because they prefer work at that level and subscribe to the goals and structure of this type of institution. Much is made of the point that in a junior college a premium is placed upon good teaching. Teacher-student relationships are generally thought to be excellent. Teachers are said to be recognized for their performance in the classroom and are not held responsible for research and publication as a basis for promotion. The general morale is considered high.

Table 7-1. Number and Percentage of Respondents in the Various Types of Institutions

Type of institution	No. of institutions	No. of staff in survey	No. of staff responding	Per cent of staff responding	Per cent response of each type
Local unified*	21	1,555	1,346	87	41
Local separate†	25	1,466	1,219	83	37
State	6	236	199	84	6
Extension centers	5	101	92	91	3
Private	17	555	418	75	13
Total	74	3,913	3,274‡	84	100

* Includes junior colleges operated by high school districts. Also includes four institutions in legally separate districts but under the same board of trustees and top administration as the local school system.

† Junior colleges with separate administration and governing boards.

‡ An additional eight respondents did not identify their institutions.

The purpose of the inquiry reported in this chapter was to learn more about the views of junior college teachers and administrators and their possible impact on the college and its program. A questionnaire was mailed in the fall of 1957 to all members of the professional staff (teachers and administrators) in 74 of the two-year institutions which cooperated in other phases of the over-all study.[1] Since it was thought that the responses might vary among

[1] A total of 3,282 (84 per cent) of the 3,895 staff members included in the survey returned completed questionnaires. This does not include the responses of 183 (5 per cent) who returned a one-page mimeographed questionnaire excerpted from the larger printed instrument.

types of institutions, the data will be analyzed by forms of control.[2] Table 7-1 shows the number of colleges in each type, together with information concerning the total number of staff members and the number of respondents in each type.

Response from the staff in many of the institutions ran 90 per cent or more, and in some colleges 100 per cent.

CHARACTERISTICS OF THE STAFF

Many data obtained on the background of the respondents will be published later, but the following brief description of those returning the questionnaire should be helpful in identifying the two-year college instructor:

The staff is composed mainly of full-time teachers, but also includes full-time administrators and counselors, in addition to persons who hold combined positions. Full-time teachers accounted for more than 68 per cent of the respondents, full-time administrators for 6 per cent, and full-time counselors 1 per cent. Almost 8 per cent of the group held combined teaching-counseling responsibilities and another 8 per cent were classified as combination teachers and administrators. Various other combinations accounted for the remainder of the group.

Almost 72 per cent of the respondents were men. More men appear to enter teaching at the junior college level than at the high school level. Only 47 per cent of the secondary classroom teachers in the United States are men.[3]

Approximately three-fourths (74.3 per cent) of the respondents held a graduate degree. More than 64 per cent held only a master's degree—of these, more than 60 per cent a master of arts degree. Seven per cent had earned a Ph.D. and 2.7 per cent an Ed.D. More than 9 per cent were working toward a master's degree and more than 10 per cent toward a doctorate.

[2] More detailed analyses of the data are to follow in articles prepared for educational periodicals. In addition, a book dealing more comprehensively with the sociological background of the two-year college staff member is in preparation by Dr. Herbert Maccoby, associate research sociologist at the Center for the Study of Higher Education.

[3] *Estimates of School Statistics, 1958–59*, National Education Association, Research Report 1958-R6, table 3, p. 20.

Almost 93 per cent held at least a bachelor's degree. This means that only 7 per cent did not hold a first degree, although more than a hundred teachers indicated they were working toward it.[4]

It is interesting to compare data on degrees with similar information gathered by Koos in 1941–42 on 1,458 teachers in 48 local public junior colleges in California and in eight states in the Middle West and the South.[5] Although the sample studied by Koos was somewhat more restricted than that of the current study, the data are strikingly similar, considering the time elapsed between the two studies.

	Per cent of staff with various degrees	
	Present study	Koos study
Doctorate	9.6	6.3
Master's	64.6	63.6
Bachelor's	17.0	26.8
No degree	6.7	3.3
Indeterminate or unclassified	2.1	0.0
Total	100.0	100.0

More than 64 per cent of the group had formerly taught in secondary or elementary schools or in both, mostly, however, in secondary schools. Almost half of the teachers in the local unified colleges had taught in secondary schools as had about a third of the staff in local separate districts. Very few of the staff in state junior colleges and even fewer in extension centers had had secondary school experience. The large number of teachers with experience at the secondary level confirms the general belief that high school teachers tend to move into the junior college. This is most likely to happen in unified systems where the central administration is empowered to make such transfers and where the staff is likely to regard the move as a promotion in status. The same progression occurs to a lesser degree in the local separate junior colleges where teachers in nearby high schools are likely to apply for junior college positions.

More than a fourth of the group (27 per cent) had once at-

[4] Teachers without degrees may be approved in many two-year colleges for instruction in vocational courses. In such cases other appropriate training and experience are allowed to stand in lieu of a baccalaureate degree.

[5] Leonard V. Koos, "Junior College Teachers: Degrees and Graduate Residence," *Junior College Journal*, vol. 18, pp. 77–89, October, 1947.

tended a junior college. This percentage is surprisingly high in view of the relatively small number of college graduates who would have attended a junior college during the time that the present generation of teachers was in training. It would suggest that long-term recruitment of junior college teachers may well begin with the present generation of junior college students.

Most of the staff come from "white collar" or farm-family backgrounds. Almost 53 per cent of the group reported that their fathers were managers or professional, sales, or clerical workers; 20 per cent were farmers; and the rest were craftsmen, operatives, and service workers. About 4 per cent of those whose fathers were professionals reported that the fathers were in the field of education.[6]

THE REFERENCE POINT OF TWO-YEAR COLLEGE TEACHERS

Before proceeding with a report of the basic attitudes of the staff members toward their role in the junior college and toward the role of the junior college in higher education, it may be useful to lay an interpretive background that will be explored further near the end of the chapter. This interpretive context is the "reference group theory." According to this theory, a person may not be identified primarily with the occupational, social, or economic group of which he is a member. Instead, he may more readily adhere to the views of another group, presumably a group to which he aspires to belong or one with which he wishes to be identified in his own mind or in the minds of others. Sociologists point to the familiar tendency of some people in lower-income groups to identify with and emulate standards of middle-class life.

Certain junior college staff members may identify themselves with groups outside the college. More particularly, the attitudes of junior college teachers may reflect the educational values or attitudes of teachers in four-year colleges and universities. Another possibility is that the relatively new and inexperienced teacher in the junior college will retain a close identity with the graduate school or department from which he recently came and thus visualize the role of the junior college in terms of graduate standards and

[6] The question which elicited this information read as follows:
"What kind of work did your father do for a living when he was your age (or if he was deceased by then, or retired, what was it just before that)?"

procedures. Still another possibility is that junior college teachers who once taught in high school may retain that perspective after they transfer to junior college teaching. A junior college teacher may have many reference points; he may see himself through several different projections, each one of which may influence his thinking about the junior college.

This possibility would suggest that junior college teachers not committed to the two-year college as an institution with distinctive purposes may be more likely to evaluate it in the light of the activities of scholars in their teaching field or in terms of the values associated with the older, more familiar, and higher prestige-carrying senior college.

HOW DO TEACHERS REGARD THE JUNIOR COLLEGE AS A PLACE TO WORK?

In one item the staff was asked to indicate how satisfied they were with their present position. The five categories of satisfaction and the number and percentage of the total group responding to each category were as follows:

	Number	Per cent
Completely satisfied	801	24.4
Well satisfied	1,792	54.5
Neither satisfied nor dissatisfied	269	8.2
A little dissatisfied	328	10.0
Very dissatisfied	45	1.4
No answers and indeterminable responses	47	1.5
Total	3,282	100.0

One might speculate on the reasons why 10 per cent of the group were "a little dissatisfied" and a few "very dissatisfied." It is possible that local situations may account for the negative feeling in some instances. It is also possible that some of the respondents were fundamentally not in accord with the purposes and nature of the junior college.

Only slightly more than 11 per cent of the group registered any degree of dissatisfaction with their situation. However, there was a different response to another question which asked the teachers to indicate the type of institution in which they would prefer to work if they had their choice and if "salary schedules, promotion opportunities, retirement benefits, job security, etc., were equal in each type of institution." The returns were summarized both for the total group and by types of two-year colleges in which the respondents were employed. Of the total group approximately one-half indicated that, if other conditions were equal, they would prefer teaching in a four-year college or university. About 46 per cent said they would still prefer a junior college. More than 2 per cent indicated the high school as their preference. The preferences of the group varied, however, among the staffs in the different

Table 7-2. Types of Institutions in Which Two-year College Teachers Would Prefer to Teach, in Per Cent*

College in which employed	Preference as to type of institution for employment		
	2-year college	4-year college or university	High school
Local unified junior college	41	54	3
Local separate junior college	51	45	1
State junior college	63	37	—
Extension center	34	66	—
Private junior college	41	52	4

* Since the percentage of no answers or unusable responses is omitted from the table, not all totals add up to 100.

types of two-year colleges. Table 7-2 shows the preferences of teachers employed in the five types of institutions.

Staff members in local separate junior colleges were somewhat more content in their positions than those in local unified junior colleges. The high preference for the two-year college among those in the state junior colleges in the sample may be partly accounted for by the fact that some of the state institutions were technical institutes in which many staff members would have neither the qualifications nor the inclination to teach in a senior institution. Only about a third of extension center staff members indicated their preference for the two-year institution, a smaller proportion than for any other group, probably because their aspirations are toward employment on the main campus of the university rather than in one of its branches. It is possible that even though many teachers

are happy in a two-year college they would still prefer a position
in a higher institution because of its status and because teaching
loads in four-year colleges are considered to be lighter than in two-
year colleges.

Although not a measurement of personal work preference, a
third question sought to gain an idea of the value which respondents
attached to the junior college by their expressed willingness to have
an able son attend it.[7]

Fifty-five per cent of the respondents preferred to send their
sons to a four-year college or university for four years, forty-one
per cent said they would have a son attend a junior college first,
and four per cent either gave no answer or one that was in-
determinate. Undoubtedly, some were influenced by the prestige
of the four-year college or university. Also, the example was that
of a boy qualified to complete a four-year degree program from a
family financially able to send him to a four-year college. Had
there been any question about either factor or had the boy not
been interested in a baccalaureate degree, the results would have
been different.

The responses on preferences do not reflect as high a degree of
enthusiasm for the junior college on the part of its professional staff
as would ordinarily be presumed. Unfortunately, there are no data
permitting a comparison of satisfaction of junior college teachers
with teachers in high schools and in four-year institutions. The advocates of the two-year college frequently claim that most of its
teachers are there because they want to be—that they prefer the
emphasis on teaching in such a college. That this is true on the part
of many teachers was substantiated by the number of respondents
indicating their satisfaction; that it is not true of all teachers was
indicated by the number who said they would like to be elsewhere
or who would send their sons elsewhere. To be sure, the fact that
a two-year college teacher may wish he were in a university does
not necessarily mean that he is ineffective in his present position.

[7] The specific question asked read as follows:
"Assume that you have a son who wants, and is competent, to complete
four years of college education. Assume further that finances are no problem.
Now all things considered, which of the following alternatives do you lean to?
"He attend a four-year college or university for four years. . . . "
"He attend a junior college for two years and then transfer to a four-year
college or university for the final two years. . . . "

More important is his belief concerning the nature and functions of the two-year college.

Many factors affect the staff members' feelings about working in the junior college. Among them are faculty-administrative relationships, working conditions, and the extent of in-service training and orientation. It is well to acknowledge certain dissatisfactions and to temper the statements often made about the enthusiasm which teachers have for the junior college. Beyond that lies the responsibility of teachers, administrators, and governing boards to work together in helping to reduce the cause for dissatisfaction.

IS THE STAFF IN AGREEMENT WITH THE GENERAL PURPOSES OF THE JUNIOR COLLEGE?

Since most two-year colleges and particularly the local public junior colleges are multipurpose institutions, the question frequently arises as to whether teachers are in harmony with the several functions of the college. If they rate one function much higher than others, such differences could well reduce the institutional effectiveness with which the various functions are fulfilled.

Numerous items in the questionnaire sought responses which would reflect attitudes on the purpose, program, and general effectiveness of the two-year college. In one section the respondents were asked to rate on a 3-point scale the degree of importance which they attached to each of several listed programs. In another section they were asked to indicate on a 4-point scale how strongly they agreed or disagreed with each statement on a long list about the junior college and its role in American higher education. Other questions related to the balance between vocational and general education and to admission requirements. Still another section asked the staff to indicate agreement or disagreement with each of a series of statements which are often heard either in favor of or in opposition to the two-year college, particularly when it is compared with a four-year college.

The respondents almost unanimously agreed that the two primary educational programs which the junior college should offer are: (1) the first two years of traditional college education and (2) specialized terminal vocational education. The two types of programs were given almost equal rating by the respondents—97 per cent rated transfer work and 92 per cent vocational-technical work as either "very important" or "important."

The respondents were less well agreed on other stated functions of the two-year college. For example, 28 per cent indicated that it was "not important" for the junior college to offer remedial high school level courses for students whose academic record makes them ineligible to enter directly into conventional college courses. Nineteen per cent said it was not important that the junior college offer supplementary study opportunities for students who show weaknesses in such subjects as English and mathematics. There were also some minority expressions against having the junior college offer certain programs for adults. A fifth of the respondents thought it not important for the junior college to offer vocational or in-service classes for adults. Ten per cent opposed the offering of broad, general educational courses for adults, and thirteen per cent thought it not important for the junior college to sponsor such events as public forums, concerts, plays, and the like.

Though these opinions of the total group are interesting, more significant differences are observed when responses of teachers of academic subjects are compared with those of applied subjects, and when the opinions of both groups are examined according to the type of two-year college in which they teach. Table 7-3 shows the percentage of each of the two categories of teachers from each of the five types of colleges who indicated the relative importance of the transfer, terminal, remedial, adult-vocational, and adult-general education functions mentioned above.

It is clear that the relative importance of the various programs as expressed by the respondents is related to the teaching field of the faculty members. For example, a higher percentage of the teachers in the academic group than in the applied group in *all* types of colleges rated the transfer function as being very important. The opposite was true in their rating of the terminal function. Also, teachers of academic subjects were more inclined to regard general education programs for adults as more important than vocational programs for adults, whereas the opposite rating was given by the teachers of applied subjects. The percentage of teachers of applied subjects who rated the remedial function as very important was consistently higher than that of the academic staff. A higher percentage of the academic group than of the applied group said the remedial function is not important.

The differences between the academic and applied group also varied in degree among the types of two-year colleges. For example, teachers of academic and applied subjects in the state junior colleges were less inclined to consider the transfer programs very

Table 7-3. Faculty Opinion on Importance of Educational Programs in Two-year Colleges, in Per Cent*

Institution	No.	Transfer			Vocational-technical			Remedial			Programs for adults					
											Vocational			General academic		
		VI	I	NI†	VI	I	NI†	VI	I	NI†	VI	I	NI†	VI	I	NI†
Local unified:																
Academic	557	83	15	1	59	36	5	19	48	32	23	53	22	38	53	8
Applied	310	71	28	1	87	12	1	27	48	24	43	44	13	25	61	13
Local separate:																
Academic	509	79	18	2	53	42	4	26	44	27	26	55	18	46	48	5
Applied	311	68	28	4	76	14	—	30	50	18	46	43	10	29	56	14
State:																
Academic	51	65	33	2	57	35	6	22	43	33	24	59	16	41	51	6
Applied	80	46	36	15	89	9	2	40	33	26	31	56	13	11	59	28
Extension center:																
Academic	45	93	4	—	20	53	24	11	29	58	9	51	38	58	36	4
Applied	21	71	29	—	62	33	5	33	38	29	14	52	33	5	71	24
Private:																
Academic	194	83	14	2	41	42	15	20	40	36	9	37	48	28	49	17
Applied	53	64	34	2	62	28	8	32	36	28	19	38	42	21	57	19
Total academic	1,356	80	16	4	58	35	5	21	44	31	22	51	25	40	49	10
Total applied	775	67	29	3	80	14	1	30	47	23	40	46	13	24	58	15
Grand total	2,131	75	21	2	65	27	3	24	44	28	28	48	20	34	52	10

* Since the percentage of no answers or unusable responses is omitted from the table, totals do not add up to 100.

† VI, very important; I, important; NI, not important.

important than their counterparts in the other types of colleges. A larger percentage of both groups of teachers in extension centers rated the transfer program as very important, and a smaller percentage of them rated the terminal program as very important than did their counterparts in other types of public instructions. Academic teachers in the extension centers were also much less inclined to consider remedial work important than teachers in any other type of college. The teachers in the local separate junior colleges were inclined to rate remedial work slightly higher than the teachers in the local unified colleges, although, aside from this difference, teachers in the two types of local colleges were substantially in agreement.

Analyzed also, though not reflected in Table 7-3, was the effect of other variables on the response of the staff to the importance of functions. Where teachers preferred to teach had some effect on their response. Those who indicated that they preferred to teach in a junior college were much more likely to rate terminal vocational training as very important than those who said they preferred to teach in a four-year college. Those who preferred to teach in a junior college were also much more likely to consider a remedial program as very important. The factor of whether a teacher had previously taught in a secondary school seemed to make for no consistent pattern of responses on the matter of functions. Likewise, there were no consistent differences among teachers with different family backgrounds.

In addition to the opinions concerning the relative emphasis on transfer and terminal programs, some data on the attitudes of the staff about emphases on general and vocational education are worth noting. Information on these phases of the program was obtained through several questions. A general question first sought an opinion on the statement that "the junior college should offer a flexible program which can be adjusted to the needs of society, unhampered by conventional notions of what constitutes higher education." One-third of the group "strongly agreed" with such a statement. Slightly more than a third "agreed," and about a third either "disagreed" or "strongly disagreed." The fact that two-thirds of the staff believe the two-year college should disregard tradition in higher education would appear to make it easier for the junior college to develop programs less orthodox than those of four-year colleges, and this would have a bearing on programs for general and vocational education.

But disregarding tradition apparently does not, in the opinion of the staff, mean that the transfer program should be scuttled in favor of a vocational program. Nor does it mean that there is general agreement on the place of unusual vocational programs in the junior college or on a desirable balance between general and vocational education. Table 7-4 reports opinions of teachers of academic and of applied subjects according to the different types of institutions on certain questions related to this balance. The headings in the three major columns of the table are condensations of

Table 7-4. Faculty Opinion Concerning Emphasis on Vocational Education in Two-year Colleges, in Per Cent*

Institution	No.	Main emphasis should be on vocational education				Programs such as cosmetology have no place in junior college curriculum				Approximate per cent of vocational-technical program which should be devoted to general education ‡		
		SA	A	D	SD†	SA	A	D	SD†	25	50	75
Local unified:												
Academic	557	1	5	46	48	19	31	41	6	27	54	12
Applied	310	9	16	52	22	10	20	50	16	44	46	4
Local separate:												
Academic	509	1	5	43	51	18	30	43	7	30	53	12
Applied	311	5	21	47	24	6	25	49	15	52	40	2
State:												
Academic	51	2	10	57	29	20	37	35	2	37	53	10
Applied	80	16	26	38	19	13	29	50	6	59	30	1
Extension center:												
Academic	45	2	—	29	67	47	27	22	—	36	38	16
Applied	21	14	10	33	43	24	48	24	—	43	19	5
Private:												
Academic	194	2	5	43	48	34	41	16	3	20	52	16
Applied	53	6	15	53	26	28	38	25	4	34	40	19
Total academic	1,356	1	5	44	49	21	31	37	5	28	52	12
Total applied	775	8	19	48	23	10	25	47	13	48	41	4
Grand total	2,131	3	10	45	34	17	29	40	8	35	47	9

* Since the percentage of no answers or unusable responses is omitted from the table, totals do not add up to 100.

† SA, strongly agree; A, agree; D, disagree; SD, strongly disagree.

‡ Other proportions omitted from table since 90 per cent or more of the responses clustered around 25, 50, or 75 per cent.

the statements in the questionnaire. The figures are the percentages of those who agreed or disagreed with the statements.

Note in the "disagree" and "strongly disagree" subcolumns in column 1, the overwhelming extent to which teachers said that the main emphasis of the junior college should *not* be on vocational education. The academic teachers were more united in their opposition than the teachers of applied subjects, but in *all* types of colleges even the teachers of applied subjects were much opposed to the statement. The largest group which strongly agreed or merely agreed with the statement was the teachers of applied subjects in the state junior colleges. The largest group of both academic and applied subject teachers expressing strong disagreement with the statement was in the extension centers.

Column 2 of Table 7-4 shows the rather evenly divided opinions on the statement that "programs such as cosmetology have no place in a junior college curriculum." Cosmetology was chosen as an example only because it represents a type of vocational training much debated in educational and lay groups. Those who oppose such a curriculum contend that it and similar subjects make a "trade school" out of the junior college. Although in the total group the response was almost equally divided between those agreeing and those not agreeing with the statement, there were again major differences by groups of teachers and among types of institutions. As would be expected, academic teachers in all types of colleges were most likely to be opposed. The highest percentage of opposition to cosmetology by both groups of teachers was in the extension centers and private junior colleges, with state junior colleges next in order. The two groups of teachers in the local unified and local separate junior colleges again agreed very closely —the academic teachers in the unified checked with their counterparts in the local separate colleges, and the same was true of the teachers of applied subjects.

Since the balance between general and vocational education is much debated, an item was included in the questionnaire which elicited the opinion of the staff on this matter.[8] The gist of the

[8] "Many junior college students are in a terminal technical-vocational program. Approximately what part of their curriculum would you like to have devoted to general education (e.g., the humanities, the social sciences, the natural sciences)?

"   No general education
    25% general education
    50% general education
    75% general education
    100% general education
Other (What?........)"

faculty response in the different types of colleges is shown in column 2 of Table 7-4. Since 90 per cent or more of the responses clustered around the three proportions of 25, 50, or 75 per cent, only the percentage of responses in these categories are shown in the table. The academic teachers recommended a considerably heavier proportion of general education than did the applied teachers. In fact, in all types of two-year colleges except the extension centers slightly more than 50 per cent of the academic teachers thought that general education should comprise at least one-half of the technical program. In the extension centers and the private colleges a greater percentage than in the other colleges thought that the proportion of general education ought to constitute at least three-fourths of the total program. In all types of colleges the teachers of applied subjects were more likely than the academic teachers to suggest that only a fourth of the program be general education.

It is clear that, as a group, teachers of academic subjects stressed the preparatory and general academic functions more than they did the vocational and remedial functions. Teachers of applied subjects tended to take the opposite point of view. All teachers in extension centers and private junior colleges were more likely to restrict the functions of the two-year college than were teachers in the other three types of colleges. There were few differences in the basic beliefs regarding program and function between the staffs of local unified colleges and local separate colleges.

The responses indicate that the staff in extension centers and in private junior colleges is less in accord with the comprehensive two-year college concept than the staff in the other types of two-year institutions. In all institutions, however, teachers of academic subjects are less inclined than teachers of applied subjects to subscribe to the comprehensive institution.

ATTITUDES TOWARD ADMISSION AND SCREENING PRACTICES IN JUNIOR COLLEGES

Most *local* public two-year junior or community colleges generally admit any high school graduate and even that requirement is often waived for students over eighteen. But although practically all students may be admitted to the college, not all are admitted to certain courses or even to certain curricula unless they meet prescribed requirements. Some state junior colleges have somewhat higher general admission requirements than local colleges. Extension centers usually follow the requirements of their parent university campuses.

Since some junior college teachers contend that the low admission requirements militate against appropriate academic standards, an attempt was made to measure the extent of such feelings. One question asked whether the group agreed with the statement that "scholastic entrance requirements for junior colleges are too low for the most part." Surprisingly, the respondents were evenly split in their opinion—43 per cent agreed, 44 per cent disagreed. The academic teachers were more likely to agree than the teachers of applied subjects. The only exception to this was in the local unified colleges where well over 50 per cent in both groups of teachers—a higher percentage than in any other type of college—indicated they believed the standards were too low. Generally, the staff in the extension centers was inclined to disagree with the statement or to indicate indecision. Well over half of the staff in the state junior colleges disagreed. In each of the different types of colleges, teachers who had indicated their preference for teaching in a four-year college were more likely to believe that entrance standards were too low than were those who had preferred the junior college. Also, except in the private colleges, those who had not taught in secondary schools were more likely to subscribe to this belief than those who had taught there.

Another question asked whether admission requirements to the junior college should be the same for technical-vocational and transfer students, and if not, whether the requirements for the technical-vocational students should be higher or lower. About half (48.7 per cent) said they thought admission requirements should be the same for both groups. Almost 43 per cent said that requirements for the technical group should be lower. Teachers of academic subjects were more likely to suggest higher entrance requirements for the transfer group than teachers of applied subjects.

A related question sought an opinion on whether the admission requirements for transfer students should be the same as those imposed by the state university. Two-thirds of the group said "yes." Only about a fifth thought they should be lower.

Another question asked if admission to certain standard freshman level courses in such fields as mathematics and English should be based on minimum ability and aptitude tests. More than three-fourths of the staff responded affirmatively. Here there were no major differences of opinion among groups of teachers or by types of institutions. However, despite the tendency to insist on high entrance standards, there appeared to be general staff agreement that admission requirements should be flexible. Almost three-fifths of the group indicated they would admit, provisionally, a young adult who had not graduated from high school but whose record showed he was a good student. Another 36 per cent said they would admit him if he were given special tests and the results indicated he was capable of pursuing junior college work. Only 5 per cent said they would not admit him under any circumstances.

It would appear, then, that the staff in the junior college is by no means in complete accord with the general principles of admission applying in most junior colleges. The group was evenly divided on the general question of whether requirements are generally too low. It was divided evenly, too, on whether there should be different requirements for transfer and terminal students. A high majority recommended screening tests for certain subjects. The response of the staff in the private junior collges and extension centers to the particular questions asked might not have been surprising in view of the tendency in some of these institutions to apply some measures of selectivity. But it is significant that the division of opinion prevailed so definitely among teachers in the local public junior colleges which generally do not impose academic admission requirements. Perhaps the staff in the institutions where most any student can be admitted is most likely to feel the pressures of the great range of abilities. It is only natural for most teachers to prefer to teach more able and homogeneous groups of students, and thus to register a protest against lack of selection when the opportunity arises in a questionnaire.

The data would indicate that teachers are particularly concerned about the requirements for the admission of transfer students. Presumably many staff members feel that a student whose record does not predict success as a candidate for a baccalaureate degree should not be admitted to a transfer program. While this is a normal reaction, both in terms of a desire to avoid misappropriation of effort and of a hope that transfer students will "show up well" in the next institution, it ignores certain problems. For example, it is not always possible to identify the transfer student upon entrance. Furthermore, the criteria for predicting success in the junior college are not infallible; some students may be able to pursue some parts of a transfer program well, but may do less well on other phases of it. Clearly, the large number of teachers indicating that special tests should be used as screening devices for certain courses implies selection by these means for parts of the transfer program.

A final observation should be made about teacher attitudes toward admission policies. Despite the opinion of at least half of the teachers that greater selection should take place, the other half subscribed to the situation as it now exists. The situation, then, is not such that the great majority of staff members are in opposition to generally nonselective standards. On the other hand, the division of opinion creates a problem for junior college administrators, for they must in some way reconcile the differences in opinion held by the staff. If the public two-year college in particular is to continue to be considered the vehicle for giving *any* high school graduate the opportunity of proving himself capable of carrying some type of program after high school, the pressure to move toward institutional selective admission is obviously not in the right direction. Undoubtedly, however, the pressure will be increased with mounting enrollments. Thus, the problem of determining what role the two-year college is to play and the types of students it is to admit must receive serious consideration by all members of the staff.

ATTITUDES TOWARD COUNSELING

Faculty members were asked two questions on counseling. One was whether in their opinion educational and vocational counseling was more important, equally important, or less important than instruction. Two-thirds of the group indicated that counseling and instruction were equally important. A few (3 per cent) said counseling was more important, and 32 per cent said it was less important than instruction. In all types of institutions many more teachers of applied subjects than of academic subjects ranked counseling as equal in importance with instruction. A considerably heavier percentage of both types of teachers in the extension centers than in any other type ranked counseling as of less importance than instruction. The private junior college teachers were second in the tendency to rank counseling lower. In all types of colleges those who preferred to teach in junior college were more likely to consider counseling as important as instruction than were those who preferred to teach on the university level.

Junior colleges are sometimes criticized for too much counseling. In responding to a question on this point, almost three-fourths of the staff said they did not believe students were "overcounseled." Only 13 per cent thought there was too much counseling; 15 per cent either did not know or did not answer. On this matter, differences between the two major groups of teachers or among types of institutions were relatively minor. However, more of those who preferred teaching in a four-year college than those who preferred teaching in a junior college tended to agree that students were overcounseled.

The fact that the two-year college staff seems, on the whole, committed to the importance of counseling can be considered an asset of the junior college. But, if counseling is to be effective in an institution, it should have the support of the entire staff. If there is a difference in the educational philosophy between those who regard counseling as important and those who do not, no junior college will have a staff whose members are equally committed to counseling. However, the administrator has the responsibility of developing among all staff members an awareness of the importance of counseling in an institution with great diversity of students and programs.

ATTITUDES TOWARD ADVANTAGES AND DISADVANTAGES COMPARED WITH FOUR-YEAR INSTITUTIONS

Another series of questions was grouped around a comparison between junior college and four-year college, seeking the staff's attitude about two points: (1) the *relative* effectiveness of the two-year college and (2) the degree of influence exerted by the four-year college on the two-year college program.

Table 7-5 summarizes the response. Column 1 records the extent to which the faculty agreed with the statement that "junior college instruction is usually as good as or better than lower-divi-

Table 7-5. Faculty Opinion on Advantages and Disadvantages of the Two-year College Compared with Four-year College or University, in Per cent*

Institution	No.	Junior college instruction is usually as good as or better than lower-division teaching			The junior college is diluting the standards of American higher education			The administration of a junior college is more likely to give recognition to good teaching than is a four-year institution			Four-year colleges and universities play too great a role in determining junior college programs		
		A	D	DK†	A	D	DK†	A	D	DK†	A	D	DK†
Local unified:													
Academic	557	85	9	6	20	70	8	22	49	27	26	57	16
Applied	310	84	8	6	12	79	9	21	47	31	35	47	16
Local separate:													
Academic	509	84	9	6	19	71	9	30	39	29	23	58	17
Applied	311	87	7	5	5	89	5	31	42	26	26	53	19
State:													
Academic	51	90	8	2	8	86	6	45	31	22	45	31	22
Applied	80	73	14	14	5	93	3	34	40	26	45	38	16
Extension center:													
Academic	45	73	16	11	22	58	20	29	33	38	13	60	27
Applied	21	81	14	5	5	85	10	57	19	19	38	52	10
Private:													
Academic	194	83	9	8	9	82	8	25	43	31	21	63	16
Applied	53	81	11	4	8	91	—	38	42	17	34	55	9
Total academic	1,356	83	9	6	18	72	9	26	43	28	24	57	17
Total applied	775	84	9	6	8	85	6	28	43	27	33	49	17
Grand total	2,131	82	9	6	14	76	8	26	42	28	27	53	17

* Since the percentage of no answers or unusable responses is omitted from the table, totals do not add up to 100.

† A, agree; D, disagree; DK, don't know.

sion teaching in most four-year colleges and universities." By far the majority (almost 80 per cent or more) of the teachers in all types of two-year institutions agreed with the statement. Those who had said they would prefer to teach in the junior college and those who had taught in secondary schools were the most likely to agree with the statement. Apparently, the staff has no doubts that its instruction is just as competent as instruction elsewhere. It may well be that this particular response was due in part to a natural reluctance of any group to admit that it is less effective than any other group. On the other hand, the response may have been due to a genuine feeling that junior college instruction *is* good.

The staff further verified its belief in the quality of the junior college by disagreeing in substantial majority (76 per cent) with the statement that "the junior college is diluting the standards of American higher education" (see column 2, Table 7-5). Teachers of academic subjects were the most likely to agree.

The staff also generally (82 per cent) agreed that the junior college is less of an "educational factory" than the four-year college or university. On this point there were few differences among teachers of different subjects.

However, there was less general agreement on *recognition* of good teaching. Column 3, Table 7-5, lists the responses to a statement in the questionnaire which read: "The administration of a junior college is more likely to give recognition to a good teacher than is a four-year college or university." Only 31 per cent agreed with the statement, 40 per cent disagreed, and the rest did not know. There were no major differences of opinion according to the subjects taught. Surprisingly, the teachers in local unified colleges were the most likely of all groups to doubt the recognition given by local administration. The instructors further revealed their feelings about recognition in response to a somewhat similar statement which read: "The instructor usually has less opportunity to advance his own intellectual development in the junior college than in the four-year college or university." To this, a majority (62 per cent) agreed; about a third disagreed. The fact that many teachers disagreed may reflect the lack of intellectual stimulation in the junior college staff itself. After all, few staff members are engaged in scholarly work, and this fact alone would tend to reduce the climate of interest in scholarly affairs and stimulating exchange of opinion. Also, the respondents were doubtless influenced by the difference in the work situation in the two types of institutions. In the junior college a teacher typically teaches 15 or more hours per week and is given neither time nor credit for research and publication activities, whereas in most four-year colleges the teaching load is lighter and the opportunity for other activities greater.

Further, such privileges as sabbaticals and official leaves for teachers are likely to be more restricted in junior colleges than in four-year colleges. On the other hand, the one-third who did not believe that junior college teachers are more limited in the opportunity for personal development must also have had a rationale for their belief. They might have been influenced by the stimulus that results from a local situation where a premium is placed on good teaching and where there is encouragement through in-service training and other media of professional development. Nonetheless, the high percentage of the staff who consider developmental possibilities in the junior college to be few poses a problem of concern to those responsible for the operation of two-year colleges.

Inquiry was made about the extent to which four-year colleges and universities tend to determine the junior college program. Critics of the junior college often claim that it is merely a "little university," that it has little personality of its own, because of the influence and pressure constantly exerted on it by its four-year sisters. However, more of the staff (mostly academic teachers) disagreed with this contention than agreed with it (column 4, Table 7-5). The entire staff in the state junior colleges were the most likely to agree. Further analysis showed that those who preferred to teach in senior college were the most likely to believe that the four-year colleges do *not* exert undue influence.

ATTITUDES TOWARD ORGANIZATIONAL CHARACTERISTICS

The staff's feelings about the two-year college are likely to show best in answer to the question of whether it should either become or at least assume some of the characteristics of a four-year college. The questionnaire contained four items on how teachers feel about administrative autonomy, conversion of the two-year college into a four-year institution, professorial rank for junior college teachers, and single- instead of multiple-purpose junior colleges.

Attitudes toward Autonomy for the Junior College

Should the junior college be administratively autonomous? This question has meaning primarily for the local junior college. Should it be part of a school district responsible for other segments of local public schools, or should it be maintained by a separate district with its own board of control?

Column 1 of Table 7-6 shows the responses on a four-point scale by groups of teachers and by types of institutions. As a group

Table 7-6. Faculty Opinion on Organizational Characteristics of the Two-year College,* in Per Cent

Institutions	No.	A junior college should be administratively autonomous, having its own board of trustees				Would you like to see your college become a four-year college?		Should there be different teaching ranks in the junior college comparable to the ranks in four-year colleges?		
		SA	A	D	SD†	Yes	No	Yes	No	Don't know
Local unified:										
Academic	557	30	39	27	2	43	54	30	52	18
Applied	310	26	37	29	3	32	66	22	56	22
Local separate:										
Academic	509	39	51	6	1	40	56	41	38	20
Applied	311	38	52	6	1	29	65	36	45	18
State:										
Academic	51	12	33	39	14	31	67	71	24	6
Applied	80	18	45	29	4	25	74	66	24	9
Extension center:										
Academic	45	11	44	31	4	36	56	69	13	18
Applied	21	—	67	28	5	33	67	57	43	—
Private:										
Academic	194	39	54	3	—	45	47	43	36	19
Applied	53	34	55	6	—	32	66	32	43	23
Total academic	1,356	33	45	16	2	41	54	38	41	18
Total applied	775	30	46	18	2	30	67	34	47	18
Grand total	2,131	31	45	17	2	37	58	36	43	18

* Since the percentage of no answers or unusable responses is omitted from the tables, totals do not add up to 100.

† SA, strongly agree; A, agree; D, disagree; SD, strongly disagree.

the respondents definitely favored the idea of autonomy; 76 per cent either "strongly agreed" or "agreed" with the statement that the junior college should be autonomous. The principal differences of opinion were by types of institutions. About a third of the teachers in state junior colleges and in extension centers registered opposition to autonomy. Presumably they were satisfied with the nonautonomous plan under which they were operating, since extension centers are under the direction of the parent university and state junior colleges generally under some over-all state board. By the same token, apparently, the teachers indicating in greatest proportions their preference for autonomy were those in autonomous institutions—the local separate colleges and the private colleges. The most significant response came from the staff in the local unified colleges, in which only a third of the teachers favored the unified arrangement. More than a fourth of the respondents from the unified colleges checked the "strongly agree" column. Thus, in the very institution for which many educational arguments for unification have been made, the faculty renounced the plan. Presumably the protest was founded on some of the commonly expressed disadvantages of unified organization—that in such a system the junior college often becomes a "stepchild" with resulting impairment to such factors as finance, recognition of junior college problems, and personnel policy. Some may also have felt that an autonomous institution is more of a college than one closely related to elementary and high schools. Whatever the reason, the great majority of the teachers in unified systems believe autonomy is preferable.

Attitudes toward Conversion of the Junior College to a Four-year College

There is often agitation to convert two-year institutions into four-year colleges, indicating an assumption that most junior college teachers would be happy about it. However, the returns did not substantiate this. Of the total group, only slightly more than a third (37 per cent) said they would like to see their institution become a four-year college (column 2, Table 7-6). The academic teachers were more inclined to favor the four-year idea than the teachers of applied subjects. Some would personally prefer to be in a four-year institution, but still subscribe to the idea that their own institutions should remain two-year colleges. In all types of two-year colleges a higher percentage of the respondents said they would prefer to teach in four-year colleges than see their own colleges turned into four-year institutions.

Attitudes toward Professorial Rank in Junior College

The teachers' attitude toward adoption of a system of professorial rank comparable to that in most four-year colleges is not directly related to organizational structure but has a bearing on their concept of the two-year college. Teachers who believe the rank system should prevail in the junior college would seem to want the junior college to have some of the earmarks of the four-year institution. A person's feeling about professorial rank may also be governed by his preference of junior college or senior college as a place to teach. On this subject, teachers were more divided in their opinion than on many of the other matters: 43 per cent were opposed to teaching ranks, 36 per cent were in favor, and 18 per cent did not know (column 3, Table 7-6). The teachers in extension centers and state junior colleges were by far the greatest contenders for rank. This is natural, since in both types of institutions the system is generally used. Teachers in local separate colleges were more inclined to favor rank than were teachers in local unified colleges. Interestingly, of the group in the local unified colleges who preferred to teach in junior college, 64 per cent opposed the rank system; but of those who preferred to teach in a four-year college, only 47 per cent opposed it. In the local separate colleges the corresponding percentages were 49 and 37. Those who had taught in secondary schools were also more inclined to oppose rank by about ten percentage points over those who had not worked at that level.

It is not surprising that some teachers favor a system of rank. Prestige for both themselves and the institutions they represent would cause many to favor it. However, the teachers in the sample who subscribed to it were in the minority; and it is perhaps more surprising that more did not recommend it. At the moment at least, teachers do not appear greatly concerned about the question.

The practice of assigning rank to teachers in junior college is largely confined to institutions in a state system of higher education and extension centers of universities. Since the degrees held by junior college teachers and the relative emphasis on teaching and research are so different in junior and senior colleges, it is difficult to visualize the implementation of the plan in comprehensive community colleges on the same basis as in four-year colleges. Further, the question can be raised as to whether a system of rank would tend to obliterate further the differences between two-year and four-year colleges.

Attitudes toward Splitting the Junior College

Another question on junior college structure was whether two kinds of two-year colleges would be desirable—one to offer traditional lower-division college work and the other semiprofessional and vocational training only. The large majority of the staff members indicated that they did not believe in the single-purpose institution: a third of the group "strongly disagreed" with the idea, and more than 43 per cent "disagreed"; only about 22 per cent thought well of the plan, including 10 per cent who indicated strong agreement.

There were, however, differences of opinion by groups of teachers in types of colleges. Thus, the majority of academic teachers in extension centers and private colleges were in favor of separate institutions. In state colleges 40 per cent of the applied teachers and 26 per cent of the academic staff indicated their preference for two types of colleges. It was, however, in the local junior colleges that the strongest opinion against splitting the functions prevailed. Only a very small per cent of either the academic or the applied subject teachers in both the local unified and the local separate colleges recommended two types of colleges. This fact seems significant because, if there are severe handicaps to a multipurpose institution, the staff should be most aware of them and most likely to recommend a change.

The widespread opinion that the junior college should not be split has a bearing on the alternative between organizing technical institutes or vocational schools as separate institutions and having the vocational-technical function performed in a general two-year college. Elsewhere in this report other arguments are presented in favor of the multipurpose institution. Here, however, the extent is noted to which faculty opinion supports comprehensiveness of purposes in single institutions.

ATTITUDES TOWARD REQUIREMENTS FOR JUNIOR COLLEGE TEACHING

Since there are strong differences of opinion about the extent to which there should be special professional requirements and state certification for public junior college teachers, and since these requirements vary considerably throughout the country, it was decided to find out how the teachers themselves feel about the question.

A substantial majority (62 per cent) of the total group of respondents favored state certification. However, there were, as usual, differences among the various groups of teachers. Those who preferred to teach in junior college were generally more likely to recommend certification than those who preferred to teach in senior college. This was especially true of the teachers in both types of local colleges. Most teachers in local and state junior colleges were in favor of certification; most of those in extension centers and private junior colleges were opposed. Of all groups (by type of institution), the teachers in the local unified districts were most likely to favor certification. A greater percentage of applied subject teachers than of academic teachers declared themselves in favor of it. Also, more of the teachers who had taught in secondary schools recommended it than did those without that experience.

Since one of the common requirements for a state credential is practice teaching supervised in part by the teacher training institution, the opinion of the staff was sought on this matter. A majority (58 per cent) believed that such a requirement should be imposed. Academic personnel were less prone to favor practice teaching than teachers of applied subjects. But even academic teachers varied according to types of institutions: in extension centers, 78 per cent were opposed to the requirement, in the state junior colleges 57 per cent, in private junior colleges 53 per cent, in local separate colleges 45 per cent, and in local unified colleges 39 per cent. This variation would suggest that the response was conditioned by the requirements which the respondents were likely to have had imposed on them. The two groups most likely to have had to conform to such a requirement were the teachers in the local unified and local separate colleges, and they were the only groups in which a majority recommended the requirement. Teachers in extension centers, on the other hand, are least likely to have had to meet a practice teaching requirement, and the great majority of them were opposed to it. Probably, too, the differences among the types of institutions suggest a hierarchy of opinion concerning the prestige of the two-year college. Those who believe that it should resemble a four-year college are most likely to contend that such a requirement as practice teaching is not necessary because it generally is not a means of preparing four-year college teachers. This possibility is further strengthened by the fact that a higher percentage of those teachers who indicated that they preferred to teach in senior college opposed the requirement than was true of those who preferred to teach in junior college.

An important and interesting related question, much debated in educational circles, is where teachers feel practice teaching should be done. About half of the 58 per cent who recommended practice teaching significantly said it should be done in a junior college. A small number said it should be done in a four-year college. The others either said it made no difference or suggested other alternatives, such as the high school or a combination of institutions.

The foregoing report on teacher opinions concerning state certification and practice teaching requirements suggests that the majority of the staff would temper agitation against such requirements.

ATTITUDES OF ADMINISTRATORS AS COMPARED WITH THOSE OF TEACHERS

The attitudes of junior college administrators on the philosophy and policies of junior colleges are important because the position of leadership which they hold makes them powerful agents in shaping the nature of the institution. Obviously, the administrator is not the only one concerned with policy—the governing board and the faculty are equally concerned. But he is the catalyst who must not only make recommendations but also see that policies are implemented; he influences the faculty and is influenced by it. The extent of agreement between administrator and faculty on basic institutional policies indicates unity and institutional direction; if there is basic and continuous disagreement, the institution is not maximally successful in the discharge of its responsibilities.

The extent of agreement between administration and teaching staff on basic philosophy and policies is not always easily determined, especially in individual institutions where many factors may subdue outspoken differences of opinion. For this reason the present study on staff attitudes sought the opinions of administrators on the same points as those asked of the faculty. Obviously, the sample of administrators in the study was materially smaller than that of teachers and could not be as finely divided into categories. Due to the small sample it was not even feasible to establish a category for administrators in extension centers, and care must be taken not to generalize unduly on the opinions of administrators in private junior colleges and state junior colleges, where the numbers were also small.

Since teachers tend to vary in their opinions according to the subject matter they teach, it is clear that administrators could not possibly agree with all teachers. They tend on some matters to agree more with teachers of academic subjects and on other matters more with teachers of applied subjects. On some points, they fall between the two groups of teachers; on other points some of them take a position more extreme than either of the two teacher groups. Their opinion depends also in part on the type of two-year college in which they hold their position. However, the following generalizations may be made on the comparison of attitudes of administrators and faculty:

Administrators were more prone than teachers to favor a comprehensive educational program in the junior college. It will be recalled that academic teachers rated the transfer program as more important than the terminal program, whereas the reverse was true of the teachers of applied subjects. Administrators regard both types of programs as equally important. Administrators, particularly those in local junior colleges, were also more likely than teachers to rate remedial work highly. A higher percentage of them were inclined to believe that a subject like cosmetology should be included in the curriculum. In all but the private junior colleges the administrators were more likely than the teachers to show concern for adult education of all types.

Administrators were more inclined than faculty members to rate junior college teaching highly. A higher percentage of them than of the teachers agreed with the statement that "junior college instruction is as good as if not better than lower-division teaching in four-year colleges and universities." The administrators in both types of local junior colleges also were more agreed than the faculty in believing that the good junior college teacher is more likely to receive recognition than the four-year college teacher. In private junior colleges, however, the position of the administrator on this question was approximately the same as that of the teachers.

The administrators were more prone than the faculty to believe in liberal admission requirements for junior colleges. In all types of junior colleges a smaller percentage of administrators than teachers agreed with the statement in the questionnaire that "scholastic entrance requirements for junior colleges are too low for the most part." On this point, however, administrators in different types of colleges differed: 33 per cent of administrators in local unified colleges agreed with the statement, but only 14 per cent in local separate colleges, and 25 per cent in private junior colleges. The fact that the administrators in the local unified colleges were less liberal than those in local separate colleges is surprising, and especially so in view of the fact that the local unified administrators were the most liberal of all teacher and administrator groups in believing that a young adult who is not a high school graduate should be admitted. A possible factor accounting for the difference may be the familiarity which the local unified administrator has with young people in the local high schools who do not do well in high school, yet frequently enter the junior college.

Administrators tended to agree with the faculty on certification and practice teaching. As to certification, the variation in percentage among administrators by types of schools was about the same as among the teachers from the different types of schools. Administrators in local unified colleges were by far the largest group in favor of certification (79 per cent), whereas administrators in private colleges were substantially opposed to it. Only a bare majority of the administrators in local separate and state junior colleges were in favor. As to a requirement of practice teaching, the administrators of each type of college approximated the opinion of the teachers in each type.

With certain exceptions, the administrators were substantially in agreement with the faculties of their own colleges on the organizational structure of the junior college. They followed the pattern of the faculty in believing that the junior college should be administratively autonomous. In local unified colleges, more than two-thirds of the administrators were in favor of a separate governing board for the college. The two groups of administrators most in favor of autonomy were those in local separate colleges where only 4 per cent opposed the idea, and in private junior colleges where only 7 per cent opposed it.

The administrators also generally followed the beliefs of their teachers on the matter of faculty rank in junior colleges, with a few exceptions. While in local unified colleges most staff members were opposed to the idea of rank, the percentage of administrators opposed was greater than the percentage of teachers opposed. In local separate colleges the administrators and the teachers of applied subjects were more opposed to the idea than teachers of academic subjects. In private colleges considerably more administrators (54 per cent) were opposed than the teachers.

A general conclusion on administrator-teacher agreement is that, except on a few specific questions, the two groups tend to think alike in their own types of institutions. Where they differ the administrators tend to represent more nearly the comprehensive, unique junior college idea than do the teachers. For example, a greater percentage of the administrators than of the total teaching group appeared to be in favor of the different programs that characterize a comprehensive college and to be more liberal in admission requirements. The fact that there is general agreement between teachers and administrators is good, provided, of course, the *status quo* philosophy does not prevail to the detriment of progress. The fact that administrators take a somewhat more liberal view with respect to the comprehensive college idea than teachers is perhaps better than if the reverse were true because, without administrative leadership, the goals of the comprehensive college would be difficult to achieve.

SUMMARY AND CONCLUSIONS

The data presented in the preceding pages of this chapter, clustered around certain questions on which it is important to know staff attitudes, were necessarily detailed. It is now desirable to review the salient facts and attitudes ascertained by the study in a way that will assist in portraying the junior college staff member and in identifying certain conclusions and implications.

Variation in Responses

It is clear that the staff has no stereotyped view of the junior college. Attention hardly needs to be called to the great variation in the responses. In fact, the frequency with which the respondents were divided rather evenly in their opinion on a number of items may cause the reader to wonder whether members of the staff in two-year colleges have *any* ideas in common.

It is clear that the opinions and beliefs of those cooperating in the study varied considerably according to their position in the college, their preference as to the type of institution in which they wished to work, their previous teaching experience, and the type of two-year college in which they were employed. Furthermore, the various groups of staff members were fairly consistent in their response to the different items. For example, teachers of academic subjects were inclined to reflect a conservative attitude toward the junior college, which leads to the impression that they favored its assuming some characteristics of the traditional four-year college. The same point of view was also frequently expressed by those who admitted that they would prefer to teach in a four-year college, those who had not taught at the secondary level, and, by and large, those employed in extension centers and in private junior colleges. Conversely, the groups least likely to agree with this concept of the junior college were teachers of applied subjects, those who preferred work in a junior college, those with some secondary experience, and those in public junior colleges. Differences were also noted among administrators according to background and type of institution, as well as between them and the teaching staff. It should never be forgotten, however, that these are generalizations which, by definition, do not necessarily apply to individual members of the group. Thus, it would obviously be dangerous and unfair to characterize *any* teacher of academic subjects as being more in favor of the traditional college aspects of a junior college than of some of its unique functions. It would be equally hazardous to assume that any teacher of applied subjects is opposed to high-level academic work.

But why is there such great variation in the responses? At this point it seems appropriate to return to reference group theory for a possible interpretation. The responses give some indication that junior college staff members do orient themselves to different reference groups. The fact that more than half of the total group indicated their preference to teach in a four-year college and the tendency for certain groups of teachers to be more inclined than others to favor the more academic type of junior college may well mean that some teachers make the four-year college their frame of reference. Some of these teachers were undoubtedly interested in professional mobility. Others were bound to the disciplines of their major fields which are best preserved in the four-year college. Others were only recently students in a graduate school, and they related more to how, what, and by whom they were taught than they did to lower-division teaching in an entirely different institution.

Some of the identification of junior college teachers with four-year colleges may result from what Stouffer calls "relative deprivation."[9] A junior college teacher may simply feel "put upon" by reason of a heavier teaching load and what he considers to be his lower status and smaller opportunity for self-improvement, with the result that he identifies more closely with the higher status senior institutions.

Students of reference group theory have extended it further to suggest that members of a group, in evaluating their opportunities for promotion, recognition, and the like (and their consequential attitudes toward the organization), tend to be more dissatisfied in situations in which the chances of recognition and promotion are great than situations in which such chances are more limited.[10] The theory behind such a paradoxical finding is that opportunity for recognition induces excessive hopes and aspirations among members of the group so that frustrations are more likely to occur. This theory suggests that those who express dissatisfaction about aspects of the junior college, such as lack of recognition for good teaching or lack of opportunity for intellectual development, may in fact be pointing to relatively good chances for recognition and development.

More facts are needed before a conclusion can be reached on what is cause and what is effect in the attitudes of junior college

[9] S. A. Stouffer et al., *The American Soldier*, Princeton University Press, Princeton, N.J., 1949, vol. I.

[10] *Ibid.*, p. 236.

teachers. It seems logical, however, to explain some of the responses by the extent to which the persons making them were oriented to patterns of education outside the junior college.

Points of Substantial Agreement

Despite the diversity of responses, on certain aspects of the junior college the respondents substantially agreed. If instances of two-thirds agreement with no subgroup deviating radically from the general group can be considered as substantial agreement, the staff showed accord in the following ways:

There was general recognition of the place and value of the junior college in American higher education. Almost 80 per cent said the junior college is closer to the educational needs of the community than the four-year college. Further, two-thirds of the staff agreed that the junior college should offer a flexible program unhampered by "conventional notions of what constitutes higher education." The respondents contended that the junior college is less an "educational factory" than the four-year college. When given an opportunity to say whether they would favor converting their junior colleges into four-year institutions, two-thirds of the group said "no." As such responses are reviewed, they suggest that, despite wide differences of opinion on certain matters, those who teach in two-year colleges believe that the junior college has a definite role to play in American education after high school.

The great majority of the staff indicated that they were satisfied with their positions in two-year colleges. Almost 80 per cent said they were either well satisfied or completely satisfied. The fact that half of the group said that, even if other things were equal, they would prefer to work in the two-year college rather than in the four-year institution is further indicative of general satisfaction.

There was strong agreement on the fact that the junior college must perform multiple functions. Despite differences in the degree of emphasis, the staff almost unanimously agreed that the junior college should be *both* a preparatory and a terminal institution and that it should offer programs for both purposes. Furthermore, they agreed that both purposes should be discharged in the same institution—in other words, that the junior college should be a dual- rather than a single-purpose institution. The counseling function was regarded highly by the group. Two-thirds of the staff rated counseling as important as instruction; three-fourths dismissed the notion that junior college students are "overcounseled."

There was agreement that the quality of instruction in the junior college is high. Eighty per cent of the group considered the quality of instruction in the junior college to be at least as good as or better than instruction in the four-year college. The group strongly denied that the junior college is diluting standards in American higher education. On other items the response was such as to reflect the nearly uniform belief that quality does prevail in junior college instruction.

The group strongly believed that a junior college should be administratively autonomous. The fact that almost 80 per cent of the entire group expressed the belief that a junior college should have its own governing board and its own chief administrative officer directly responsible to that board is particularly significant in view of the many questions that are being raised concerning the best organizational pattern for junior colleges.

Extent of Agreement with the Concept of the Community College

As indicated in Chapter 1 and elsewhere throughout this report, the comprehensive community college is regarded as one which (1) offers a variety of educational programs of an academic and an occupational nature, day and evening, for full-time and part-time students, (2) provides an opportunity for students to make up educational deficiencies, (3) has a liberal admission policy, (4) emphasizes a well-developed guidance program, (5) performs a variety of special services to the community, and (6) insists on its rights to dignity on its own merits without attempting to resemble a four-year college.

If these are the characteristics of a comprehensive community college, which groups of the staff members were most in accord with the description? Although the following summary would not characterize every individual in the groups designated, it would appear that the five groups most likely to support the objectives and program of the community college are: those who teach in applied fields, that is, teachers of nonacademic subjects; those with administrative responsibilities; those who indicate a preference for teaching at the junior college level; those who have had secondary school teaching experience; those who are employed in public junior colleges rather than in extension centers and private junior colleges.

Some Implications

The findings of this study suggest the following implications for those who have a concern for the two-year college:

The administrator of a two-year institution must know and understand the points of view of the various groups in the faculty. Though this is desirable in any institution, the responses in this study revealed more than ordinary disagreement among the staff concerning the role, program, and policies of the two-year college, particularly the comprehensive community college. The administrator must realize the potential situation where opinion about fundamental issues is split and often pulls in opposite directions. He should encourage participation and lead the faculty in studies pertaining to the purposes of the two-year college and how best to achieve them. This further suggests the continuous accumulation for use by the faculty of information about (1) trends in education after high school generally and in the particular state and (2) the characteristics of the students served by the college and their outcomes after admission and departure.

Programs for the preparation of junior college administrators and teachers should help them to understand the two-year college and to participate in the development of its purposes and policies. Teachers need to know a great deal about the students served by the two-year college. Administrators need broad understanding of the process of working with groups. They need a broad educational background in other disciplines as well as in professional education. The special and difficult problems of orienting teachers and administrators to a more complex and less-well-understood institution such as the junior college may suggest the merits of internship experiences for both prospective teachers and administrators.

Agencies responsible for planning higher education in any state should consider thoroughly the specific tasks to be performed by two-year institutions and, therefore, the type of such college most likely to accomplish those tasks. Staff attitudes revealed in this study would indicate that, if the job to be done requires the services of comprehensive colleges, the public junior college is more likely to be conducive to the execution of the job than is the university extension center.

There is need for a thorough study of the advantages and disadvantages of each of the two types of local junior colleges. With more than two-thirds of the staff in unified districts recommending autonomy, it is inferred that from the teachers' point of view, there are disadvantages to operating the junior college as part of the unified district.

There is need for a study of attitudes of the professional staff in other types of collegiate institutions so that comparisons may be made between these data and the data from this study.

The Two-year College in the Various States—Its Development, Financing, and Problems

This chapter summarizes the development of public two-year colleges in the past and future plans for them in selected states. Information came from several sources, primarily from interviews in each state with persons in coordinating agencies and two-year and four-year institutions. Such interviews were supplemented by correspondence and by the study of various documents. In many instances recent studies on higher education yielded valuable data. The summary statement on each state was checked for accuracy by state officers and college administrators.

The following pages contain sections on each of the 15 states included in the original sample, plus 3 additional states in which significant recent developments occurred. These additional states are Florida, Indiana, and Washington. Attention is drawn to the following topics: (1) types of districts empowered to maintain local junior colleges, (2) provisions for financial support, (3) methods of the state to exert leadership, (4) special problems in the development of the system, and (5) the role of the system in the entire program of higher education in the state.

The states are discussed in alphabetical order.

CALIFORNIA[1]

This state with the largest number of public junior colleges and enrolled students operates its junior college system as a legal extension of secondary education. This does not mean that junior colleges in California operate differently or have different declared functions than in other states. They were made an extension of secondary education to integrate them closely with the high schools. Local school districts which maintain and largely support junior colleges come under the jurisdiction of common school laws of the state and have certain responsibilities to the state department of education and its executive officer, the superintendent of public instruction.

Enabling legislation in California permits two types of local districts to establish junior colleges.[2] One is the unified district, which maintains and is responsible for all units of the local schools from kindergarten through high school, or through the junior college if one is established. The other is the special junior college district, which may be created in one or more high school districts by a vote of the people in the proposed district. A district must meet certain legal criteria to be eligible for the establishment of a junior college. Approval must be procured from the state department of education, and is given only after a survey of the district.

In early 1959, 56 districts maintained 63 day junior colleges in the state. Of these 56, 12 were unified districts, 16 high school districts, and 28 separate junior college districts.

Financial support for California junior colleges comes mainly from two sources—local taxes and state aid. In the past the state has contributed approximately one-third of the total expenditures for junior college operation, but with the rapid increase in enrollment accompanied by an increase in cost per student, the proportion of cost borne by the state is decreasing. The local property tax rate may be set by the board of trustees at no more than 35 cents per

[1] For a more complete description of California junior colleges, see Hugh G. Price, *California Public Junior Colleges*, California State Department of Education, Sacramento, 1958.

[2] It was previously possible for high school districts to establish junior colleges, but recent legislation prohibited this. However, high school districts which had already established junior colleges may continue to operate them.

$100 valuation, but the rate may be increased by a vote of the people in the district. Local bonding capacity is 5 per cent of the assessed valuation. State aid is computed principally on two bases, as for other segments of the public schools. An apportionment is first made to each district on the basis of the average daily attendance (ADA) for the previous year, calculated on a complex accounting formula. The amount for each unit of ADA is $125, apportioned with certain exceptions on the basis of units accumulated in classes for adults and for regular freshman and sophomore students. State aid is also available through the state's educational foundation program: in junior college districts in which the assessed valuation is so low that a required tax rate plus the ADA apportionment will not provide a total income of $410 per unit of ADA, the state makes up the difference. Other state funds are available to junior colleges for such items as transportation and unusually rapid growth, but none for capital items, such as site acquisition and buildings.

The California program permits a student from any area to attend any junior college in the state. There are, however, some limitations. If the student lives in a district that maintains a junior college, he must procure a permit from that district to attend a junior college elsewhere. If the permit is granted, the two districts make an agreement about costs and state aid. If the student does not live in a district that maintains a junior college, he may, by complying with certain regulations, attend any junior college. The county of residence is required to levy a junior college tax to pay for the cost of instruction and the use of facilities[2a] for all students from the county who attend junior colleges. Thus, areas which do not maintain junior colleges are nevertheless subject to a tax for junior college purposes.

California junior colleges generally have comprehensive programs. Their curricula lead to transfer or employment, and they have developed large-scale adult education programs. These functions have not only been agreed upon by the institutions themselves, but they also have the tacit approval of the Legislature (which accepted reports of two important studies in higher educa-

[2a] Use-of-facilities cost was increased by the 1957 Legislature from $150 to $300. The increase appears to be having the effect of enlarging junior college districts because there is no material finanical advantage for communities to remain outside a nearby junior college district.

tion in which differential and yet overlapping functions were recommended for the different segments of education after high school).[3]

The legal requirements for admission to California junior colleges as set forth in the education code are as follows: "Any high school graduate and any other person over 18 years of age who . . . is capable of profiting from the instruction offered." In October, 1958, a total of 300,079 students was enrolled in these institutions. Of this number about 91,000 were classified as full-time students, 54,000 as part-time, and 155,000 were enrolled in classes for adults.

The junior college program is coordinated in a number of ways. Legally, the department of education, operating through its divisions of instruction and public school administration, is concerned with standards of instruction, approval of courses, and financial control in the junior colleges. A newly created bureau of junior college education, directly under the division of instruction, will henceforth be the clearing and service agency for the major phases of state and local relationships. Obviously, local controls are in the hands of the governing board of the district, and a high degree of autonomy prevails. The districts and institutions do much coordinating themselves through a highly organized state junior college association.

The development of this system of junior colleges has taken a long time.[4] The first enabling legislation came in 1907 when the Legislature authorized high school districts to offer postgraduate courses, but no financial aid was provided by the state. Fresno City High School, in 1910, was the first such district to organize these courses. In 1917 came the first state aid legislation, and in 1921 the law authorizing the formation of junior college districts. Each successive legislative session brought new laws relating to establishment, district responsibilities, finance, and similar matters.

[3] T. R. McConnell et al., *A Restudy of the Needs of California in Higher Education*, California State Department of Education, Sacramento, Calif., 1955.
   Monroe E. Deutsch et al., *A Report of a Survey of the Needs of California in Higher Education*, University of California Press, Berkeley, Calif., 1948.
[4] For a brief history of California junior colleges, see Frank B. Lindsay, "California Junior Colleges: Past and Present," *California Journal of Secondary Education*, March, 1947; and H. A. Spindt, "Beginnings of the Junior College in California," *College and University*, Fall, 1957.

The size of the junior college program in California results in many local and state-wide problems—problems of finance, control, facilities, staff, relationships with other phases of the state's educational program, and understanding on the part of the public.

The financial problems of junior colleges in California are similar to those in other states. The local taxpayers in California have been willing to assume a considerable tax load for junior college purposes. They did this undoubtedly because of the values accruing to a community from an institution which enables young people to continue their education while living at home, and also because of the many special services rendered by such an institution, particularly to adults. However, increasing costs and competition for the local tax dollar may in the future cause the public to be less willing to support a junior college program unless an increasing share of the costs are borne by the state. Some observers believe that the state should not only assume a higher share of current operations, but should also assist local communities with funds for junior college building and other capital outlay purposes. Since the junior colleges enroll approximately 73 per cent of all full-time freshmen and sophomores in California public higher institutions, it is considered unfair for local communities to have to assume more than 60 per cent of the operating costs and the full amount of the capital costs. Obviously, if the students now in junior college were enrolled in the state colleges or the university system, the state would bear most of the entire cost. Legislation introduced in the General Assembly in 1957 and again in 1959, designed to provide state aid for capital purposes, was not successful. Such legislation introduced in 1959 had the endorsement of both the state board of education and the Board of Regents of the University of California.

Problems concerning control of California junior colleges center on the question of whether they should be operated by the governing boards and administrations of the elementary and high schools, or by separate junior college boards. Unfortunately, there are no adequate empirical data on the extent to which vertical integration is effected and unit costs are lowered when a junior college is maintained by a high school or unified district in comparison with a special junior college district. Even more unfortunate is the fact that cost data in high school and unified districts are particularly difficult to obtain because some districts fail to segregate in their accounting the income and expenditure for each segment of the system.

Another problem is to find the best way to encourage and provide additional junior college opportunities. Educational leaders in California agree that with increasing numbers of college-age students, adequate junior college opportunity should exist in all geographical areas in the state. The state department of education, with the sanction of important organizations and agencies, is working toward the goal of having each high school in the state included in some junior college district, with the possible exception of high schools in certain outlying and sparsely settled areas. Such areas would be served by sending students to junior colleges in other communities and paying the costs. Areas in need of new or additional junior college facilities have been identified.[5] Furthermore, the state board of education and the regents of the University of California jointly have agreed on a policy that neither a new state college nor a new campus of the university should be established in a community that has not first established a junior college.

Nevertheless, certain areas identified as badly in need of junior colleges have made no move to establish them. Indeed, some of these areas have strongly pressured the Legislature to establish four-year state colleges. In fact, the 1957 session of the Assembly did provide funds for a new state college in one such area, despite the policy enunciated earlier by the state board of education and the regents. Perhaps citizens of some of these areas believe that by creating fully state-supported four-year colleges rather than junior colleges, the local community may shift the entire financial burden of education after high school to the state. Such a belief would be erroneous because without junior colleges many youths would go unserved. A recent study showed that with selective admission practices in the California four-year public institutions, 56.4 per cent of California high school graduates met neither the University of California nor state college requirements.[6] Besides, many special services rendered by junior colleges to the community and to adults are not rendered by four-year colleges.

[5] H. H. Semans and T. C. Holy, *A Study of the Need for Additional Centers of Higher Eucation in California,* California State Department of Education, Sacramento, 1957.

[6] *Ibid.,* p. 156.

Greater financial aid by the state, particularly for building and other capital outlay purposes, would probably reduce much of the reluctance of local communities to establish junior colleges. Despite the lack of such assistance, several communities in the state in 1957 and 1958 either established junior colleges or took first steps by requesting a survey by the state department of education.

The California junior college program is so well established as an integral part of the entire state program of public education that it is generally accepted by the public and even by those who are frequently critical of the cost of education. Nevertheless, interpretation of the junior college program to the public is never-ending, even in a state that has generously provided extensive free public education through the fourteenth grade.

There is one problem which the junior college in California has not had to contend with—inadequate understanding and support from other colleges and universities in the state. Much of the impetus given the junior college movement in the state at the time of its inception came from such men as Alexis F. Lange, dean of the School of Education at the University of California, and David Starr Jordon, president of Stanford University. During the 50 intervening years, officials in both universities and in other four-year institutions in the state have testified by word and deed to their belief in the junior college. Furthermore, the public higher institutions, including the junior colleges, are closely integrated through carefully designed liaison machinery and committees. The assistance and support given the junior college by its sister institutions have meant much in enabling it to accomplish its mission. Also, public pronouncements concerning the junior college made by officials in other colleges and universities have assisted materially in the status accorded it by the lay public. The attitudes toward the junior college expressed by those who speak for four-year institutions are a crucial factor in the development of the two-year college of any state.

FLORIDA

This state has taken bold strides in large-scale planning for junior colleges. Four areas have for years been supporting public junior colleges, but recent legislation has provided for a well-defined system of such institutions to serve the entire state.

The 1955 session of the Legislature began this move by providing capital outlay funds for the existing Florida junior colleges and by authorizing the appointment of a community college council, composed of seven lay and three professional members, to make recommendations to the state board of education concerning a long-range plan for junior college development. This council, working with a full-time professional director with offices in the state department of education first set about determining the elements of adequate legislation for the state which would put the program on a sound financial basis and encourage the orderly establishment of junior colleges. A thorough community survey was made in each county to determine the need for, the interest in, and the probable problems connected with the establishment of such a college. On the basis of an extensive review of the individual surveys, the council recommended the priorities with which institutions would be established if proposed legislation were enacted.[7]

In the meantime, another study group, the Council for the Study of Higher Education in Florida, established in 1953 by the Board of Control for Florida Institutions of Higher Learning, after approval from the 1953 Legislature, studied other segments of higher education. The two councils worked closely together; and in the report of the Council for the Study of Higher Education in Florida in July, 1956, a strong recommendation was made to develop a system of public community colleges in the state to provide a broad range of educational programs.[8]

With strong backing from these two major study groups, as well as interest and support from many segments of the population in the state, bills for improving and extending junior college education were introduced in the 1957 Legislature. The major proposals were adopted by both houses, and, on May 29, 1957, the Governor signed into law a plan that will undoubtedly be studied with care by those interested in state systems of locally controlled junior colleges.

[7] Community College Council, *The Community Junior College in Florida's Future*, Florida State Department of Education, Tallahassee, 1957.

[8] A. J. Brumbaugh and Myron R. Blee, *Higher Education and Florida's Future*, vol. I, University of Florida Press, Gainesville, 1956.

Basically, the plan makes the community junior colleges a part of the local public school systems. The plan also provides for their establishment or acquisition by a single county board of public instruction or by the county boards of any two or more contiguous counties, if the state board of education approves. Florida operates under the county unit system for its entire public school program. This arrangement makes the junior college a part of the county school system and specifies the county board of public instruction of the county in which the college is situated as the governing board of the institution. If two or more counties establish a college, the legal controlling district is the county in which the institution is situated. The law stipulates that the college shall be directed by a president who shall be responsible through the county superintendent to the county board.

To provide for over-all administration of education, an interesting system of advisory bodies has been established. For the state as a whole, the state Advisory Council on Education advises the state board of education. Further, the law provides for each junior college the appointment of an advisory committee of five lay members when the college is operated by one county board and not more than nine members when more than one county board is involved. The members are appointed by the state board from a list of persons recommended by the county board or boards. The law specifies that the committee shall meet regularly and, after consulting with the college president, shall make recommendations to the county board on such matters as curricula, personnel, finance, and general policies. It may meet with the county board, but its members do not vote.

Florida's public junior colleges are supported mainly by what is called the Minimum Foundation Program for Junior Colleges. This is an amount of money based upon a formula. The minimum amount of money required is based on the total average daily attendance (full-time student equivalent based on a 15-semester-hour load) divided by 12 for the first 420 students and by 15 for all above this number. The units derived by this formula are valued at different amounts according to the training of the instructors. In addition, special units for administrators and student personnel services are included. Also included are amounts for current operating expenses and for the salary of the president.

The local county is required to contribute an amount not to exceed one-half of the operating budget, the exact amount depending on the wealth of the county. After subtracting the amount contributed by the county from the total amount required, as determined by the above formula, the state then supports the college to the extent of the difference. The local share of the Minimum Foundation Program varies from 10 per cent to 50 per cent of the current operating budget.

In addition to the Minimum Foundation Program, local counties contribute additional amounts to the junior college budget. These funds may come from the budgets of the county commission or other local sources. The state also furnishes funds for capital outlay based on a formula designed to provide eventually 148 square feet of space per student. Local areas are required to furnish the sites.

The third source of money for operation is tuition and fees set by the local institution but limited by the state board regulations. A tuition fee may be charged only to out-of-county and out-of-state residents. However, a matriculation fee of $37.50 per semester is charged to all students, and this, along with other fees, is in essence a tuition charge.

Because legislation is so recent, it is impossible to project the functioning of the Florida plan over many years ahead. The plan is characterized by apparently adequate financial support, particularly from the state, and a high degree of over-all planning. As to the latter, the division of community junior colleges in the state department of education is the responsible agency for the state. A major responsibility of this division is to promote the orderly development of junior colleges and to serve as a professional arm for the state board.

The Community College Council has designated 31 areas in potential need of junior colleges. In 1959, 16 were already in operation and the establishment of 6 additional ones was authorized. Others will be recommended for approval as population growth and sufficient finances make them feasible.

The important place of the junior college in Florida is evidenced by the fact that, in the counties served by a local public junior college, 75 per cent of the students enrolling in college for the first time in 1958–59 chose the junior college.

GEORGIA

Georgia was included in this study because (1) four of its junior colleges were operating in 1956 as parts of the state's university system (explained below), that is, as autonomous units of the system; (2) two local junior colleges and two local military junior colleges, operating without state aid, were also in existence, thus making for a diversity of plans; and (3) there was a general feeling that the state should review its responsibility to local junior colleges and to other communities which were becoming interested in two-year colleges. The state thus afforded opportunity to examine the functioning of junior colleges operating under a *system* of higher education and at the same time to report whatever recommendations were to grow out of the concern over the expansion of the junior college program.

The four state junior colleges in operation at the time the study began (as reported later in this section, three additional ones have since been added) were originally part of the area's secondary agricultural school program and were converted into colleges as the agricultural program waned. They are all situated in comparatively small communities in the southern half of the state, and each has residential facilities. There is some difference in their enrollments, but all tend to fall within the range of four hundred to five hundred full-time students. Except for a tuition charge accounting for approximately 25 per cent of the institutional budgets, each is fully supported by the state with no assistance from the local community. Three of them emphasize the standard preparatory program with a scattering of vocational programs. The transfer program is offered in the fourth college, but this is primarily the junior college agricultural institution for the state and thus concentrates on this phase in both day and extension activities.

These colleges are separate two-year units each with its president who is responsible to the board of regents, the governing board of all state-supported higher institutions. In fact, a constitutional provision makes these institutions with the one governing board the entity known as the University System of Georgia. The system operates under the direction of a chancellor, elected by the board of regents, who with his staff coordinates all institutions through budget controls and other supervisory procedures. In this plan the junior colleges thus operate in the same manner as the University of Georgia and other state institutions. From what could be observed, the principal function of the central system and its board is to review the current operating and plant budget requests of the individual institutions, to examine the need for the amount requested, to present a total budget to the Legislature for appropriation purposes, and to administer an accounting of funds for the entire system.

A certain amount of program coordination is automatically carried on through budget control. Some coordination is also accomplished by an advisory council composed of representatives from the various units in the system and by the frequent communication between the chancellor's office and the institutions. It appears, however, that program coordination and control are achieved more through informal techniques than through a structured procedure within the chancellor's office and that, aside from budget restrictions, the junior colleges develop their own curricula and plan their own programs of counseling and guidance. Questions of policy on such matters as the functions of the individual institutions, entrance standards, degrees offered, and faculty standards are determined by the regents and implemented by the chancellor's office through the junior college presidents.

Instructors in the junior colleges are employed and promoted through a system of academic rank; however, salary brackets for each rank are somewhat lower than in the four-year units of the university system.

When additional types of two-year institutions are considered, the state picture becomes somewhat more complex. Mention has been made of two local junior colleges—one in Augusta, fully supported and controlled by the local county, and the other in Savannah, supported by the city from municipal funds and endowments and controlled by a special college commission (not the local board of education). These two colleges were essentially community-centered institutions. Armstrong, in Savannah, in 1956 served a full-time student body of approximately 430 in transfer and vocational classes and, in addition, enrolled approximately 850 in an extensive evening program. Although these colleges are now a part of the university system, at the time of the visit to the state they were struggling for some means of state aid to local colleges. The two locally controlled and supported military colleges are municipal institutions, and each has a preparatory school connected with it. Their fees are high and, obviously, they serve a special clientele from many geographical areas.

Other dimensions of the post-high school program in Georgia with implications for the junior college program are the extension activities of the University of Georgia, a two-year technical institute operated as a branch of Georgia Institute of Technology, and the vocational program under the jurisdiction of the state board of education. The university's extension activities and continuing education programs are far flung. Eight centers have been established in the state, in which the total average full-time-equivalent enrollment per quarter for 1956–57 was 1,277, a figure roughly comparable to the average enrollment in the state junior colleges. These centers operate with a full-time administrative staff and some full-time teachers. Most centers offer two-year programs; but, due to regulations of the Southern Association of Colleges and Secondary Schools, only one year may be counted towards a degree.

Serving a somewhat different purpose is a two-year extension center of the Georgia Institute of Technology, established at Chamblee near Atlanta in 1948 under the name of Southern Technical Institute. The major curricula offered at this center are strictly of the technical institute type, such as warrant accreditation by the Engineers' Council for Professional Development. An average of approximately 750 students are in attendance. A fairly high percentage of those enrolled in the past have been veterans, but non-veteran enrollment will probably increase.

For the training of tradesmen and skilled workers of lower than the technical institute type, the state, as part of its vocational education program operating through the state department of education, has established two area trade schools which are entirely controlled and financed by the state. One of these is at Americus, where one of the four junior colleges is also situated. This vocational school has residential facilities and extends over a 400-acre campus. It offers numerous courses in such areas as aviation, radio and television, diesel mechanics, practical nursing, business, and automotive mechanics, which run from nine months to two years. Since 40 per cent of its students are high school graduates and 90 per cent are eighteen years of age or more, it, in effect, serves a junior college function.

This was the complex of post-high school institutions of a nonbaccalaureate type in Georgia at the time of the visit to the state in early 1957. For years there had been a difference of opinion as to how the junior colleges should be financed and controlled. In 1949 the regents of the university system contracted with George D. Strayer and his research staff to study the system. One of the recommendations of the group was that the junior colleges be disassociated from the university system and made part of the common school system, controlled and supported by local districts with financial aid from the state, and under the general supervision of the state board of education. The recommendation was apparently not regarded favorably by many in the system, particularly by the staff and constituents of the individual junior college units. The regents of the university system rejected the proposal, and the Legislature passed a resolution commending the regents for doing so. But unrest and indecision continued because the two local colleges performed the same functions as those in the state system, yet had to do so at local expense. Some local colleges contended that they should continue to operate locally but should receive state assistance; others petitioned to be made part of the university system. Communities without any junior colleges pressed hard for such facilities.

The pressure for a solution was so great that the 1957 Legislature authorized an interim legislative committee to study the situation. In the report to the Governor in late 1957 the committee reviewed the potential future college enrollment in the state and made this statement: "With the increases in number of applicants for admission to colleges as projected for the next five years, it is very doubtful that existing institutions of the University System, even with the projected expansions of state appropriations, can make provision for all the young people of Georgia who will soon be seeking the privileges of a college education. It seems desirable and even necessary, therefore, for Georgia to consider the advisability of establishing junior or community colleges in other areas of the state." The committee recommended:

That appropriations for present junior colleges (as well as other higher institutions) be increased

That the state undertake at once to make available in its over-all budget an appropriation for the operation of junior or community colleges

That the regents of the university system be designated as the state agency under whose direction and supervision the junior colleges would be established and operated

That authority be given to "any county, counties, independent school system and other political subdivisions with taxing power within the state of Georgia to either singly or in combination with any other such political subdivision" to establish junior colleges under standards and criteria prescribed by the regents and that state aid amounting to not less than $300 per year for each full-time-equivalent student be made available for the operation of these colleges

That the present junior college units in the university system be continued on the basis on which they are now operating

Following the committee's report, the General Assembly early in 1958 approved legislation permitting local communities to maintain junior colleges according to the provisions enumerated above with state aid and with responsibility for coordination vested in the university system. However, the legislation requires the regents of the university system to resolve annually that all needs of the system have been met before allocating funds to local junior colleges. This provision can well serve as a deterrent to the establishment of colleges under the 1958 law.

In fact, no colleges have been established under the new legislation. Instead, the local colleges in Augusta and Savannah have been admitted to the university system and a former extension center of the state university at Columbus has been changed to a junior college operating as a unit of the university system. Thus, as of 1959, there are in Georgia seven two-year colleges operating as fully state-supported and state-controlled institutions. Despite enabling legislation, it would appear that the idea of local community colleges is a long way from being implemented in the state.

ILLINOIS

Illinois is considered the birthplace of the public junior college and ranks third in the number of students enrolled; hence it might be assumed that the state had taken advantage of its early beginning in the field and had strongly promoted the cause of the public two-year college. However, the number of junior colleges outside Chicago and enrollments in them have not increased as rapidly as could have been expected.

In the state, local control is established exclusively. In 1957–58, 12 districts maintained 17 junior colleges, the Board of Education of Chicago having established 6 branches of the Chicago City Junior College.[9] Present legislation provides for the establishment of junior colleges as a part of the public common school system and specifies the general conditions under which they may be established by "the board of education in any school district maintaining and offering a four-year high school course of study."[10] In Illinois this could mean either a unit district maintaining both elementary and high schools or a special township or high school district. Of the districts, including Chicago, which presently maintain junior colleges, five are unit districts and seven are high school districts. Any district that wishes to establish a junior college must first seek approval of the state superintendent of public instruction. Upon the receipt of such a request, the superintendent makes a survey of the district and the area it serves and, in accordance with legally established criteria, determines the needs and the ability of the district to maintain a junior college with adequate standards. If the superintendent approves the proposition, it is submitted to the voters of the district. Thus, no new junior college is established without the expressed approval of the people.

Separate junior college districts were legalized for the first time by the 1959 Legislature. Any contiguous or compact territory, no part of which is included within any school district maintaining a junior college or any junior college district unless all of such district is included, having a population of not less than 30,000 and not more than 500,000 persons and an assessed valuation of not less than 75 million dollars may petition to establish such a district. A study of the proposed district is then made by the state superintendent of public instruction. If it is recommended that a

---

[9] A projected junior college plan for Chicago provides for the eventual maintenance of seven branches of City Junior College.

[10] For districts with fewer than 500,000 inhabitants, thus excluding Chicago, which operates under special legislation.

district be formed, the proposition is submitted to the voters in the proposed district.

Financial support of Illinois junior colleges comes from three possible sources: nonresidence tuition (which may not exceed the per capita cost of maintaining the junior college attended), local taxes, and state aid. The maximum rate of the local tax in districts outside Chicago is 17½ cents per $100 valuation for operating purposes, and 7½ cents for building purposes and site acquisition. In Chicago there is no special tax for junior college purposes because the amount of local money necessary to maintain the college comes from the general revenues of the school district's over-all levy. The maximum tax rates for the newly legalized separate junior college districts are 5 per cent of the assessed valuation for operating purposes and 1 per cent of the assessed valuation for building purposes and purchase of school grounds.

Until the 1959 session of the Legislature it was illegal for an Illinois junior college to charge tuition to students in the district maintaining a junior college. In that session, however, a bill was passed which permits a junior college to levy tuition in an amount not to exceed one-third of the per capita cost of maintaining the college. Questions have arisen concerning the legality of this legislation and it may be some time before the issue is clear.

State aid for junior colleges, which has for the last biennium been $200 for "each resident student in attendance," was changed in the 1959 legislative session to $7.60 per credit hour for students who complete one-half or more of any term. This will result in a slight increase in state support. Also by 1959 legislation, the local district is eligible for state aid on enrollments in summer classes and in television classes. There is no foundation program in the state aid provision for junior colleges, nor is there any aid given by the state for capital outlay purposes.

A provision of the law entitles a district not maintaining a junior college to levy a maximum tax of 0.175 per cent for use in paying the tuition of its residents qualified to attend a junior college in the state. The law also makes it possible for a student living in a district maintaining a junior college to attend another junior college and for his tuition to be paid by his district of residence.

In any description of the enrollment and program phases of Illinois junior colleges, it is necessary to refer to the Chicago City

Junior College separately from the area outside the city. Of the 17,629 regular freshman and sophomore students enrolled in Illinois junior colleges in 1956–57, 13,659, or almost 80 per cent, were in the then five branches of City Junior College. This indicates a small enrollment in the other junior colleges of the state which in 1956–57 ranged from slightly more than 100 to more than 560 regular students, with an average of approximately 250 students. Most junior colleges outside Chicago share the buildings and frequently also teachers and facilities with the high schools. Their programs consist mainly of the subjects normally required in the first two years of a liberal arts or preprofessional college program, with some terminal offerings in the field of business and occasionally limited offerings in other terminal fields. The junior colleges outside Chicago vary in the extent of their adult and community service programs. However, most of them provide a minimum of such activities, and several of them have developed comparatively large and unique community service programs.

Services in the Chicago City Junior College are more comprehensive. As a supplement to the transfer and terminal programs, courses designed to meet the objectives of general education are emphasized. The terminal offerings in the six branches of the college are restricted somewhat by the fact that the board of education maintains many of its vocational-technical programs in its vocational schools and its technical high schools. Thus, even in the City Junior College programs leading directly to employment are limited to such fields as business (including the secretarial and merchandising fields), medical technology, and drafting. The college has an extensive evening program of regular college offerings. Typical noncredit adult classes are offered by the evening programs in the high schools instead of in the junior colleges. A large-scale television program is in operation in the college—a program in which in September, 1957, more than fifteen hundred students enrolled for credit and six thousand without credit in nine conventional college courses broadcast daily and nightly.

It is helpful to review briefly the history of the junior college movement in Illinois. After the initiation of a post-high school program at Joliet in 1902, a number of school districts followed the example and thus, in effect, began a junior college program without specific legal sanction. The first enabling legislation, enacted in 1931, gave Chicago permission to operate a junior college program as a part of its school system. Legislation validating existing down-state junior colleges and permitting the establishment of new ones came in 1937. This was followed in 1943 by definite regulations with regard to local taxes for the support of junior colleges.

In the meantime, lay and professional leaders became concerned about the future of the junior college in the state, and primarily about the fact that local communities which had established junior colleges were having to bear the entire cost of their operation. In several independent and state-authorized studies the situation was analyzed and recommendations made for strengthened legislation and for state aid.[11] Beginning in 1945 and continuing with each following session of the General Assembly, strong but often fruitless efforts were made to obtain greater recognition of the two-year college. In the closing days of the 1951 session, the General Assembly went so far as to recognize the junior college as a part of the public common schools but still refused to include it in the program of state aid. Finally, in 1955, provision was made for $100 state aid per student per year.

Early in 1957 the Higher Education Commission, established by the General Assembly and appointed by the Governor in 1955 to study the problems of higher education in the state, rendered its report, in which a major part was devoted to the community junior college.[12] The commission recommended (1) the extension of a system of tuition-free junior colleges enabling all high school graduates to be within commuting distance of such an institution; (2) the study of legislation permitting the organization of special junior college districts to include two or more high school districts; (3) the immediate increase of state aid to $200; and (4) the provision, by high school districts not maintaining junior colleges, of free tuition for students to attend college elsewhere. The commission further identified several communities in the state in which potential enrollment, financial ability, and other factors would

[11] Previous studies on higher education and the place of the junior college in Illinois include C. R. Griffith and H. Blackstone, *The Junior College in Illinois,* University of Illinois Press, Urbana, Ill., 1945; and *The Report of the Commission to Survey Higher Educational Facilities in Illinois,* 1945. (George A. Works was director of the survey; the junior college phase of the study was done by Leonard V. Koos.)

[12] *Illinois Looks to the Future in Higher Education,* Report of the Higher Education Commission to the Governor and Legislature of the State of Illinois, 1957.

indicate the desirability of establishing junior colleges, provided sufficient state aid were available.

With this report as background, and doubtless as a result of the vigorous campaign carried on by the Illinois Association of Junior Colleges and the office of the superintendent of public instruction, the Legislature passed a bill providing for $200 state aid and for other improvements in junior college legislation. With this step another milestone was reached in the state.

The history of these legislative efforts best illustrates the major problem common in many states—the lethargy of many people and agencies about the development of local two-year colleges. Outside of Chicago a few communities struggled for many years to carry on small programs. The need for junior college facilities in numerous other communities was recognized, but most of them were so burdened with taxation for elementary and high school education that they were unwilling to add the full cost of a junior college to the tax load. Chicago established a junior college program, but the fact that the full cost of it was borne by the city made the college a target for various economy-minded groups with the result that it was frequently subject to questions and restrictions. At one time it was discontinued and the staff assigned to high school positions; at another time two branches were suddenly moved from their permanent campuses into temporary quarters. Such conditions obviously did not facilitate continuity of planning or staff security.

Early endeavors to obtain state aid were made by junior college administrators and lay people, including legislators from the communities maintaining junior colleges, with endorsement by a limited number of organized professional and lay groups. Other groups representing educational interests do not appear to have given the junior college legislation any help, but there was no evidence that they openly lobbied against it. Certain business groups openly opposed the idea of state aid to junior colleges. In recent legislative sessions numerous organizations and institutions, some of which had not supported the idea earlier, now advocated financial aid for the junior college in their own legislative platforms and took a favorable stand in committee hearings on junior college legislation.

The situation in Illinois has been further complicated by lack of coordination and a strong competition among other public higher educational institutions. Only one factor of this situation is considered here—that of extending the parent campuses of four-year institutions into outlying areas by establishing branches. The University of Illinois has been offering a two-year undergraduate program in Chicago since 1946. The Higher Education Commission in its report recommended the continuation and strengthening of the program but not its extension to four years.[13] This under-graduate program is the only actual extension of the university into another community, and its presence in a metropolitan area has not appeared to restrict the services of the local city college—probably because the latter is so well established. If there were no junior college in the city, it would be doubtful whether one could be started with a University of Illinois branch at hand.

Southern Illinois University, serving the southern section of the state (and under a board of control and administration separate from the University of Illinois), has proposed to extend its services through a major center in the East St. Louis area and through other smaller centers. An outside consultant has recommended a branch in the St. Louis area, and in 1957 Southern Illinois University took over the campus of a discontinued four-year college in Alton. These proposals have elicited sharp criticism from those who believe that extension of lower-division opportunities should be achieved primarily through local junior colleges.

In summary, it appears that two situations have retarded the development of public junior colleges in Illinois. One is the lack of a coordinated, over-all plan for post-high school institutions which would identify the role to be played by different types of institutions, and which would include a state policy on how and by whom additional colleges are to be established. The other is the previous apathy of many groups toward a system of junior colleges.

INDIANA*

The only two-year public colleges in Indiana are the extension centers operated by Indiana University and Purdue University. The

[13] *Ibid.*, p. 174.

* Because Indiana was not one of the 15 states originally selected for intensive study, the report of its two-year program is purely descriptive and somewhat more limited than that of certain other states.

former maintains nine off-campus centers located at Calumet, Fort Wayne, Gary, Indianapolis, Jeffersonville, Kokomo, Richmond, South Bend, and Vincennes.[14] Purdue maintains centers at Hammond, Michigan City, Fort Wayne, and Indianapolis. For the most part the centers maintained by Indiana University stress liberal arts and business education of a standard lower-division nature, together with offerings of a noncredit nature for adults in personal development and the cultural and creative arts. Some upper-division and graduate courses are offered also. Purdue offers a substantial amount of freshman work in several fields and an increasing amount of sophomore work in engineering and science. In addition, each of the four Purdue centers provides several two-year programs of study for engineering technicians as well as various noncredit courses. Further details concerning the policy and nature of the extension program conducted by each of the universities are briefly reported in the following sections.

Indiana University

University officials report that a goal of higher education in Indiana is that there be some type of college, public or private, within a 25-mile radius of every individual in the state. The declared policy of the university, therefore, is to make college opportunities available in communities in which there is no other college within the 25-mile zone. The university generally does not establish centers in communities in which another college offers evening work.[15] It may, after conferring with a local college and often in cooperation with it, establish a center in the community for the purpose of offering services and programs that do not duplicate those offered by the local college. That the centers tend to serve in a regional capacity is evidenced by the fact that in most of them one-third of the students live outside the immediate community in which the center is located.

Student fees are the principal source of revenue for both operation and capital outlay in the centers. For the academic year 1958–1959 only 22 per cent of the operating budget came from

[14] Centers in Richmond and Vincennes are operated in cooperation with Earlham College and Vincennes University, respectively.

[15] In Indianapolis the university center was established before Butler University began its evening program.

state funds and the remainder from fees. Except for the donation of free sites for building purposes, the local communities are not asked to contribute toward the support of the centers. Students enrolled for lower-division work in the centers are charged tuition at the rate of $12 per credit hour as compared with $7 per credit hour on the Bloomington campus. Two of the twelve dollars are earmarked for building purposes. New plants have now been constructed in several centers and others are being planned. Those built since 1955 have been financed by the $2 per credit hour earmarked for the building fund.

Although the centers are set up to serve both full-time and part-time students, the number of part-time students is much greater than the number attending full time. In the first semester of 1958–59 a total of 1,214 students enrolled on a full-time basis in the nine off-campus centers as compared with over 8,000 part-time students in courses bearing university credit and more than 5,200 part-time students in noncredit courses. Three of the centers, all relatively new, enrolled only a few full-time students. In each of the remaining six centers full-time enrollment ranged from 143 to 229. Enrollment in part-time credit work was highest in Indianapolis, where more than 2,200 students were registered, and in the Gary and South Bend centers, in each of which more than 1,100 students were attending part time. By far the greatest number of the noncredit enrollment was in the South Bend center where almost 3,300 students were attending noncredit classes. Enrollments in all categories in the fall of 1958 represented an increase over 1957.

Admission requirements for courses bearing university credit are the same in the centers as those on the Bloomington campus. However, no data are available on the characteristics of students attending the centers as compared with those who enroll initially at Bloomington. Neither is there information on the number of center students who transfer to another institution, or if they transfer to Bloomington, how long they tend to remain in the centers before transfer. It was reported, however, that only a limited number of students complete the equivalent of two years' work in the centers before transferring.

Responsibility for the over-all center operation program rests in the Division of University Extension under the direction of a dean and appropriate staff. The staff in each center includes a director, a limited number of full-time teachers, and a greater number of part-time teachers. Full-time teachers are employed with the same rank and salary as the staff on the Bloomington campus. In the fall semester, 1958, approximately 72 per cent of the center staff were instructors or lecturers, 20 per cent were assistant professors, 6 per cent were associate professors, and 2 per cent were full professors. Part-time instructors are paid by the credit hour.

All members of the teaching staff must be approved by the appropriate teaching department on the main campus as well as by the dean of extension and the director of the center. The center credit courses are taught from the same texts and are presumed to be identical with those on campus. Manuals for many of them are supplied center faculty members for the purpose of helping them maintain comparability of courses.

Library services in each of the centers are under the general direction of a center faculty library committee.

A counselor is employed at each center. In addition to doing regular counseling work, this person does the necessary testing of students and generally teaches at least one class.

Purdue University

Since Purdue is the land-grant institution in the state, its offerings reflect an emphasis on engineering, science, agriculture, technology, and home economics. Three of its centers are in communities in which there are also Indiana University centers.

The standard lower-division courses leading to a degree are the same as those offered on campus and are supervised by the heads of schools and departments on campus. Enrollment in a center is enrollment in Purdue.

As of 1958 a total of eight curricula for the preparation of technicians had been developed, of which four were accredited by the Subcommittee on Technical Institutes of the Engineers' Council for Professional Development. In addition, several one-year programs of a like nature were available. Two-year programs lead to associate technical aide diplomas and one-year programs to technical certificates.

As in the case of Indiana University, the Purdue extension programs are supported mainly by student fees. These fees are set for each course within the technical curriculum but they tend to total between $225 and $265 per semester for a full-time load.

More than 4,500 students were enrolled in the four centers during the fall semester, 1958—2,221 in lower-division, degree-credit classes and 2,315 in technical institute programs. Full-time students were not reported separately. University officials report that during the school year 1957–58, a total of 426 students completed either one or two years of work in one of the centers and transferred to the Lafayette campus to continue their work.

The foregoing account of the extension programs in Indiana is descriptive only. The expressed point of view of university officials is that existing institutions can and will be expanded to meet the state's college enrollment growth and that no new institutions will be needed. Presumably, this means that as far as public institutions are concerned, existing and additional branches of the two universities will care for the needs.

It would seem as if two questions would eventually be raised in the state. One relates to the inevitable competition and duplication of effort that result when the universities both maintain centers in the same community, as is the case in the Calumet area, Fort Wayne, and Indianapolis. The duplication applies especially to transfer courses. The other question is whether or not the majority of either the potential terminal or the potential transfer students will be served when tuition rates are as high as those charged by the two universities.

IOWA

Long known as a state with many small junior colleges, Iowa has to cope with the problem of providing junior college education in an agricultural state with relatively few heavily populated areas.

The 16 public two-year institutions in the state are controlled by a local school system, which in Iowa means either an independent or a consolidated or a community district. The population of the districts maintaining the colleges varies from forty-five hundred to thirty-four thousand, with seven of the districts having fewer than ten thousand residents. With districts of this small size it is not surprising that the colleges are also small. In fact, the total full-time freshman and sophomore enrollment for all 16 colleges as of September 15, 1957, was only 2,402 students. Enrollment in the individual colleges ranged from 39 to 419, with 13 enrolling fewer than 200 students. Only 3 colleges have separate buildings, and even they share some facilities with the local high school. For the school year 1956–57, only 16 per cent of the teachers taught full time, the remainder taught both in the college and in the high school. The curriculum in the colleges is limited by their size and by the comparative lack of industry in the state, which limits the demand for vocational programs. Hence the Iowa colleges primarily emphasize lower-division transfer work, although in most of them a few students who expect to go directly into employment are enrolled in various business classes. Two of the colleges have a relatively large number of part-time students enrolled in regular college classes during evening hours. All but one offer some noncredit adult courses at night, and in three of the institutions enrollment in these programs tends to run higher than one thousand students per semester. Several of the colleges also make their facilities and staff available to four-year colleges for extension work, and in one of them enrollment in such programs approximates five hundred students.[16]

The history of Iowa junior colleges is marked by a slow and painful struggle. Thirty-five institutions have been established but only sixteen are now in operation. Five colleges were closed, then reopened, and closed once again. Of those now in operation, five have been closed once since their original establishment. All this has occurred since 1918 when the Board of Education of Mason City established the first college—one of the 11 junior colleges in continuous operation since their establishment. At the time Mason City began its college program, there was no legal recognition of post-high school work in the state. It was not until 1927 that the General Assembly passed the first enabling legislation, which simply provided that a local board, upon approval of the state superintendent and authorization by the voters, could establish and maintain a junior college. A law in 1931 prohibited the establish-

[16] For a more detailed description of Iowa junior colleges and a recommended plan for reorganization, see James A. Starrak and Raymond M. Hughes, *The Community College in the United States*, Iowa State College Press, Ames, Iowa, 1954, part 3.

ment of junior colleges in districts with fewer than twenty thousand inhabitants. In 1941 a further law provided that junior colleges could be established only if the proposition were approved by at least 60 per cent of the voters in the district.

Financial support for Iowa junior colleges has until recently largely been borne by the local community. Tuition is charged in all colleges, and in 1956–57 ranged from $60 to $90 per semester. There was no state aid until 1949 when a bill was passed providing for 25 cents per day per student carrying 12 or more hours. This amounted to $45 per full-time student per year. In 1956–57 the total state aid received by the colleges amounted to slightly less than 10 per cent of the total income budgeted for them that year. However, in the 1957 session of the Legislature, after much debate and as a result of tireless efforts by many friends of the junior college in the state, an appropriation bill for the next two years was passed amounting to $1 per day per student, or $180 per year.

To be eligible for such aid, a district must levy a school tax for the general fund of at least 15 mills for the year preceding the receipt of state aid and must meet standards established jointly by the state board of public instruction and the state board of regents. The Iowa Association of Public Junior Colleges serves in an advisory capacity to these boards.

The increased state aid enacted in 1957 should result in the partial solution of some of Iowa's problems. It should, for example, lead to improved facilities for junior colleges, to richer programs, and to better instructional aids, including library holdings.

State aid alone, however, cannot solve all problems that confront Iowa in its junior college program. Many of these problems stem from the size of the colleges, which in turn is a reflection of the size of the districts and the population distribution in the state. Except for Des Moines (which has no junior college because of the general feeling that Drake University, a private institution, through its lower-division and extensive part-time programs serves the junior college function), there are only 11 cities of twenty-five thousand or more. Only 5 of them maintain a junior college. The low enrollments resulting from small districts have precluded any breadth of program, with the result that most Iowa junior colleges offer a straight (and small-scale) university parallel program.

The problem of offerings and finance in the Iowa colleges

would be partly solved by increased enrollments resulting from larger districts. Two measures would make larger districts possible. One would be a cooperative effort by contiguous school districts in the maintenance of a junior college. The other would be legislation permitting the creation of separate junior college districts. Larger districts, however, have certain drawbacks such as long commuting distances for some students and the increased difficulties in inclement winter weather. In this study no analysis was made of local school districts in the state and of the extent to which they might be enlarged.

Iowa is over one hurdle with increased state aid, but there is still no aid for capital outlay and hence no real encouragement for districts to establish junior colleges or to acquire facilities for them. The problem of size still remains and must soon be studied if the state is to realize a legitimate return on its investment in these institutions. It is possible that a more concerted attack on the problems of the junior colleges may be necessary and feasible in the years immediately ahead when higher school enrollments and increased competition for the tax dollar may force the state to look more accurately at the junior colleges as a segment of higher education and at the same time to ascertain their place in the public school system. The Coordinating Committee of Registrars of the Iowa State Board of Regents has projected total college enrollments, indicating that they will probably increase from 44,000 to 47,300 by 1962, to 60,000 by 1966, and to 72,600 by 1970; yet there seems to have been no over-all, state-wide attack on how the junior colleges are to fit into the total program of higher education. The favorable action on state aid taken by the Legislature in 1957 may be an indication of a prevailing attitude by the public which would lead to early consideration of the over-all problem.

MASSACHUSETTS

The Commonwealth of Massachusetts was for three reasons included in the list of states studied: (1) it is a state in a section of the country where the early development of private institutions has set a pattern of higher education now questioned in view of increased demands for college opportunity; (2) the size of the state's population and industry has raised the question as to whether existing educational opportunities and services are comparable to those in similar states; (3) although a system of public junior colleges was recommended for the state more than thirty years ago with little development in the meantime, a renewed effort has recently been made to determine the possible role of this type of institution. In fact, since the study began, there has been new and significant junior college legislation in the state.

Historically, private education at the college level has been predominating in the state. In 1956, only 17 of 93 higher institutions were public and 76 (81.7 per cent) were private. In 1950, Massachusetts ranked third among the states in resident private junior college enrollment. For the most part, the private junior colleges offer basic transfer programs with a sprinkling of vocational offerings, although some of them, and particularly the one at Worcester, resemble community colleges with numerous terminal offerings and a large adult education program. Both the public and the private colleges enroll large numbers of students from outside the state. In 1950, Massachusetts ranked second among the states in which in-migration exceeded out-migration of undergraduate students.[17]

Only three public junior colleges are in operation in Massachusetts—all maintained by the school districts in their respective cities under enabling legislation enacted in 1948. While each is small, they all appear to be growing gradually. The 1948 legislation was little more than permissive, and simply provided that the school committee in any city or town could submit to the state department of education a plan for "a course of school instruction beyond the regular high school course" and, provided the plan was approved in writing by the department, the course could be maintained on the junior college level with public funds appropriated for the purpose and in conformance with standards set by the state department. The law also provided that the state department of education could on its own volition establish and maintain a junior college in any community. In 1956 the state authorized the opening of a pilot institution in one of the teachers colleges.

The cost of maintaining the local colleges has been met by tuition charges and local taxes. However, in 1957 the Legislature provided for state aid to the extent of one-half the cost after

[17] *Higher Education in the Forty-eight States,* The Council of State Governments, Chicago, 1952, p. 188.

deducting tuition receipts, but stipulated that such aid could amount to no more than $100 per student per year.

This small beginning of junior college operation in Massachusetts does not reflect the considerable interest that has prevailed in the state for many years. For information on the history of junior college consideration the author is indebted to Dr. Stanley F. Salwak of the University of Massachusetts.[18] Dr. Salwak traces that history to 1911, when a special committee of the state board of education pointed out that many communities were not provided with collegiate opportunities and that secondary and higher education were not in balance. In 1915 another study group called attention to the fact that many worthy youths were unable to go to college at existing costs. In 1923 George F. Zook completed for a committee a study of the state in which he confirmed the conclusions in the earlier studies regarding lack of opportunity.[19] In the study industry was also surveyed and the need for semiprofessional training programs identified. Zook recommended the establishment of not more than 12 local junior colleges and identified 11 regions in immediate need of them. Interestingly enough, Salwak reports, the 1950 census shows that by then 70 per cent of the state's population was in these 11 regions, and 90 per cent of the population was in the region that would have been served by 8 of the junior colleges had they been established. Salwak concluded that in terms of its per capita wealth, Massachusetts was not adequately supporting education at all levels; that the public was little aware of the value of the junior college; and that the old and established colleges constituted a deterrent to the development of junior colleges because they offered a prestige value in the mind of the public.

Some of Salwak's conclusions may explain why no action was taken on Zook's proposal. In fact, nothing was done until 1941 when the state again authorized a study of junior colleges and created a commission for that purpose. This commission recom-

[18] Stanley F. Salwak, "Some Factors Significant in the Establishment of Public Junior Colleges in the U.S. (1940–45) with Special Reference to Massachusetts," unpublished doctoral dissertation, Pennsylvania State University, University Park, August, 1953.

[19] *Report of a Fact-finding Survey of Technical and Higher Education in Massachusetts*, House Document No. 1700, Dec. 26, 1923.

mended the legislation previously described, which was adopted in 1948. In August, 1956, another special commission was created by the Legislature for the purpose "of making an investigation and study relative to the operation and structure of junior colleges in the commonwealth." This commission rendered a brief report on December 31, 1956, which made some tentative estimates of the gaps between available facilities and need, but concluded that a thorough state survey was essential before any specific recommendations could be made.

The detailed study was assigned to a newly created agency, the Special Commission on Audit of State Needs. In the meantime, during 1957, interest in public junior colleges seemed to increase despite the commission's recommendation to make a thorough state survey before action was taken. Several bills were introduced in 1957. One of them would have empowered the University of Massachusetts to establish and operate a branch on "a junior college level" wherever buildings and other facilities were furnished without charge by the school committee of a city or town. The pattern proposed was similar to that in operation in Wisconsin and Pennsylvania. Another bill provided for junior colleges in nine of the largest cities to be operated by the department of education. Another urged the establishment of junior colleges in at least six teachers colleges. However, no action was taken on any of the proposals. Meanwhile, various groups began vigorously to declare themselves in favor of various patterns of junior college organization, including university extensions, junior colleges operated through the state department of education, and local institutions with state aid.

In August, 1957, the special commission published its first quarterly report, devoted exclusively to the needs of Massachusetts in higher education. Among the significant data in the report are those showing (1) shortages in higher education and facilities and space needed for the state (in nine different regions) by 1967; (2) the state's needs for engineers and technicians by areas; (3) the relatively low percentage of high school graduates, by regions, who go to college; and (4) that Massachusetts ranks forty-eighth among the states in the per capita support of all public higher education, and thirty-fifth in its support of junior and community colleges.

These and similar topics were deliberated at the Governor's Conference on Higher Education in late 1957, and at a later hearing held by the Special Commission on Audit of State Needs.

On January 1, 1958, the Governor in his annual message called attention to the fact that the state's system of higher education suffers from a lack of concerted and coordinated attacks on such problems as junior college education and announced that he would ask for an informal coordinating committee composed of the leaders of the various public institutions to work together for some solution of this problem.

In looking toward a solution, the state board of education through the department of education announced its policy on providing junior college opportunities. It recommended (1) the establishment of industrial, technical, and semiprofessional programs in the state teachers colleges to be operated during late afternoons and evenings (such as the experimental program now in operation at one of the teachers colleges), and (2) additional local community colleges with supervisory services coming from the department of education.

As in other states, the policy of the state university was involved. University of Massachusetts officials in published statements and in informal conferences have declared that their interest lay in seeing action taken and that the university would offer all its resources in the planning and development of policy. In a published statement included in the report of the 1956 special commission, the university declared itself in favor of comprehensive community colleges. However, the university continued that it could not support them without additional budget support; that the local property tax could not assume the added burden; that the anticipated unit costs of such a program should be the average cost prevailing at the university "less any . . . costs locally provided"; and that leadership and policy for junior colleges should be developed and coordinated at "the college and university level rather than from or within the secondary programs of the commonwealth."

In July, 1958, Governor Furcolo followed the earlier recommendation of the audit commission with a special message to the Legislature entitled "The Responsibility of the Commonwealth in Higher Education." This message reiterated the arguments presented in the previous report, and urged a rapid acceleration of the existing capital plan for the existing state colleges, plus the creation of a state-wide community college system. The total capital outlay recommended by the Governor, in the form of a bond issue, was $111,594,750 over a three-year period, including $24,-000,000 for the planning and construction of the community college system.

The Legislature voted approval of the new Massachusetts Board of Regional Community Colleges, and later voted 1 million dollars for the initial planning and development of the system.

The law providing for the community colleges establishes a Massachusetts Board of Regional Community Colleges, consisting of 15 members and including the president of the University of Massachusetts, the commissioner of education, a president of 1 of the 10 state teachers colleges (elected annually by all presidents), and a president of 1 of the 3 state technical institutes (elected annually by all presidents). Of the other members of the board appointed by the Governor for overlapping terms, 1 shall be a president of a private college or junior college in Massachusetts.

The board appoints a chief administrative officer, known as the president of the Massachusetts Regional Community Colleges, and fixes his duties and those of staff members. The president, under the board, has the responsibility of developing a plan for a system of community college education throughout the commonwealth. "Community college" is defined to include the usual college courses of the freshman and sophomore years, vocational-technical education, and adult education.

The board is empowered to appoint the dean and faculty of each college established. Although it is understood that facilities for the colleges will soon be constructed, existing buildings may be used in any town at the discretion of the board.

Each regional community college shall have a local advisory board of 10 members.

While the law did not specify either the number of colleges or their locations, this being left to the discretion of the board, the previous study had shown that eight or nine colleges could be located so as to serve most of the state's population.

The new board began to function soon after its creation. It employed an executive director, sought the advice of outside consultants, set up procedures for determining priorities for location of colleges, and agreed on organizational steps. Despite this good beginning, however, the budget submitted by the board was not passed by the 1959 Legislature. The board has a nominal budget to continue a minimum of research and planning but any program of action pertaining to community colleges has been indefinitely postponed. Thus, after a long-delayed but optimistic beginning on an expanded community college program, the future of such a development in Massachusetts is still unknown.

MINNESOTA

Minnesota is an example of a state that has shown considerable interest in the public junior college but where various factors have restricted its maximum development.

The state's nine existing public two-year colleges are exclusively locally controlled and operate as an integral part of the public school system. Enabling legislation provides that the school board of any independent or special school district may make application to the state board of education to establish and maintain a junior college. If, after making a legally required survey to determine the need for additional college facilities and the financial ability of the district to provide them, the state department approves the proposition, it is then presented to the voters. If the proposition is approved by a two-thirds majority, the local board may establish the college as a part of the district's school system. The junior college thus comes under the jurisdiction of the local school board, with the city or district superintendent responsible for the over-all district program. In each case a dean who reports to the superintendent is selected to administer the junior college. Until recently, all junior colleges were housed in a section of the local high school plant and shared certain facilities, such as auditoriums, gymnasiums, and libraries. However, two of the colleges are now housed in separate buildings. To some extent the colleges and high schools share teachers, particularly in special subject fields, although most of the colleges have many full-time teachers.

Minnesota junior colleges are now financed through combined state and local efforts, but until 1957 support for them came entirely from local taxes and tuition. No special junior college tax is designated in the local district, the total allowed tax rate supplying the funds needed for operating all units in the system. Tuition charges have ranged from $30 to $105 per semester for resident students and more for nonresidents. The 1957 session of the Legislature, in passing the first state-aid bill for junior colleges, provided that the state board of education shall distribute to each district maintaining a junior college $200 annually for each student in average daily attendance. This amount was increased to $250 in the 1959 Legislature. The act further provided that no such aid would be paid to any district that establishes a junior college within 36 miles of any existing junior college or state teachers college.

Minnesota junior colleges are established in small communities, and the institutions themselves are small. The population in the service area of each junior college is somewhat greater than that of the community of location; the estimated population in junior college districts ranges from two thousand to thirty-five thousand in Rochester. The number of full-time day students reported in the fall of 1956 for each of the junior colleges ranged from 98 to 390,[20] and the total full-time enrollment in all junior colleges accounted for less than 5 per cent of total enrollment for all Minnesota colleges.

Although each junior college includes among its purposes vocational education for students not planning to go on for advanced study, the majority of students are enrolled in preparatory programs. Rochester is an exception to some extent, because it has specialized in the preparation of students for semiprofessional and technical fields associated with the healing arts.

Apparently, Minnesota faces many crucial problems concerning the junior college, and they will become intensified as far greater numbers of the state's youths seek a college education. Some of the problems are outlined in the report of the Governor's Committee on Higher Education issued in December, 1956.[21] This report of a lay committee, appointed by the Governor early in 1956 to study Minnesota's current problems in higher education and to make recommendations and projections for the future, gives considerable space to the junior colleges. It designated as the basic

[20] *Minnesota's Stake in the Future—Higher Education, 1956–1970*, Governor's Committee on Higher Education, Minneapolis, December, 1956.
[21] *Ibid.*

problem the fact that the junior colleges were inadequately supported, particularly because of the lack of state aid, and recommended that the Legislature appropriate $200 per student per year —the figure later approved. Need for financial stability had also been identified in earlier studies, including the report of a study made by the Minnesota Commission on Higher Education in 1950.

This lack of response to a recognized need would suggest the existence of political forces in the state which were opposed to necessary legislation, or simply lack of concern by the people. A hint of political pressure was made in one of a series of articles in the *Minneapolis Tribune* in April, 1956, when staff writer Richard P. Kleeman stated: "Opposition to expansion of Minnesota's public junior colleges—and to state aid for them—has come from men who say they don't oppose junior colleges as such— but doubt that they are 'right' for Minnesota." Mr. Kleeman went on to report interviews with certain college administrators and a long-time legislator who expressed this point of view.

An indication of general lack of concern about Minnesota's junior colleges was borne out in a poll made in 1956 of a sampling of the state's population, which showed that most Minnesotans have only a limited knowledge of the nature and purpose of the junior college and think little about its future development. This apathy is more forcefully illustrated by the fact that no new junior colleges have been established since 1940—not even with the emphasis given them in the state studies of higher education. While this could be caused by lack of funds, it would also seem to represent a general lack of interest.

The position and influence of the state university in any state is important in achieving adequate legislation and status for the junior college system. Minnesota has only one university, which in 1956 enrolled more than half of all full-time students in all higher institutions and approximately three-fourths of the full-time students in *public* higher institutions. When any institution holds such a dominant position, it has many followers who often find it difficult to orient themselves to the needs for other types of colleges. This attitude can result in lethargy or opposition by those who influence legislation, including organized pressure groups, university alumni, individual regents, and legislators. In such a situation it is desirable for university leadership to voice a strong opinion in support of junior college needs and to place them alongside those of the university when appropriations are being made by the Legislature. This is not to say that the University of Minnesota has not shown interest in the junior colleges. Interestingly enough, it was President Folwell who in 1869 was among the first educational leaders in the United States to advocate junior colleges. President Morrill has declared himself in favor of Minnesota's junior colleges and state aid for them. A number of able people on the university staff have over the years given strong leadership to the junior college and by their statements and studies have expressed their full interest in its further development.

In considering the future of junior colleges in Minnesota, certain other problems must be resolved, even though state aid has become a reality. One is to determine areas or districts of sufficient size to warrant the establishment of such institutions, particularly in view of the lack of population concentration except in a few areas of the state. In the studies of 1950 and 1956 several possible locations for junior colleges were identified. Eventually, the state may find it desirable to legalize combinations of districts or separate districts for the maintenance of sufficiently large junior college units.

Another still unsolved problem relates to educational facilities in the Twin Cities area. Whether Minneapolis and St. Paul and their extensive suburban areas continue to be served exclusively by the university becomes both a state and local matter. The general college of the university in a sense serves as a public junior college for the area because of its less stringent admission requirements and its broad type of curriculum. Approximately 90 per cent of its students live locally, and the general college offers them some terminal work, though not of the technical type. The Governor's committee in the 1956 study recommended serious consideration of the establishment of junior colleges in the area to relieve the pressure on the university for lower-division education. Some suburban areas are reported to have indicated interest in establishing such junior colleges, but apparently no great interest has been shown in either St. Paul or Minneapolis. The university in 1957 acquired land across the river from the main campus to expand its lower-division facilities, which must be greatly enlarged regardless of whether new junior colleges are founded in the area. But opinion is sharply divided on the question of whether the university should expand sufficiently to carry the full local load in the 1960s and beyond. Since the local area will be reluctant to pay its share for junior colleges if the university continues the services, it would seem wise for the university to announce policies in definite terms.

Still another facet to the situation is the question of what should be done about the five university-sponsored secondary agricultural schools scattered throughout the state. With the exception of the one in St. Paul, all are in rural, sparsely settled areas. These schools appear to have fulfilled their usefulness, and their future utilization is now a problem. Since each has dormitory space and other capital facilities, it has been suggested that they become extension centers of the university. If the schools are converted into two-year extension centers, two types of such institutions will then exist in the state—the extension centers and the local public junior colleges. The result may well be a retardation of the local junior college movement, because many communities already are hard pressed for school funds and may see in the extension plan an opportunity to procure local college offerings at no local cost. This attitude would be partly offset by increased state aid for junior colleges and state assistance for capital outlay as well as for operation.

The final solution of the problem of serving the Twin Cities area and the outlying rural sections depends on state policy. The present observations should not be interpreted as recommendations. They are enumerated simply to show that what is done will substantially affect the junior college movement in the state. If junior colleges are provided on a wider scale, the state may develop the policy of assigning differential functions to its different public institutions, and the larger the number of warranted junior colleges in the state, the greater will be the likelihood that the public junior college movement in Minnesota can be put on a sound operating and financial base.

MISSISSIPPI

When observers select a state as an illustration of over-all planning for a junior college system, they often point to Mississippi. A total of 16 public junior colleges—14 for white students and 2 for Negroes—are now in operation in the state. Of the colleges for white students, one is a municipal institution maintained by the school system of Meridian, which operates on a 6-4-4 plan. The remaining 13 in a sense are area junior colleges, and it is their development and the planning for them which constitutes the example frequently characterized as unique in state planning. A brief description of the development of these institutions, the means of coordinating them, and their present structure and program is thus in order.

The area junior colleges in Mississippi grew out of county agricultural high schools—approximately fifty in number—which dotted the state in the early part of the century at a time when local public high schools were nonexistent except in urban centers and when roads made commuting difficult. As these schools became relatively less important because of better transportation, organization of local high school districts, and other factors, the question arose as to whether some of the schools might not offer certain college level courses. In 1924 the Legislature first approved such post-high school courses, and by 1928, 10 of the high schools were offering some kind of college program. The interest in many of the other schools in adding college classes led to the first junior college law, which provided that a separate school district or an agricultural high school meeting certain criteria might establish a junior college. The law also provided that school districts and county agricultural high schools might unite with other school districts or other counties in the establishment of junior colleges.

Just as important as the enabling legislation was the creation of a Junior College Commission with authority to place and approve institutions. This commission consists of seven members: the state superintendent of education; the chancellor of the University of Mississippi; the presidents of Mississippi State College, Mississippi State College for Women, and of three junior colleges. One of the first steps taken by the first commission was to identify areas that would meet certain criteria adopted by the commission as necessary to qualify for a junior college. These qualifying areas were designated as "zones," and 13 of them were originally identified. By 1948 a junior college had been established in each zone. In 1950 the junior college laws were completely rewritten. One provision made it mandatory for the Junior College Commission to divide the state into districts or zones[22] within which junior colleges could be established and to fix the territorial boundaries of each zone.

The Junior College Commission has wide powers in determining criteria for establishing new institutions and in setting up standards to be met by colleges before they are eligible for state appropriations. These standards specifically relate to such matters as tax base, internal organization of the institution, curriculum, training of teachers and administrators, instruction, physical plant and equipment, library, laboratories, admission requirements, minimum enrollment, financial report, student activities and student personnel, student records, quality of work, self-evaluation, and general stability of the institution. The commission also has a working relationship with the Mississippi Commission on College Accreditation, which accredits all higher institutions in the state.

The legal and financial arrangements for junior colleges in Mississippi add to the story of cooperative efforts and state-wide planning. As noted above, the law makes it possible for two or more counties to join in the support of a junior college, even though the institution itself is located in the facilities used by the original agricultural high school in one of the counties. At present, 58 counties are included in the districts involving the 15 colleges (exclusive of Meridian) and are thus contributing to their support.

Mississippi junior colleges are financed jointly by the local districts and the state. The law provides that the local districts may levy a tax up to 3 mills on the assessed valuation for support and 3 mills for enlargement and improvement of plant.[23] Provision is also made for bonding for capital construction. The state makes an appropriation each biennium for junior college support, dividing the amount into two categories: (1) support and maintenance of junior colleges and (2) support, maintenance, and equipment of vocational-technical departments in junior colleges. The total appropriation for these items for 1956–57 was almost 4 million dollars. The ratio of local support to state support for maintenance tends to be one to one. Generally it is up to the local community to acquire,

---

[22] The terms "zone" and "district" appear to be used interchangeably with "district," the legal term always used when two or more counties unite to support a junior college.

[23] None of the districts presently levies the maximum tax allowed.

construct, and improve the plant, although on three occasions the Legislature has also appropriated money for this purpose. There is no tuition for resident students. Some of the college students in the county colleges (Meridian has no housing facilities) are housed and fed in dormitories, but an increasing number of them commute. Cost of attendance is small; charges for board and room approximate only $35 per month, and there is no tuition for resident students.

The Mississippi junior colleges have shop facilities for teaching some 25 to 30 vocational and technical courses and agricultural facilities, such as meat curing and processing facilities, grade A dairy and pasteurizing plants, forestry plots, nurseries, and locations for the study of general farm operation. There is a partial policy of allocation of functions whereby certain colleges specialize in one or more unique vocational or technical programs for which demand is limited, such as horology, office-machine repair, barbering, and building technology. Such courses draw students from wide areas. Enrollment figures show that from a total of 8,932 students enrolled in the 15 colleges in 1956–57, 2,002 were in vocational-technical classes of some kind. Observation in the state caused the author to conclude that a high percentage of students in the vocational programs were veterans and adults, and that only a limited number of recent high school graduates enroll in such programs. Conversely, these younger, typical college-age youths comprise a high percentage of the academic parallel program. Evening programs for adults are organized in some of the colleges, but the small size of most communities limits the possibilities. This is not true at Meridian, which has a large evening program, or at Hinds in the Jackson metropolitan area.

Coordination among the junior colleges and between them and the senior institutions is accomplished in a number of ways. A person in the office of the state superintendent of public instruction is designated as supervisor of junior colleges; in addition to the usual responsibilities of such supervision from the state's point of view, this person serves as secretary of the Junior College Commission and of the state Junior College Association, which means that he is a central figure in terms of communication, information, and advisory relationships. As in other states, the Junior College Association is active and automatically makes for a certain amount of coordination. There is also continuous informal coordination with the four-year colleges, both through state conferences planned for junior and senior colleges and through the office of the executive secretary of the Board of Trustees of Institutions of Higher Learning, which is the coordinating agency for public higher institutions other than junior colleges. It was reported that for the most part the junior and senior colleges stand together on requests for legislative appropriations, each group lending support to the other.

The impression should not be left that the Mississippi junior colleges have no problems. They have many, particularly those of financing adequate educational programs in a state with a relatively low per capita income. The absence of a legal requirement for state assistance means that at each legislative session the colleges must press for sufficient appropriations, which not only requires much time and effort but also results in uncertainty of the amount finally to be appropriated. Other problems relate to the desirability of additional junior colleges so that other segments of the state's population could be served and to the proximity of a few colleges that may be so close to each other that each one is hindered in its growth and in its support. The state presumably will have to face the problem of whether junior colleges should be situated in centers of population concentration even if other institutions are in the same community. At present it is not the policy to place them in the same area, but with the growing number of college-age people to be served and with the desirability of extending opportunities to groups not now served, the policy may be in need of review.

There can be little doubt that Mississippi affords an example of planning which provides opportunities despite economic barriers and peculiar population distribution. It has chosen to accomplish its objectives by what its leaders call the grass-roots approach by means of local colleges rather than by state-controlled institutions. This, together with the element of over-all state planning, constitutes the example worthy of note in this report.

NEW YORK

Much has been said and written about the New York plan for community colleges, and an unusually significant development has been predicted for them.

Before the current program of two-year college operation in New York is described, it is necessary to discuss two frequently mentioned state agencies, which, because of their titles and responsibilities, are confusing: one is The University of the State of New York and the other is the State University of New York. The former is an agency of long standing and is responsible for all education, public and private, at all levels. It has a governing board, the board of regents, whose administrative agency is the state education department. The University of the State of New York is roughly comparable to the department of public instruction in most other states, except that it is concerned with all private as well as public schools and colleges.

The State University of New York was created in 1948 on a recommendation by the Temporary Commission on the Need for a State University. In general, the State University is a decentralized entity which embraces all state-supported institutions of higher education and is responsible for their operation. There is no centrally located state university in New York similar to that of other states. Instead, the university is an amalgamation of individual public institutions including teachers colleges, professional colleges, medical colleges, and certain other types of institutions under one system.

The working relationship between these two bodies is such that the State University is recognized as "occupying a position within The University of the State of New York corresponding to that of the trustees of private colleges and universities.[24] Subject to budget restrictions and to supervision from the regents on curricula and standards, the Board of Trustees of the State University has freedom to administer and coordinate its various units, which include technical institutes and community colleges.

Of the 17 public two-year institutions in New York which were in operation in 1957–58, 6—the agricultural and technical institutes—were fully controlled and financed by the state and the remaining 11 had their separate boards of control in their local communities. Of the latter group 7 were in effect technical institutes offering primarily technical terminal programs.

The community college law provides that in individual com-

[24] Oliver C. Carmichael, Jr., *New York Establishes a State University,* Vanderbilt University Press, Nashville, Tenn., 1955, p. 311.

munities a "local sponsor" may, by following the standards prescribed by the Board of Trustees of the State University, establish a
community college and assume for the taxing body, which the
sponsor represents, the community's share of the financing. Plans
for the establishment of community colleges are recommended for
approval to the board of regents by the Board of Trustees of the
State University of New York. A local sponsor is defined as "any
city, county, intermediate school district or school district approved by the State University trustees." The law requires for each
sponsoring agency a board of trustees. In communities outside New
York City this board consists of nine members—five appointed by
the local legislative body of the sponsoring agency, including one
person who is a member of this local body, and four local residents
appointed by the Governor. All appointments are for nine years on
a rotation basis. In New York City the governing board may be
either the city board of education or the board of higher education.
Of the eleven local colleges in operation in 1957 the sponsor for one
was a municipality, for six a county, and for four (including those
in New York City) a school district.

Basically, these institutions are financed by state and local
agencies sharing equally all expenditures for capital outlay, and
each bearing one-third of the annual cost of operation, with the remaining one-third coming as tuition from the students. Legislation
permits the local agency to bear as much as two-thirds of the operating costs and to require less or no tuition, but so far no agency
has exercised this option. The only partial exception is the Fashion
Institute of Technology in New York City, where tuition is waived
because of extensive scholarships and subsidies from the industry it
serves. Another important provision of the financing plan permits a
local agency to charge back to the county of residence an allocable
portion of the local sponsor's share of operating costs for nonresident students.

The original master plan completed by the university and approved by the Governor and the board of regents in 1950 contained
a blueprint for community colleges and, in addition, identified certain "economic" areas in the state which were considered to be in
need of such institutions.[25] However, the identification of eligibility
and need is a continuous consideration and necessitates constant

[25] *The Master Plan*, State University of New York, Albany, 1950.

study by the board of regents and the State University. Once a community is identified or once a group of people in a community on their own initiative becomes interested in a community college, it is generally the responsibility of the community to seek the advice of the State University and the state education department on the next steps. State University officials maintain that their responsibilities are to advise, approve, and coordinate, and not to initiate the establishment procedure.

If a community is interested in establishing a community college, certain criteria must be used by the community, the State University, and ultimately the board of regents in determining whether approval is to be given. These criteria include enrollment potentials, occupational needs (local, state, and national), local facilities already available, and financial requirements.

Once a community college is established, broad powers are left to the local sponsor, although approval and supervisory responsibilities reside in the state agencies that make for coordination and control. The local board of trustees is empowered to appoint a president for the college, subject to approval by the State University trustees, and to appoint (or delegate to the president the appointment of) other members of the staff. The local board adopts curricula, subject to the approval of the State University trustees; prepares a budget for approval by the local legislative body or board or other appropriate governing agency; and, subject to the general supervision of the State University trustees, discharges such other duties as may be appropriate for the effective operation of the college.

The technical institutes—the six operated by the state and the seven local ones operating under the community college law—serve almost exclusively students preparing for vocational-technical occupations. Each of the four comprehensive community colleges also offers a number of technical programs in addition to regular preparatory work, although, as usual, enrollment is higher in the preparatory courses.

Because the current plan is somewhat different from what it was only a few years ago and because of the confusion resulting from various laws and terminology applied to New York's two-year institutions, the historical development of the program is briefly reviewed here. Before 1946 only the six state-owned and state-operated agricultural and technical institutes, organized between 1906 and 1913, existed. These were small residential schools concentrating on the agricultural and technical programs of most application to the area they served.

When the veterans returned after World War II, the state set up three emergency two-year colleges. Before this, however, a study on the problem of long-term postwar needs was begun. In their report to the Governor on postwar needs late in 1943, the regents proposed the establishment of 22 new institutes of applied arts and sciences—11 in New York City and 11 outside—and a broadening of the program of the already existing agricultural and technical institutes.

The proposal elicited considerable discussion in and outside the state. A commission was appointed in 1945 which held hearings throughout the state, and a number of cities petitioned the board of regents for the establishment of an institute in their particular area. Finally, in 1946 the Legislature authorized the establishment of five of the proposed institutes (referred to as "institutes of applied arts and sciences") on a five-year experimental basis at Binghamton, Buffalo, Utica, Brooklyn, and White Plains. All were fully supported by the state.

No sooner had these institutes been established than a new commission was created to consider the need for a state university. This commission called attention to the existing need for two-year programs of technical and general education in the state and to the discrepancy between expected need and available facilities by 1960. With the creation of the university in 1948, the five existing experimental institutes of applied arts and sciences, as well as the six agricultural and technical institutes, were made part of the university program.

The same act that created the State University also authorized the establishment of community colleges of the type described earlier and in accordance with the mentioned master plan. The first such colleges to be specifically authorized were in Orange County and in Jamestown. Thus, at this point, three types of public two-year institutions were operating in the state.

As the five-year experimental period for the five technical institutes approached the end, the problem of their continuance arose. After considerable controversy arising from political and economic considerations, it was decided to transfer the institutes to the local communities. It then became necessary for some local governmental unit to become the sponsor of the institute in each of the five communities and as such to assume responsibility for one-third of the operating costs and one-half of subsequent capital outlay costs of the institute. This transfer, effected in 1953, was not without much frustration. The position taken by the state made it necessary for each community to find a sponsor or lose the local institute. Since no community was willing to give up its institute, each found a way of maintaining it.

Like other states, New York has in recent years been planning intensively for the coming wave of college-age students. After numerous studies, the regents published, on December 21, 1956, a statement and a series of recommendations which had far-reaching implications for the two-year colleges.[26] One recommendation was to change the formula for state aid to the community colleges so that the state would provide one-half of the operating cost. A bill to accomplish this did not get to the voting state in the 1957 Legislature. A second recommendation was to establish several new community colleges in New York City, Nassau and Suffolk Counties on Long Island, and in several other designated communities throughout the state. A third recommendation was to allow six of the technical institutes still operating with restricted technical terminal programs to offer transfer programs as well, at the option of the local sponsor. Legislation in 1957 made this possible.

An additional statement published in June, 1957, further set forth state policy on two-year institutions indicating that the state would probably serve more lower-division students in the two-year colleges and would expect these institutions to play a larger role in the state.[27]

The New York community college program is characterized by a number of complex factors which are of interest to those who study state-wide plans for two-year colleges.

[26] *Statement and Recommendations by the Board of Regents for Meeting Needs of Higher Education in New York State,* The University of the State of New York, Albany, 1956.

[27] *Regents Position on Additional Higher Education Facilities on Long Island: A Supplemental Statement on Meeting the Needs of Higher Education in New York State,* The University of the State of New York. Albany, 1957.

The first such element is the complex organizational plan involving two state agencies and usually two local agencies. It will be recalled that the university must approve the curriculum of the local institution before application for curriculum registration is made to the state education department. Inquiry on this point did not reveal any major conflict. The leadership role of the State University staff seems generally to be carried out through continuous conferences with the staff of the local institutions so that curricula and courses are generally agreed upon long before formal approval is sought from the State University. Obviously, as the number of local units increases, constant communication will become more difficult and agreements harder to reach. Obviously, too, if an offering is not approved, the local sponsor would not be free to include it unless it does so without state aid.

A second element provokes a question about the relationship between the local board of trustees and the local legislative body of the sponsoring agency. For example, if the sponsor of a community college happens to be the board of supervisors, which is the legislative body of a county unit, what is that sponsor's relationship to the body it has helped to create—the board of trustees of the college? The board of supervisors represents the taxing authority. It must, therefore, be the body which approves the college budget and which makes decisions on capital outlay, including the problems of site selection and acquisition. In the final analysis, the board of supervisors is the body which must answer to the people on tax rates and public policy. What, then, is the real responsibility of the board of trustees? In a sense it becomes an advisory board—in some respects an arm of administration. Most of its actions and recommendations must be approved either by the university or by the legislative board of the sponsor. This peculiar position of such boards, even with the quasi-legal responsibility given them, reduces their effectiveness. The general opinion in different communities was that the local boards perform an outstanding service in the system; and that their screening of practices and policies makes possible a thorough consideration of operational procedure which would not be possible if left entirely to the board of the sponsoring agency. Despite this opinion, the inherent dangers of boards on top of boards are present.

A third element is the complexity which arises when the county is the sponsoring agency. In such situations another official, the county controller, becomes important in the control of the community college, although not responsible for it.

This, together with the requirement that administrative, teaching, and nonteaching staff be classified under civil service and fit into the schedules of the local civil service pattern, creates potential though apparently surmountable difficulties in the administration of the college. Regardless of the exact type of the local sponsor, local controls are exercised over and beyond the board of trustees of the college, in addition to the controls imposed by the State University and the board of regents.

A fourth element is the number of private two-year and four-year institutions in existence, and the effect of their presence and the attitude of their staffs, boards of control, alumni, and friends toward the development of public two-year colleges. The state ranks first in the number of privately controlled junior colleges and first in the number of private four-year colleges. Although there is no objective way to measure the attitudes of those interested in such institutions or the effect of their views on the development of other institutions, it was reported by many persons interviewed that over the years representatives of private institutions had opposed large-scale development of public institutions which would compete with the independent colleges. Historically, this attitude is partly explained by the fact that public higher education in the state is legally a supplement to private education. The coordination and balancing of the scope of public and private institutions lie with The University of the State of New York and its regents, but even the university frequently appears to be in a difficult situation. Representatives of certain private colleges were frank to say that community colleges should be located only in areas not adequately served by private ones. That this attitude and the resulting pressures have been factors reducing the number of local public community colleges seems well established. Whether the independent institutions can meet the needs of certain geographical areas should properly be determined by the board of regents as the overall coordinating agency.

A fifth element in the New York situation is the existence of the six regional state institutes, some in close proximity to local two-year colleges. The different support patterns of the two types of colleges and the variation in tuition charges are reported to be confusing to the public.

Despite all these complexities, the system appears to be emerging rapidly as a result of over-all planning and coordination.

NORTH CAROLINA

North Carolina was included in the study as an example of a state in which public junior colleges are only beginning to emerge. The private junior college movement in North Carolina has had a long and interesting history. In 1956–57 there were seventeen such institutions, all but one church-related; there were only three community-supported small public junior colleges and one state-supported technical institute.

New legislation providing for the organization and operation of public community colleges in North Carolina was enacted in 1957. As in most states, legislation did not come suddenly but resulted from many years of study and ferment.

Although there had been a public two-year college in Asheville since 1927, it was not until 1946 that interest in public community colleges became widespread. As in several other states, this interest was caused by the return of veterans desiring college opportunities. Also, a general increase in population and industrial development foreshadowed the need for additional facilities in the years ahead. Higher institutions, cooperating with the state department of education, began to hold conferences and workshops on the community college. In 1950 the state superintendent of public instruction authorized a study on the need for state-supported community colleges and the projection of a plan for their development. A state-wide professional committee working under the direction of a survey director submitted its report in September, 1952.[28] The report projected the need for junior college education, set criteria for the establishment and standards for operation, suggested the necessary physical facilities, and outlined a plan of organization and finance proposing that the state pay half the operating costs and half the cost of capital outlay of the local institutions. Specific plans for

[28] *Community College Study*, State Superintendent of Public Instruction, Raleigh, N.C., 1952.

implementation called for desirable legislation, delegation to the state board of education and the state superintendent of schools the position of leadership and the responsibility for establishing standards, the appointment of a state-wide community college commission, and the appropriation by the Legislature of the necessary funds for the start of the program. In short, the plan was similar to plans in operation in other states, such as California, New York, Texas, and Mississippi, but went further than some of them by including state aid for capital outlay.

The plan received mixed reactions from various groups in the state, but failed to get sufficient support for legislative action in 1953. The three communities which in the meantime had organized junior college programs to accommodate veterans, and in which other students had begun to enroll, continued to operate the institutions on their own, but no new ones were established. In the 1955 session of the Legislature, two measures of importance to the community college movement evolved. The first was the appropriation of a small amount of state aid for operating the principle of such aid; the other was an act creating a state board of higher education for the purpose of developing a coordinated system of higher education in the state. Establishment of the board paralleled developments in several other states toward the use of an over-all agency in the formal coordination of all higher institutions. The creation of the board had far-reaching implications for two-year colleges in the state. The act establishing the board defined higher education as "all educational and instructional curricula and services beyond the twelfth grade or its equivalent." Thus in North Carolina (unlike in many other states) the board of higher education was made the coordinating agency for the junior colleges—not the state department of education, as had earlier been proposed.

In its first biennial report published early in 1957 the board set forth its philosophy on two-year programs and on vocational-technical programs of "less than college grade." It said:

> The Board considers a community college to be an institution dedicated primarily to the particular needs of a community or an area and including two divisions, (1) an academic division offering the freshman and sophomore courses of a college of arts and sciences, and the first or first and second years of work of a two-year technical institute of college grade, and (2) a division

which offers a variety of occupational, avocational, and recreational training programs, depending upon need and demand. The academic division of the community college thus contains the work of a junior college of arts and sciences. The Board is of the opinion that the contribution of the State to the operation of a community college should be restricted to the academic division.[29]

The board recommended that the three existing community colleges extend their programs to include technical institute education, that the one existing separate technical institute be made an extension center of North Carolina State College, and that another such extension center be established in some other section of the state. As to vocational terminal education of less than college grade, the board declared that such education falls within the competence of the state board of education and reported a plan of the state board to establish such programs at various places in the state to be operated by public school systems.

Two characteristics of the board's proposed post-high school program make the North Carolina two-year college program somewhat different from programs in other states. First, three types of institutions are recommended to carry out the functions: the vocational centers in the public schools; the technical institute centers of the State College; and the community colleges, which would include technical institute curricula. Second, although the board of higher education recognizes the responsibility of the community college to offer "occupational, avocational, and recreational programs," it does not propose to give state aid for them but by declared policy intends that such programs be financed from other state and federal funds for vocational education and from tuition fees and local taxes.

In June, 1957, a new community college law was passed.[30] It provides for the establishment of colleges in counties which meet approval of the board of higher education and in which the board of commissioners is empowered by a majority vote of the people to levy taxes for the local support of such colleges. It further pro-

[29] *Biennial Report for 1955–1957*, North Carolina Board of Higher Education, Raleigh, N.C., pp. 9–10.

[30] *An Act to Provide a Plan of Organization and Operation for Community Colleges*, H.B. 761, Ch. No. 1098, North Carolina Board of Higher Education, Raleigh, N.C., 1957.

vides for a board of trustees consisting of twelve members, as follows: two appointed by the governing board of the municipality in which the community college is situated, two appointed by the board of commissioners of the county of location, two members of the board of education of the municipality in which the college is wholly or partially located, two members of the county board of education, and four appointed by the Governor. The law gives bonding authority as a means of matching state appropriations for capital outlay purposes; and it provides for state appropriations for operating purposes on the basis of a specified sum per student quarter-hour of instruction *limited to courses for freshmen and sophomores in liberal arts and sciences and in first- and second-year offerings of technical institutes of college grade.* State appropriations cannot exceed the total of local funds raised for operating purposes. The law established the procedure for the necessary elections, permitting the three existing colleges at Asheville, Charlotte, and Wilmington to come under the new act.

The 1957 Legislature also appropriated money for state aid to the three colleges to the extent of $3 per quarter-hour or approximately $135 per year per full-time student on the basis outlined in the law. It also appropriated $1,500,000 for capital outlay purposes in community colleges on a matching basis, with the provision that no one college be eligible for more than 40 per cent of the amount.

It is obviously too early to predict the workability of this recent unique planning in North Carolina. The encouraging aspects of it are that coordinated planning is under way and that the state has begun to share in the financial responsibility of the community colleges. The question can be raised whether the limitation of state aid to restricted types of programs will mean that other types of training will fail to develop and that the community college will therefore not fulfill its broad functions. Also, it must yet be determined whether it is more desirable to assign individual functions to the several types of post-high school institutions than to establish more comprehensive institutions that would combine all functions of a community college. The state now will have the opportunity to apply pertinent criteria to its plan. Among the factors which should be observed are the number of communities needing colleges and willing to establish them; the extent to which the community colleges develop occupational and community service programs; the general availability of post-high school programs of all kinds to people in the state; and the extent to which young people have freedom and ease to explore programs and select the most appropriate.

OHIO

The two-year college situation in Ohio is characterized by (1) a total of 22 branches maintained by the 5 public universities, (2) no public junior colleges, (3) a history of numerous inquiries concerning the need for additional college facilities, and (4) two recent state-wide studies out of which came certain recommendations with respect to the two-year college.

In a report published in 1954, Professor D. H. Eikenberry of The Ohio State University said: "With 54 colleges and universities serving a total population of eight millions the belief has been strong among educators and laymen alike that educational opportunities on the post-high-school level are adequately provided for and that, consequently, there is no need for public junior colleges."[31] Professor Eikenberry continued, however, with evidence that Ohio's needs in higher education were not being fully met. He pointed out that the state ranked twenty-third with respect to the percentage of persons eighteen to nineteen years of age attending school in 1950 and fourteenth with respect to the number of persons per ten thousand of the population attending college in 1949–50. In both rankings, he reported, the states that stood above Ohio were in most cases states in which public junior colleges had been developed. Eikenberry also showed that there was a great variation among counties with respect to college attendance and that the lowest 22 counties did not contain a higher institution of any kind.

Reported also by Eikenberry were the summaries of five doctoral dissertations, nine masters' theses, and one seminar study (all completed between 1931 and 1952 at The Ohio State University) which were concerned with the development of public junior colleges in Ohio. Among other findings, these studies showed the great

[31] D. H. Eikenberry, *The Need for the Upward Extension of Secondary Education in Ohio*, College of Education, The Ohio State University, Columbus, 1954, p. 1.

differences within the state in the percentage of college-age youth attending college. They also showed that although approximately one-half of all seniors in Ohio high schools had the desire to pursue their education for at least two years beyond high school, distance from higher institutions and economic circumstances made it impossible for many to do so.[32]

During the early 1950s certain Ohio communities and public school superintendents became interested in establishing junior colleges as a part of the state's system of public education. In fact, enabling legislation was introduced into several sessions of the state's General Assembly, but none of the bills was passed.

Meantime, the universities began to establish branches in communities without college facilities. By 1958–59 the five public universities were maintaining branches in 22 communities. The work offered by these branches is the same as that offered on the main campuses and includes upper-division and graduate courses as well as the standard lower-division program in certain fields. Classes are available only during late afternoon and evening hours or on Saturdays. The public school systems cooperate with the universities by making high school plants available for the branches.

The prevailing tuition rate for the branches is $10 per credit hour for undergraduate courses, although in one of the branches the rate is $15 per credit hour. These rates are higher for full-time students than are the rates on the main campuses of the universities. The universities operate on the principle that the branch program must be self-supporting out of tuition funds.

Although more than eight thousand students were served by the 22 branches in the fall semester, 1958, only some twelve hundred attended full time. A high percentage of the full-time students were enrolled in a two-year cadet program for the preparation of public school teachers.

The matter of adequate college facilities in the state became a matter of over-all concern to the Ohio College Association, which in 1955 made arrangements to conduct a study of the problem. Dr. John Dale Russell, then of New Mexico, was engaged to conduct the study, and his report entitled *Meeting Ohio's Needs in Higher*

---

[32] Since 1954 two additional doctoral and seven additional masters' studies on the same topic have been completed at The Ohio State University with findings similar to the earlier studies.

Education was published in April, 1956. After reviewing the variation among the Ohio counties in the rate of college production,
Russell indicated his agreement with the opinion expressed by the
great majority of the people he interviewed in the state to the
effect that there was "immediate and urgent need for the establishment in Ohio of many more centers where higher education might
be available in an organization that might well be described as a
community college." He continued by enumerating the different
possible patterns of control for such two-year colleges and the advantages and disadvantages of each pattern. His recommendations
included a system of junior colleges under the auspices of the public
school system with state aid and coordinated through a community
college council as an adjunct to the state board of education.

Following the Russell report the Ohio College Association
requested the Governor to create a body known as the Ohio
Commission on Education beyond High School. This commission's
report, which appeared late in 1958, also dealt at considerable
length with the two-year college. Among the recommendations
in the report were the following:

> Branches of existing colleges and universities should be estab-
> lished as and where justified by local need and support, in order to
> provide additional students with the opportunity to live at home
> while extending their education beyond high school. These branch
> programs should receive similar financial support to that approved
> for two-year terminal colleges and technical institutes.
>
> The General Assembly should enact permissive legislation so
> that two-year colleges or two-year technical institutes financed by
> the State, by local funds and by student fees might be established
> either as branches or as separate institutions.
>
> Two-year terminal programs with state support should be estab-
> lished and operated under the following conditions:
> a. Each terminal two-year college should be approved separately
>   by an act of the General Assembly upon recommendation of
>   authorities of local taxing areas and by the proposed Interim
>   Commission.
> b. Each institution should have a board of nine trustees, three ap-
>   pointed by the governor and confirmed by the Senate, and
>   six appointed by some locally elected body or bodies.
> c. On an experimental basis outstanding students should be given
>   consideration for transfer to advanced programs.

Each two-year institution should be operated under the supervision of its own trustees and the proposed Interim Commission or some unit of state government. These institutions should be financed as follows:

a. Capital outlays and equipment: one-half by taxing area, one-half by state.

b. Operations: one-third by taxing area, one-third by fees, one-third by the state.[33]

The commission's intent is not made entirely clear in these recommendations. At least three types of two-year colleges are recommended—university branches, two-year colleges, and technical institutes. If the "two-year terminal colleges" referred to in the recommendations are considered as separate institutions, they constitute a fourth type. The wording of the first paragraph of the recommendations suggests that university branches should be financed in the same manner as other two-year colleges yet it is not made clear as to what the relationship of the local community and the university would be under these circumstances.

Presumably, the commission wished to make its recommendations broad so that they could be implemented in one or more ways. It remains to be seen whether such a general approach to the problem gives enough guidance to those who must suggest and vote on new laws pertaining to college expansion.

The commission further recommended the creation of a five-year Interim Commission on Education beyond High School which, among other responsibilities, would implement the more specific recommendations pertaining to the two-year college.

A bill permitting any city, county, or school district to establish a technical institute to be supported by the state, the local community, and out of tuition funds, was approved by the 1959 Legislature. However, the bill was vetoed by the Governor because it did not carry an appropriation for the state's share of support and because it was considered in conflict with another act providing for the interim commission to continue study on the state's needs in higher education.

Much must yet be accomplished in Ohio before the two-year

---

[33] *Ohio's Future in Education beyond the High School*, Ohio Commission on Education beyond the High School, June, 1958, pp. 9–10.

college problem is refined and clarified. There is little doubt that considerable dependence will have to be placed upon this type of institution as a means of meeting enrollment demands and of equalizing educational opportunities. So far, the trend is definitely in the direction of establishing branches of existing universities. However, so long as these branches offer courses only during evening hours at high cost to students, they cannot materially extend educational opportunity. Evidence of this is the fact that full-time enrollment for the fall semester averaged less than 60 for each of the 22 branches in operation at that time. The recommendation of the commission that the state universities continue the creation of branch colleges may mean that this plan will be continued despite the commission's further recommendation that there be legislation permitting the establishment of separate two-year colleges, particularly of the terminal type. If the experience of other states is repeated in Ohio, the universities may hold onto the branches, and local communities, though made eligible to establish community colleges, may question why they should do so when other communities already have branches. The future of the recommended terminal junior colleges is uncertain because there will likely be pressure to make these institutions dual-purpose colleges so that some students attending may prepare to transfer instead of preparing for employment. If this proves to be the case, the character of the colleges will change greatly from that originally recommended. The proposed interim commission has an important and difficult charge in implementing the optimum development of the logical type(s) of two-year college for Ohio. With college enrollments in the state projected to increase from 131,000 in 1955 to 234,000 in 1965, the commission's assignment becomes crucial.

OKLAHOMA

In Oklahoma a dual public junior college system is in operation. Of the 13 public two-year colleges, 7 are under state control, and 6 are controlled and supported by school districts in local communities.

The state junior colleges come under the legal jurisdiction of the Oklahoma State System of Higher Education which comprises the University of Oklahoma, the Oklahoma State University of Agriculture and Applied Science plus its seven affiliated agricultural and mechanical colleges (five are two-year institutions), six state colleges, a four-year college for women, and two junior colleges (one is a military academy). Each of the 18 institutions has its own board (some boards having jurisdiction over more than one college). In addition, a top board, the Oklahoma State Regents for Higher Education, through its chancellor coordinates the entire program. It also is responsible for the accrediting of all post-high school institutions in the state. The five state junior colleges that are part of the agricultural and mechanical system are under the same board. Each has a president and each operates as an autonomous unit within the system. Three of the five, listed as state agricultural junior colleges, were once regional agricultural high schools which later added college courses and finally discontinued high school offerings. The other two, known as A. & M. colleges, were originally mining schools which gradually expanded into two-year collegiate institutions. For students living outside the commuting area, all five colleges have housing facilities which provide quarters for approximately 40 per cent of the regular day students. Each has extensive buildings and grounds. The A. & M. institutions offer transfer and terminal programs, but many more students enroll in transfer courses than in those leading directly to employment in agricultural or industrial pursuits.

Of the remaining two state junior colleges, one—Northern Oklahoma Junior College—was originally a preparatory school affiliated with the state university. Now, as a regional junior college, it too offers both preparatory and terminal curricula with transfer students predominating. Its residence facilities accommodate more than one-fourth of its students. The other state institution—a military junior college, the Oklahoma Military Academy—offers high school and junior college work for transfer only.

The day enrollment in the seven state junior colleges in the fall semester of 1957 averaged 685 for each institution with a range of from 280 to more than 1,200. Only one of the institutions has a substantial program for adults and only two report any considerable number of special students. With one exception the seven institutions are in rural or small-town communities and therefore do not become community colleges in the usual sense of the term.

As indicated, the financial support for the seven colleges comes from the state. On the basis of anticipated financial needs for all institutions, the regents request funds from the Legislature for the state system as a whole. The Legislature appropriates funds to the regents in a lump sum, which the regents allocate to the institutions according to their needs and functions. For the fiscal year 1957–58 the allocation of state funds for the operation of the seven junior colleges amounted to slightly more than one and a half million dollars, or slightly less than 7 per cent of the total amount allocated for *all* higher education. Although the junior colleges enrolled more than 12 per cent of the total enrollment in the system, it is recognized that the same percentage of the appropriation would not be expected because the four-year college programs are costlier. Financial support for the institutions comes from tuition fees (currently $104 per year, which is the uniform amount for all junior colleges in the system) in addition to state aid.

The first of the six local or municipal junior colleges in Oklahoma was established in 1928, the last in 1943. The legal basis for their establishment is the Oklahoma statute which, in defining public schools, states: "The public schools shall consist of all free schools supported by public taxation and shall consist of . . . not to exceed two (2) years of junior college work." All municipal colleges were established because of concern for local high school graduates who, mostly for financial reasons, found it difficult to attend college away from home. Accordingly, post-high school programs were initiated in the local high school plants, with certain high school teachers giving some time to junior college instruction. Four municipal colleges have physical facilities of their own. Three have usually enrolled fewer than one hundred students. Muskogee enrolled 178 students in the fall of 1957, most of whom were full-time day students taking a regular transfer program. Poteau enrolled 602, of whom 397 were in regular full-time day programs (mostly in transfer curricula) and the rest in part-time programs.

The municipal junior colleges are entirely locally financed. The state school laws do not preclude the charging of tuition for junior college classes, hence there is a fee ranging among the colleges from $120 to $180 per year. The local districts provide the remaining amount necessary for instruction. The local districts also provide the building facilities, usually a part of the high school plant, although two districts have recently erected new buildings for junior college use.

The fact that the seven state institutions are fully state-supported (except for tuition and fees) and the municipal ones receive no state assistance poses a question of financial equality. There have been repeated efforts to include the municipal institutions in the state system. However, the author gathers from interviews that the regents are not inclined to recommend an enlargement of the system, nor would the legislators be likely to accept such a recommendation since it would further encumber the available funds for higher education. At the same time, local school financing becomes increasingly difficult with the state administration reluctant to recommend additional taxes for more state aid to local communities. Thus, there is little hope for state aid to local junior colleges in the near future. Yet, sooner or later there must be some solution to the problem if the municipal colleges are to remain in existence.

Another inequity inherent in the dual system is the difference in the degree of leadership. In the state system an element of leadership is vested in the regents, at least in budget control and curricula. The municipal institutions, on the other hand, come under the state board of education and, while the state superintendent of public instruction has over-all responsibility for the public schools and is concerned with general standards for municipal junior colleges, two factors make it difficult for him to exert leadership. One is the lack of state aid; the other is the fact that, since the municipal junior colleges constitute only one part of the total junior college program in the state, he is not in a position to plan and coordinate an over-all state program.

What lies ahead in Oklahoma will probably depend on enrollment pressures and the extent to which junior colleges will be called upon to meet them. No recent over-all state study has addressed itself specifically to this question or to the problem of the two types of public two-year institutions.

OREGON

Oregon has given considerable thought and study to the junior college idea, yet there have been relatively few developments. When an institution is only established a long time after the need for it has been recognized, the impeding factors should be of interest for their possible relevance to other states.

At present only two public two-year institutions are operating in Oregon. One is the fully state-supported Oregon Technical Institute, just outside Klamath Falls. This institute was established in 1947 largely to provide opportunities for veterans. It enrolls approximately 1,000 students each quarter in a wide variety of technical programs. The other two-year institution is an evening community college with an enrollment of approximately 250 students which until September, 1957, was supported and controlled by the school district at Bend under the supervision of the state department of education. As of September, 1957, this institution was reorganized under new legislation, described below, and is now supported by a combination of several districts, plus tuition and some state money. Between 1946 and 1955 an institution classified as a junior college was in operation in Portland; in reality it was an extension center of the state system of higher education. In 1955 the Portland State College was established as a part of the system, and the two-year unit was discontinued.

The history of junior college discussion and action in Oregon is recent and brief. In 1949 the Legislature passed the Dunn Bill, which authorized any school district to enter into a contract with the state board of higher education for holding classes of lower-division collegiate grade, these classes to be conducted under the joint supervision of the general extension division and the local superintendent of schools. Under provisions of this act, two school districts—Bend and Klamath Falls—instituted college programs in the fall of 1949. Klamath Falls later canceled its program because of lack of funds and small enrollment. A serious limitation of the Dunn Bill was that it prevented the organization of a well-rounded junior college.

Thus, it has been only in the last decade that Oregon has taken any steps toward two-year post-high school programs. It is fairly obvious that such a move coincided with the population growth in the West and the urgency for opportunities for veterans. In fact, the concern by state officials and citizen groups over the growing numbers of people to be college-educated led to a legislative interim committee authorized in 1949 to study the problem and recommend a detailed plan for meeting the needs. Among the areas investigated was that of the junior college. For this study the committee engaged Leonard V. Koos to work with the committee's secretary, Robert E. Wiegman.[34] Most of the recommendations made by Koos were adopted by the committee.[35] One recommendation was that community colleges should be considered for at least 21 communities in the state where, for various reasons, college-age youths were not being well served. It was also recommended that the colleges be made a part of the local school systems, supported partly by the state. Criteria for establishment were set up, and general powers of supervision at the state level were given to the state board of higher education and the superintendent of public instruction. Although Koos had recommended tuition-free community colleges, the committee recommended that local districts be allowed to charge tuition not to exceed $150 per year for residents of the district.

Legislation implementing the recommendations was passed in 1951. However, by 1955 no Oregon community had taken advantage of the legislation, even though there was increasing concern about college opportunities in the state. In that year another committee was organized to restudy the problem. This was an informal body, composed of members appointed jointly by the Oregon State Board of Higher Education and the state board of education. After reviewing the Oregon situation and studying junior college legislation and finance in other states, the committee recommended that if junior colleges were established in Oregon, they should be an extension of the public school system under the jurisdiction of local boards of education and the office of the state superintendent of public instruction. Certain changes were recommended in the existing junior college law. Among them were permission to organize additional school districts for junior college purposes only, and a regulation enabling districts maintaining junior colleges to charge back to the districts of residence the net per

[34] Leonard V. Koos and Robert R. Wiegman, *A Community College Plan for Oregon,* A Report to the Interim Committee on Post-high-school Educational Facilities, Salem, April, 1949.

[35] *Report of the Interim Committee on Post-high-school Educational Facilities,* Salem, 1949–1950.

capita cost of instruction for nonresident students. Another important recommendation was to modify junior college legislation
to enable school districts to contract with the state system of higher
education (as they could under the Dunn Act) except that such
contract would terminate at the end of five years. If at the termination date a district wished to continue its college, it would have
to meet the statutory provisions for junior colleges.

Legislation embodying the above-mentioned features was
passed in the 1957 session of the Legislature. Certain changes in the
financial support of community colleges were also made then. One
change eliminated the $150 limit on tuition so that a district
could fix its tuition rate at any amount. The other change provided for a different base for state aid. Under the 1957 law a district was entitled to receive $4.17 for "each term hour of classes
approved by the State Board of Education completed by a student
in the community college who is a resident of Oregon." This
amount approximated $150 of state aid per year per full-time
student.

The 1957 act caused immediate speculation about the number
of communities that would show interest in establishing a community college. The school district at Bend applied to the state
board of education to have its college come under the new legislation as a community college.

In 1958 a legislative interim committee, among its other duties,
assumed responsibility for another study of the state two-year
college program. In its report dated October 11, 1958, the committee reaffirmed the need for community colleges in the state and
recommended that the community college law be amended to provide (1) that a district be required to have a minimum of 75 million
dollars true cash value and one thousand resident pupils enrolled
in grades 9 through 12 in order to establish a community college;
(2) that the state contribute up to one-third of the operating costs
of community colleges; and (3) that requirements regarding formation and boundaries of new community colleges be clarified.

The committee also made a number of recommendations concerning the Oregon Technical Institute which reflected certain
disagreement among members on the question of whether the
institute should be included in the system of higher education or
remain a responsibility of the state department of education.

Most of the recommendations pertaining to two-year colleges were incorporated into law in the 1959 legislative session. Minimum criteria for the establishment of a community college by a local school district were set forth; provision was made for the creation of separate community college districts; state aid was set at $200 per equivalent full-time student or one-third of the operating cost per student, whichever is lower; and the Oregon Technical Institute was placed under the jurisdiction of the state board of higher education.

For a better understanding of the possible role of the community college in Oregon, three agencies engaged in post-high school education are briefly discussed: the vocational and adult school, the Oregon Technical Institute, and the state system of higher education.

As in most states, the division of vocational education of the state board of education encourages and supervises the operation of vocational classes both in and beyond high school; in addition, it is the agency for adult classes throughout the state. Many of these offerings are made available through local school districts or through on-the-job training in industry. In Eugene and Oregon City the local school systems support vocational schools, and there is a trend in both cities to make these schools primarily post-high school institutions. To some extent these are regional schools. The Eugene school offers day programs in aircraft mechanics, automotive trades, business, diesel engines, electrical repair, machine shop, photography, radio, and woodworking. Courses are organized at the trade level, and in most of them a student may complete a basic course in one year and an advanced course in an additional year. A student fee of $10 per month is normally charged. The school district in Eugene supports the program with the customary financial aid from state and federal funds for vocational education. The program in the Oregon City vocational school is similar to the one at Eugene but somewhat more limited in scope and enrollment.

Reference has already been made to the Oregon Technical Institute, which is fully supported by state and federal funds plus tuition. The institute's purpose, as stated in recent legislation, is "to contribute to the scientific, technical, industrial, agricultural, and economic welfare of the state." Most of its programs are well beyond the trade level and include courses in applied science and mathematics as well as allowing for electives, which may be in the areas of general education.

The state system of higher education—which includes the university, the land-grant college, the four state colleges, and the general extension division—is administered by the board of higher education and has a chancellor as the chief administrative officer for the system. Its relationship to the two-year colleges is twofold. First, its program of general extension performs in many communities a function of adult college education which substitutes in part for a local community college. (This program is administered by a dean having state-wide authority, with his offices in Portland.) Second, as previously described, the state board of higher education may, for a period of not more than five years, be the supervising agency for the transfer programs of new community colleges. In this role the board will approve curricula, instructional materials, and teaching personnel. In effect, it will develop standards and serve as an accrediting agency for new community colleges until (within the five-year limit) they are accredited by the Northwest Association of Secondary and Higher Schools.

The foregoing account raises the interesting question of the probable future for junior colleges in Oregon. State and college officials in Oregon believe that not more than seven communities are likely to establish community colleges in the next several years. They base their prediction on such restrictive factors as (1) lack of communities of sufficient size to warrant separate colleges, (2) a belief that the state and private institutions perform a regional junior college function, and (3) problems in the financing of community colleges.

There is still considerable state-wide interest in the community college, which suggests that there are underlying social, economic, and political forces which keep the idea fermenting.

If, as Koos earlier reported, college-going still varies greatly among regions and socioeconomic groups, the advent of more community colleges should lead to greater college attendance, provided community college tuition does not become a restrictive factor. In the fall of 1958 the various senior colleges in the state system took the first step toward initiating selective admissions. This move may well accelerate interest in junior colleges.

PENNSYLVANIA

Pennsylvania presents the unusual situation of a state that ranks third in population in the United States yet has only one public junior college. And even this, the Hershey Junior College, is listed as public only because it admits all students from the local area and members of families in the community's principal industry and because it is administered by the Board of Education of Hershey. However, it is not financed by tax monies but supported from funds made available by the Hershey chocolate interests. To date, the other public two-year opportunities are limited to the extension program of Pennsylvania State University.

The general extension activities of the university embrace many programs which are unrelated to a structured two-year curriculum for freshmen and sophomores. Many subject fields on the parent campus are appropriately drawn upon for short courses, correspondence courses, actual duplication of campus courses in off-campus locations, and the like. In 1933 the university (in response to requests from certain communities to establish lower-division programs for students who could not afford college away from home because of the Depression) first experimented with so-called undergraduate centers. The centers have been maintained in varying numbers through the years. Enrollments, too, varied, the years following World War II being unusually heavy because of returning veterans. At present there are 12[36] locations designated as centers where some type of structured two-year program is offered. For the most part, these centers are in communities of considerable size. Until July 1, 1959, they were all administered by a division of the university known as General Extension, whose director reported directly to the president of the university. Extension had six major divisions, each with a person in charge. An administrative committee with representatives from all the colleges in the university, whose members also served in the general supervision of the subject-matter fields of their specialty, recommended general policies and procedures in the entire extension area. (Beginning on July 1, 1959, the administrative organization of the

---

[36] There are 15 center areas; but at the time of the study Harrisburg, North Central, and State College did not have full-time day programs.

center program was placed under an administrative dean directly responsible to the president of the university.)

Within this framework the centers in the various communities were organized to expedite the extension program, serving as administrative units with housing and equipment for many of the extension services. Each center has a director who not only administers the day-to-day operation but also is the university's official representative in the area for public contacts, interpretation of community needs, and related functions.

Of the twelve centers, six offer work leading to the baccalaureate degree. It is possible to take two full years of work in a center, although it is often necessary for students in certain preprofessional programs to transfer at the end of one year. In these six centers and in six additional ones programs known as two-year associate degree curricula are also offered, which are of a technical type not designed for transfer. In eight of the centers a third type of structured curriculum known as the Evening Technical Institute program is offered. It differs from the associate degree program in that it concentrates on the specific technical subjects in specific areas, such as building construction, industrial electricity, tool design, and business administration. The technical institute programs lead to a certificate or diploma and not to an associate degree. Since they are offered only during evening hours, the time it takes a student to complete diploma or degree requirements varies from two to five years. The associate degree program, on the other hand, includes structured curricula in drafting and design technology, electrical technology, metallurgical technology, production technology, medical technology, and secretarial science. These technological programs are designed for the development of engineering technicians, as defined by the Engineers' Council for Professional Development, except in medical technology. They require two years of full-time work for completion of the associate degree requirements. There are a few offerings in art, music, dramatics, and certain extracurricular activities, including athletics.

In the fall semester, 1956, 1,476 students were enrolled in center programs leading to the baccalaureate degree, 1,327 in associate degree (terminal) programs, and 2,331 in evening technical programs.

Admission of students to the baccalaureate and associate degree programs is under the jurisdiction of the admissions office on the campus of the university, and primary records are kept there. Baccalaureate students are admitted on high school application if in the upper three-fifths of their class. All others must take entrance examinations. Various curricula, including the associate degree program, also have specific high school course requirements.

The center programs are financed through various sources. Day students are charged fees amounting to $480 per year for either the baccalaureate program or the associate degree program. The university from its regular budget supports all extension programs to the extent of approximately 20 per cent of the costs. Most local center facilities are provided by local gifts and donations, usually through the efforts of a local advisory committee which conducts the necessary drives for the funds. No legal tax structure permits the expenditure of public money for such purposes. The university, on occasion, supplements local drives to facilitate the completion or renovation of buildings, but in general the community is required to indicate its interest by raising money for the major center developments. Instructional equipment and also the maintenance of facilities are paid for from university funds. The university has recently completed a study of projected enrollments in the various centers and has designated needed facilities for each center through 1970.

Most day-program teachers in the centers are employed full time. They are paid on the regular university salary schedule. In 1957, of the total full-time extension center staffs, 51 per cent were classified as instructors, 34 per cent as assistant professors, 14 per cent as associate professors, and 1 per cent as full professors. Their assignments at the centers must be approved by the appropriate university department or departments.

Members of the university departments generally supervise the instructional program in the centers. The baccalaureate courses in the centers are identical to those on the campus. The same teaching materials, including textbooks, are used. A representative of the appropriate department on campus periodically visits the centers to confer with teachers. There is not quite the same degree of articulation in the associate and terminal programs, but university staff members still approve the teachers and the general nature and content of the course and supervise the program as in the case of the baccalaureate program.

These extension services indicate the university's intention of having the centers play the role that the junior college plays in other states. To see this role objectively in the state's total post-high school context, the general situation in higher education needs to be discussed.

As in other Eastern states, private higher education plays an important part. Of the 120 institutions of higher learning, 92 are privately supported colleges and universities. Of these, 11 are junior colleges, 15 are theological seminaries, and 12 are private colleges and universities which are partly subsidized by the state. Only the land-grant institution (and its extension centers) and the 14 state teachers colleges are wholly publicly supported (except for fees and other charges to students). Because of the predominance of private institutions, they enroll approximately 45 per cent of those attending institutions of higher learning in the state.

Despite the number of higher institutions in the state, relatively few students avail themselves of the opportunities. In 1954 the state ranked twenty-seventh in the percentage of college enrollment to the total eighteen- to twenty-one-year-old population. In terms of the percentage of its own residents who attended college within the state, Pennsylvania ranked twenty-second. These relatively low ranks suggest some deficiency of opportunity in terms of a proper distribution of institutions, diversity of programs available, or costs to the student.

There have been state-wide inquiries into this situation. One was begun in 1947 under the direction of Dr. George Works. In connection with it a special study on a community college plan for the state was authorized and was completed by Koos and Martorana.[37] This study showed that college attendance varied greatly among the different sections of the state and among different socio-economic levels of the population. It recommended a state-wide system of junior colleges as a means of equalizing educational opportunities. This system would have evolved gradually, and would have been an integral part of the public school system with state

[37] Leonard V. Koos, "A Community College Plan for Pennsylvania," *School Review*, April, 1949, pp. 202–216; May, 1949, pp. 286–294.

aid to local systems maintaining junior colleges. The study recommended further to vest state supervision in the state department of public instruction, with an advisory relationship with the state council on education. However, the proposals were not adopted and no later developments in community colleges took place.

Again, in October, 1955, the Governor appointed a commission on higher education "to survey, analyze and appraise existing or proposed programs of instruction and state assistance to such programs." This commission rendered its report in February, 1957. Among the recommendations were:

1. Consider first the expansion of existing institutions, private and public.
2. Encourage the establishment of new institutions with programs of less than four years—junior colleges, community colleges, technical institutes, and extension centers of colleges and universities—to meet the needs of the state beyond 1960, with the cost to be borne by a combination of funds from the local community, tuition, and the commonwealth.

As a follow-up of the study, a bill was introduced in the 1957 session of the General Assembly enabling school districts to establish junior colleges and providing for state aid to them. The Governor in a special message to the Assembly strongly recommended the passage of the bill. A number of newspapers published favorable editorials. However, it died in committee, presumably because of political complications in the state. In the meantime, a Governor's committee has continued to study the problems of higher education, including the possibility of a system of junior colleges.

Interviews, observations made during a visit in the state, and data from the state studies on higher education lead to the conclusion that the final status of the public two-year college still has to be resolved. Some believe that junior college legislation will soon be demanded and passed. The state department of education seems to favor such a development. Higher institutions generally—both public and private—seem to have reached the point where they concede the need for some type of supplementary facility. Yet it was frequently said that adequate financial support of new institutions is a problem at both the local and state levels. Local public school districts have difficulty in financing adequate programs. It was also said that members of the Legislature were reluctant to pass legislation which would add to the state's financial burden. It may be, however, that the Legislature is simply unaccustomed to assuming full responsibility for higher education. This lack of concern is evident from the fact that although Pennsylvania in 1956 took third place among the states in population and fourteenth in per capita income, it ranked forty-sixth in per capita expenditures of state funds on higher education—obviously because of the large proportion of college students enrolled in private institutions. However, with the increasing potential in college enrollments in the decade ahead, the state will have to assume greater responsibility.

The total problem naturally concerns Pennsylvania State University. Both the state and those immediately responsible for the university must inevitably determine the extent to which the latter can spread or continue its services to local regions in the face of rising enrollments and budget demands for regular university services. Related to this question is the university's policy of selective admissions. If the university becomes increasingly selective on campus, and moves in the same direction as the centers, it creates a further lack of collegiate opportunity and an attendant possibility of a public demand for some type of institution which would provide such opportunity.

In January, 1959, the board of trustees of the university passed a resolution to unify its system of extension centers by assimilating them all into a "state-wide system of diversified Commonwealth campuses located at University Park and elsewhere, under uniform academic, financial, and public relations policies." The tenor of the resolution made clear the intent of the university to continue to expand the extension system and to provide for greater uniformity between the main campus and the campus distributed over the state. Two exceptions to the uniform policy are noted. One is that the university will expect the local areas served by a center to "subscribe to the cost of university-approved (a) land for an adequate site for a commonwealth campus, (b) construction of the required physical plant, and (c) major repairs."

The second exception is that each center shall have a separate advisory committee.

Whether the program operated and proposed by the university will satisfy the total needs and desires of the people of the state is a matter which only time will indicate.

TEXAS

Texas ranks second in the number of public junior colleges and freshman and sophomore students enrolled; the state has long been regarded as a leader in the field.

The junior college system in the state is based on the same district structure as that of the public schools, even though the colleges, because of their functions, are regarded as institutions of higher education. As of September, 1957, 31 local districts maintained 33 junior colleges. (Two districts were maintaining two institutions.) A new district opened a college in September, 1958. In addition, the Agricultural & Mechanical College of Texas—the land-grant college for the state—operates two institutions with only two-year programs, which are therefore classified as state junior colleges. Since these two institutions have no structural relationship to the district colleges, they will not be considered here.

The history of the junior college in Texas provides interesting insights on the factors which affect the development of a junior college system in a state and on trends in local district organization. Until 1949, there was no state law providing for the maintenance of junior colleges. However, between 1922 and 1929, 17 school systems apparently recognized a need for local post-high school service and established junior college programs accordingly, even without legal sanction.

In 1929 the Legislature passed the first junior college law, which validated the junior colleges already established by local boards of trustees and specified that such boards in other independent districts could establish similar institutions by meeting certain criteria. The act of 1929 went further, however, and provided for the creation of separate junior college districts in independent school districts and cities of certain size. This act and later modifications of it also provided for separate junior college districts in combinations of contiguous school districts or parts of them and in county-wide areas or combinations of counties. The laws specify minimum criteria—the constitution of the governing board, taxing authority, and the like.

The year 1929 was, therefore, a turning point in Texas junior college history, because it legalized the colleges and because it provided that they could be maintained by separate districts. Of the 31 districts which in 1957 were maintaining junior colleges, 11 were county-wide, 16 were separate districts (called "independent districts"), and 2 were local public school systems. Eight of the junior college districts used the same board that governed the local schools. One of the public school districts is that of Houston, where by special legislative arrangement the University of Houston performs junior college services in its lower division.

Texas junior colleges are financed approximately equally by local taxes, tuition, and state aid. Legislation permits each district, by a vote of the citizens, to levy an annual ad valorem tax not to exceed $1 per $100 assessed valuation for junior college operating purposes. A tax not to exceed 50 cents may be levied for capital outlay purposes, but the total tax may not exceed $1. The actual tax levied by the different districts varies greatly and reflects the differences in assessed valuation in a state where certain sections possess valuable natural resources and where there is great variation in industrial and agricultural development. For the school year 1955–56 the range of local tax rates was from 6 cents to $1. Ten districts levied a tax of 20 cents or less, and in only four did the rate exceed 50 cents.

In 1955–56 when the minimum student tuition was $50, the median charged among all junior colleges was $75. The high for that year was $376. The 1957 Legislature set the minimum student tuition per year at $100. Total tuition collections—including reimbursements for vocational rehabilitation, vocational education, veterans' contracts, and like sources classified by the state's accounting procedures as tuition—amount to approximately one-third of the total junior college income in the state.

It was not until 1941 that the state assumed some financial obligation for the junior college program. In that year the Legislature passed an appropriation act providing for $50 state aid per year per full-time student equivalent. The same amount was continued in the 1943–45 biennium, but in 1945–47 was increased to

$60, and the appropriation has since increased steadily. The calculations used in arriving at the amount for state aid are based on a sliding scale. For example, an estimate of $4,720,295 for 1957–58 was based on $230 each for the first 350 students, $175 for each additional student. Such a procedure results in a per capita appropriation that varies among the colleges according to their enrollment. For the 1957–58 biennium the amount per student was $197.24, which for the state as a whole amounted to approximately one-third of the income for junior colleges.

It is in order here to consider some of the stipulations under which state aid is made. In the first appropriation bill in 1941, the Legislature declared that a college, to receive its proportionate share of aid, must be accredited by the state department of education as a first-class junior college. The Legislature authorized the department to set up rules and provisions for the junior colleges to be eligible for state apportionment, thus introducing an element of state direction and control. It was further provided that in order to be eligible for aid, a college must offer a minimum of 24 semester hours of "vocational and/or terminal courses"—a requirement omitted in 1957; and that the junior colleges must collect tuition from students in an amount not less than that required by law for other state-supported institutions. These same stipulations continued through later appropriation bills until 1951 when a new criterion was added for eligibility: state aid would be allowed only for enrollments in courses which were affered in one or more state-supported four-year colleges. The same provision was included in all later bills. The gross effect of this provision is to limit state aid to enrollment in approved courses, which are those offered in at least one four-year college. The net effect is to place primary emphasis on transfer courses, because presumably few terminal courses can be found in one or more of the four-year institutions. Apparently this situation presents no major difficulties because the four-year colleges themselves have a wide variety of offerings, thus making it not too difficult to find in some four-year college the counterpart of a proposed junior college course.

Mention has been made of the responsibility placed upon the state department of education for the general supervision and certification of Texas junior colleges. This responsibility is delegated to the Texas Council of Public Junior Colleges, which is a division of the State Department of Education of the Texas Education Agency. The council has an executive director with a staff, and an advisory board composed of the presidents of all recognized junior colleges. The council's functions include the development of standards for institutional and course approvals, compilation of necessary records and reports on junior colleges, certification to the state of eligibility for apportionment of monies, and exploration and program planning of the junior colleges in the state.

Enrollment in Texas junior colleges for 1956–57 totaled 20,243 equivalent full-time (EFT) students. The "head count" of all students enrolled for the first semester of that year was 34,897, which, compared with the EFT figure, indicates the large number of part-time students, most of whom attend during evening hours. In 1941–42, the first year in which state support was made available to junior colleges, the EFT enrollment was 6,498 students. The enrollment growth between 1941–42 and 1955–56 amounted to almost 200 per cent, but the net number of institutions for the same period increased only 34 per cent.

Most Texas junior colleges have day and evening programs. Both academic transfer subjects and a wide variety of vocational and technical programs are offered in the evening. As in other states this evening service is increasing in popularity and serves most segments of the local community. An analysis of regular day enrollments in the Texas junior colleges indicates that most offerings and enrollments are in academic fields leading to transfer to senior college.

A study of the over-all junior college movement in Texas gives the impression that it is efficiently planned and well recognized throughout the state. Attention is being given to standards and procedures of newly established institutions to make them sufficiently strong and to prevent unwise duplication with other junior colleges or with other higher institutions. It appears to be recognized that existing institutions must comply with standards which they as a group, together with the state department and other accrediting agencies, have set for themselves.

This is not to imply that Texas junior colleges have no problems. The state board of education has authorized various studies, the last one in 1956, to identify problems and work toward their solution. A joint college study commission was created and its report was generally accepted by the state board. The areas studied included need for codification of junior college laws; a method of apportioning state aid among the junior colleges; a review of the organization, functions, and policies of the junior college system; and establishment of new criteria for the creation of new junior college districts. It appears that these recommendations merely strengthen existing practices and policies, and that no innovations were introduced.

Two questions about the state aid program suggest themselves. First, is it wise to give state aid for only the portion of a student's attendance which is in courses approved as senior college parallels? It would seem that if a junior college is to be expected to serve any high school graduate (or adult) and discharge its functions as a multiple-purpose community college, there should be financial encouragement and support from the state in equal amount and manner for students in programs leading to employment and in programs leading to transfer. It is recognized that the two programs are not mutually exclusive and that many students use approved courses for terminal purposes. Yet there surely can be no escape from the tendency to emphasize programs that meet state approval.

The author discussed with various administrators the question of whether the present plan of apportioning state aid has hampered the development of terminal programs. Most of them said "no," but expressed the view that the regular day students are not as a group interested in terminal programs except for business courses. Recognizing this to be true, it would still be interesting to witness the results if *any* bona fide junior college course were made eligible for approval. It would seem essential that administrators in the Texas junior colleges agree on a needed and desirable program for serving students not intending to transfer and for meeting the technological needs of the state's expanding economy. Once agreed, the group should then impress strongly upon the Legislature the fact that post-high school education has several facets and that other programs merit support by the state as much as the program leading to the baccalaureate degree.

A second question relative to state aid arises from the fact that there has been no legal commitment to a formula. Would such a commitment not be advantageous? As it now stands, the junior colleges not only do not know in advance the approximate amount they can expect but also have to press the Legislature for adequate appropriation. This is not to suggest that the Legislature has been ungenerous to the junior colleges. Yet, some type of built-in formula might be helpful, even if it occasionally would have to be changed to meet changing cost situations.

WASHINGTON

The state of Washington was not included among those chosen for intensive study, but a very brief description of its junior college program and of some of its problems is presented—the result of a short visit in the state and a study of materials made available by the state department of education.

Washington has 10 public junior colleges, all of which are integral parts of the local school districts and, by 1956 legislation, are a part of the extended secondary program. The colleges vary considerably in size. In the fall semester of 1957 the number of regular day students reported in each of the institutions ranged from 537 to 1,737. Most institutions also perform a community service function by enrolling large numbers of special and adult students. Most of the colleges operate on recently completed modern campuses and are closely integrated with their communities.

Since by law the Washington junior colleges are a part of the state's public school system, they are financed by combined local and state efforts. In addition, enrollment fees ranging from $90 to $100 per year are charged. Local support comes from the local school district and the county of location. State funds, which in 1956 amounted to 64.5 per cent of the total operational funds for the 10 colleges, are computed by a complicated formula on the basis of attendance and equalization. Local and county funds in 1956 amounted to 20.3 per cent and student fees to 15.2 per cent. The state also makes contributions for building purposes on a sliding scale dependent on the property tax base per pupil in the district and the number of out-of-district students served by the college.

Supervision of the junior colleges at the state level is vested in the state department of education; an administrative officer, the director of junior colleges, is assigned the responsibility for over-all coordination.

Early in 1957 the state board of education appointed a committee to study junior college operation in the state and to make recommendations to the board on possible improvements and the future of the colleges. Included on the committee were junior college administrators, school superintendents, and representatives of senior colleges, universities, and other agencies. The committee submitted its report in June, 1957, with several major recommendations.

One recommendation was to enact legislation permitting the organization of separate junior college districts. The committee observed that in 1956 only two of the junior colleges drew as much as 50 per cent of their enrollment from within the local school district and that in four instances the percentage of enrollment from outside the district amounted to two-thirds of the total. The committee expressed concern about the financial burden falling on the local district and recommended that attendance areas outside the districts maintaining junior colleges be required to share in the support of building programs. Some persons interviewed believed that legislation permitting districts to charge back to the area of residence the prorata share of both operating and capital costs of nonresident students would lessen the argument for separate districts. Others contended that control should be shared as well as costs and that legal boundaries of the colleges should be extended to include the principal service areas of each. In fact, there was a suggestion though not a recommendation on which the committee was evenly divided that by 1965 all junior colleges in the state be in separate districts. The committee also suggested, as an alternative plan, the consolidation of all school districts in the service area of each junior college into one new district.

Another recommendation, strongly made, was that the local districts be required to segregate the funds allocated for junior college purposes and activities. This recommendation was made upon the discovery that many school districts in Washington, as in some other states, do not keep such funds separated, often to the distinct disadvantage of the junior college.

Perhaps the most important recommendation was that before the number of junior colleges is enlarged beyond that permitted under the present law, a comprehensive study be made of all higher education to appraise the facilities needed for the growth of the entire state and the function which each type of institution would be expected to perform in the total program.

Some time after the committee made its recommendations, superintendents of the 10 districts maintaining junior colleges filed a report with the state board of education in which they took issue with some of the recommendations. They particularly objected to (1) the recommendation that separate junior college districts be legalized, and (2) the recommendation that junior college funds be segregated.

The rapid development of junior colleges in the state shows they are needed. However, even a short visit made the author realize that the junior college movement in Washington faces problems of finance, curriculum, relationships with other institutions, and similar matters. For example, many people interviewed expressed concern about legislation which restricts the establishment of junior colleges in counties where there is a public four-year college. This restriction precludes the establishment of junior colleges in the Seattle metropolitan area where the state university is located. No significant junior college legislation was enacted in the 1959 session of the Legislature and thus the situation in the state remains as it has been.

It seems important that studies be continued and that the role of the junior college in the post-high school program be further identified. The recommendation to undertake a comprehensive study of higher education seems pertinent. From it should come not only a clearer designation of the role of the junior college in the system but also an identification of the need for such institutions in areas where they are not now in operation.

WISCONSIN

No state is more closely identified with the idea of performing the junior college function through two-year extension centers of a four-year institution than Wisconsin. The University of Wisconsin maintains eight centers in sizable communities and designates the total operation as the Freshman-Sophomore Center program. There are no local public junior colleges in the state except for a junior college division within the Milwaukee School of Vocational and Adult Education. The centers are listed as junior colleges in the

Directory of the American Association of Junior Colleges and, although not members of the association, are frequently represented at professional association meetings where junior colleges are considered.

The functioning of the center program is best described by first examining the operation of the centers in their communities and then the central administration at the campus in Madison.

Each center is expected to have a close relationship to the community in which it is situated. In fact, the centers are established only in communities that have given evidence of interest in them. Before the university will move toward establishing a new center, it must be assured that either the city or the community is able and willing to provide and maintain a physical plant at no cost to the university. Special legislation makes it legal for a county to levy a tax for the purchase or construction of a physical plant for a center. Cities have the legal authority to provide facilities, and recent legislation (1951) has been interpreted as authorizing a combination of cities or other political units to assess taxes to provide a center building. The board of supervisors in Marathon County voted on November 12, 1957, to spend $530,000 for an additional building for the Wausau center. In addition to Wausau, one of the centers (Green Bay) is situated in a building supported jointly by a city and a county; one (Racine) is in buildings provided by the city for the exclusive use of the center; in one of the centers (Menasha) facilities are provided by a local group of industrialists and by the local vocational school; and in four centers (Kenosha, Manitowoc, Sheboygan, and Marinette) the centers are housed in local vocational schools. The local community must provide the buildings and grounds, but the university furnishes the other items of capital outlay, including laboratory equipment and its installation.

Each center has its complete staff (with the occasional exception of specialized staff members, who may serve two centers) headed by a director who, with the assistance of an adviser to students, administers the program and is responsible for community relations. Teachers are appointed and paid on the basis of regular university rank, but a higher proportion have lower ranks and salaries than those on the parent campus.

The educational program in the centers is basically the lower-division curriculum in letters and science and preprofessional areas that is offered on the campus, although the size of the centers restricts the number of offerings in the more specialized fields. This restriction tends to become acute in the smaller centers and frequently makes it necessary for students to transfer at the end of one year. Some centers offer noncredit courses, but enrollments in them are small. As would be expected, the centers also become the arm of the university for general extension activities; and each, in a sense, is an administrative unit for a phase of the university program, apart from that of the freshman-sophomore program. Thus, when lectures, forums, institutes, workshops, demonstrations, and the like are made available to the general public or to special groups, the director of the center makes the arrangements and center facilities are ordinarily used. In addition to regular extension services emanating directly from Madison, some centers, using staff and instructors available in the community, conduct a limited number of evening courses for adults. A limited number of regular standard transfer courses are offered during evening hours in some of the centers.

The center program is not large in terms of the students it serves. The total enrolled in the regular day program in all eight centers in the fall semester of 1958 was 1,711 students. Of this number, 1,374 were full-time and 337 were part-time students. In addition, the eight centers were offering 14 credit classes in the evening in which approximately 400 students were enrolled. Some 2,000 students were enrolled in noncredit classes for adults.

The same academic admission requirements apply in the centers and in Madison. University authorities estimate that 25 per cent of the students entering the regular lower-division program transfer to the main campus at the end of the first year, and 20 per cent at the end of the second year. Since the Freshman-Sophomore Center program is administered as an autonomous college within the framework of the university, the rules governing the transfer of students between the various colleges within the university are applicable to those transferring from the centers to Madison. In general, a student must have a C average in the semester immediately preceding his transfer unless the administration of the college which the student wishes to enter grants special permission.

Over-all responsibility for the operation of the centers is

vested in the university extension division, which, as in most universities, is also responsible for correspondence study, noncredit activities of many kinds throughout the state, and special credit classes outside the sphere of the freshman-sophomore extension activity. Directly responsible for the Freshman-Sophomore Center program (and for other credit classes) is a full-time director, who in turn is responsible to the director of the extension division. The director of the center program thus becomes the liaison officer between the university and the centers on all matters of personnel, program, facilities, finances, standards, and general policies. In this position he has two important relationships with over-all university operation and policy—those of academic requirements and budgeting.

To assist the over-all director in the supervision of the instruction program in the centers, a close liaison has been established with the 20 principal instructional departments on the Madison campus. Each department designates one of its members to serve as chairman for the center classes in his field. He is to spend from 10 to 25 per cent of his time on center activities, which include selection and orientation of center staff, supervision of instruction, assistance in the selection of instructional materials, and general advisory services to the director. Thus, in essence, the center classes are tied in with the instructional departments to about the same extent as are campus classes. Faculty employment, promotion, and dismissal must be approved by the center administration, general extension administration, and the department chairman.

The budget and financial operation of the centers is a part of the over-all extension division budget. However, the funds budgeted for the Freshman-Sophomore Center program are designated as instruction and are not transferable to other extension activities. In operating the budget, it is required that approximately one-third of the cost of instruction in the centers be accounted for by tuition and fees.

Before the freshman-sophomore centers are discussed further, another type of post-high school education in the state requires attention—the vocational and adult school program under the over-all direction of the state board of vocational and adult education, operating through vocational and adult boards in local communities. Wisconsin is unique in the organization of its vocational program, because it has a state board of vocational and adult education separate from the state department of public instruction. The statutes also provide that every town, village, and city with a population of more than five thousand *must*, and with less than five thousand *may*, create a local board of vocational and adult education for the purpose of establishing and maintaining programs of vocational and adult education. This local board is also separate from the local board of education. The advantages and disadvantages of this dual arrangement have been widely argued. The important fact is that emphasis on such education is manifested in many ways and in different types of programs. The following description is limited to that phase which involves the typical post-high school program and which thus operates at the junior college level.

There are 60 vocational and adult schools in the state, of which 42 operate full-time day and evening schools. Eighteen operate in the evening only. These schools offer the usual range of vocational programs for younger students and adults but have also a number of structured programs of one or two years in length, primarily for high school graduates. The enrollment in the spring semester, 1959, included more than five thousand students who were high school graduates or over eighteen years of age and pursuing courses with a definite vocational-technical terminal objective. The board has also established standards (patterned after the standards recommended by the Engineers' Council for Professional Development) for technical institute types of programs, and some of the schools have established such programs.

The largest vocational and adult center specifically designed as a technical institute is in Milwaukee; it operates as a unit of the long-established Milwaukee Vocational and Adult School. In this institute, which requires high school graduation or its equivalent for admission to any of the programs leading to an associate degree, are two-year curricula in business, graphic arts, industrial technology (six options), telecasting, and restaurant and hotel cookery. In each of these fields the courses are also arranged in evening programs which generally permit completion in six years. Equipment and facilities of the institute are modern and complete. Enrollments reported for 1956–57 in the various day programs were as follows: 210 students in various industrial technology programs, 21 in the graphic arts, 61 in business education, 7 in retail distribution, 378 in professional nursing, 196 in practical nursing, and 292 in the general junior college division.

In 1957 the Legislature passed a bill permitting the creation of vocational and adult education districts on an *area* basis. This plan is optional; it leaves to the local municipal or county governing boards the decision of whether to organize a new and larger district, but makes possible a combination of contiguous school districts, cities, or counties for vocational and adult school purposes. The establishment of area vocational and adult school districts is reportedly being considered by a number of counties in the state. The major deterring factor in the establishment of such districts at present is said to be the limited amount of state support available.

Vocational and adult schools in the state are financed by a local tax levy generally accounting for 85 per cent of the cost of operation, state aid appropriated by the Legislature amounting roughly to 3.75 per cent of costs, and federal aid, sales, fees, and tuition for nonresidents making up the rest. Nonresident tuition under state law may be charged at a rate not exceeding $1.50 for each day or 75 cents for each evening of attendance.

A third segment of the state's two-year post-high school program (after the eight university extension centers and the vocational and adult program) is composed of the county teachers colleges (not to be confused with the state four-year colleges). The county colleges were established, under the name of county normal schools, in the late 1800s and the early 1900s to train teachers for common schools. Legislation enables individual counties or a combination of counties to organize and maintain the county colleges and to receive financial assistance from the state for their operation. At present, 23 of them are in operation, each with a very small enrollment ranging in 1955–56 from 30 to 121 students. In some instances county colleges have been considered comparable to junior colleges; but because of their limited function and enrollment, this would seem incorrect.

The machinery for over-all coordination of higher education in Wisconsin is of special interest. Under legislation passed in 1955 a coordinating committee of 15 persons drawn from the boards of regents of the university and state colleges, together with four citizens and the superintendent of public instruction, was established for the purpose of determining programs in the various institutions, reviewing budgets, establishing policy on plant utilization and construction, and studying the needs of higher education in the state. This important step is mentioned because the coordinating committee will be involved in any consideration of the extension of two-year institutions in the state.

Wisconsin thus far has been proceeding on a basis of specialized two-year institutions rather than on the comprehensive junior college plan found in certain other states. This direction appears well established both by the legislative enactments and the inevitable entrenched interests characteristic of any system that operates over a period of time under sponsoring agencies. A study on the need and desirability of junior colleges in the state was made by Fowlkes and Ahrnsbrak at the University of Wisconsin in 1947.[38] The conclusions stated were that Wisconsin had need for "some junior colleges which will offer freshman and sophomore years of work of a four-year letters and science program" and that "it seems sound that the new junior colleges be established and operated by the University of Wisconsin through the Extension Division." The report also contained a recommendation that "terminal liberal education combined with vocational work . . . should be offered by properly qualified vocational schools to be designated as terminal junior colleges." It is evident that this is the direction the program has taken except that the extension centers have not been designated as junior colleges. It is doubtful whether local boards of education could legally establish public junior colleges without new legislation. Even if they could, there would still be the question of jurisdiction over the vocational-technical phase of the program which, as at the high school level, would fall within the province of the vocational board. Nevertheless, bills for the establishment of local junior colleges have been before the Legislature at various times. One such bill was introduced in 1957; the Legislature did not act on it, but indicated that it expected the coordinating committee to study the situation and recommend a policy on the provision of educational opportunities at the two-year level.

As a result of general observations and of interviews in the state, certain problems may be identified. One problem is the fact that opportunity for the discussed level of education is not entirely

[38] John G. Fowlkes and Henry C. Ahrnsbrak, *Junior College Needs in Wisconsin*, Bulletin of the University of Wisconsin, Madison, 1947.

uniform throughout the state. Only eight extension centers are in operation, and not all vocational and adult schools have definitely structured two-year post-high school programs. University officials point to the fact that with the eight centers the state has provided publicly supported colleges in all but one of the state's urban areas. Whether this constitutes adequate coverage for the entire state could be decided only through a careful analysis. Recent studies made by the coordinating committee have shown that the percentage of high school graduates who go to college ranges in the various counties from 15.9 to 49.

Another problem concerns the state's principle of dualism which in effect means that students must choose between a public two- or four-year college and a vocational and adult school. Undoubtedly many students who enroll in adult and vocational schools would not meet entrance requirements in the two- or four-year colleges. On the other hand, many others would qualify. Those who do must make the choice. The question then arises whether it is wise to operate two completely separate institutions, making it impossible for students to change from one type of educational program to another as they can do when both programs are in the same institution. Besides, even students who do not meet college admission requirements at the time of graduation from high school would more likely find it possible to make up deficiencies and also make sounder vocational and educational choices if a comprehensive institution were available to them.

The university and the state board of vocational and adult education have vigorously moved ahead with plans for their two-year programs. Each agency has announced that it will extend opportunities when, as, and where needed. Conceivably, if a community feels the need for an extension center and is willing and able to provide facilities, the university would, if the need were verified, establish the center. The board of vocational and adult education is actively attempting to meet technical needs, and a staff member of the board has full-time responsibilities for developing the phase of the program at the state level. Both the university and the board advance the argument that, while in reality their programs are separate, an effort is made to coordinate them. In several instances the extension centers are in the plant owned and operated by the vocational and adult school. Even when they are not so housed, there

appears to be a fairly high degree of communication and cooperation between the director of the local center and the vocational
and adult school. A special committee, including representatives of
the state board of vocational and adult education and the extension
division, is at work on a plan of state-wide development of technical education through cooperative action of the two agencies.

But although the extension division and the vocational and
adult board are evidently able and willing to extend and integrate
their services, some problems still remain unsolved. One is the apparent inequity in the financial structure of the two programs. As
has been indicated, the local community bears 85 per cent of the
cost of vocational and adult schools, yet for the extension centers
the state pays all instructional costs over and beyond student tuition.
If it is true that the communities must spend more for one type
of post-high school training than for another, some adjustment may
eventually have to be made.

Another possible problem is that as college-age population
grows and as demands for service increase, the university will have
difficulty in extending itself both at Madison and in all the communities that would demand its extension center service. If the
university should eventually come to the point where the budget
is tight and accusations of overextending itself are made, embarrass-
ment and retrenchment could result. In fact, at one time in the past
it was rumored that the university was considering discontinuation
of the centers, whereupon the Legislature, reflecting the wishes of
the citizens in the communities affected and cognizant of the fact
that the state supports degree-credit programs in institutions in
nearly all other urban areas of the state, passed resolutions "advising" the regents to continue the centers.

In early 1959 the coordinating committee announced several
decisions relating to collegiate programs of less than two years in
length. One was that at the present time there is no need for establishing any different kinds of public institutions of higher learning
in Wisconsin and that the Legislature therefore not encourage any
new institutions of this type. It recommended that "pending further
investigation and determination any additional needs for publicly-
supported educational opportunities of the community college type
be met in the field of technical education by the schools of vocational and adult education, and in the field of collegiate education

by extension center programs to be developed either by the state colleges or the university."

The coordinating committee further recommended that in order to assist the committee to formulate plans for the development of post-high school programs of less than four years, a special planning committee, comprised of representatives from several educational agencies, be appointed. The function of this committee would be "to evaluate current programs in the light of the interests and abilities of high school graduates, to suggest improved means of cooperation between existing programs and to plan for the orderly and economical development of additional programs, including the development of suggested criteria for the establishment of additional collegiate type institutions. The committee should give special attention to the problem of college-going in northern and northeastern Wisconsin."

CHAPTER 9

The Next Ten Years

Thus far this report has considered primarily the present status of the two-year college in America. But how important will it be in the next decade? How is it to play its role? What major issues and problems will it face? What conditions are necessary for it to discharge its functions adequately?

For many reasons the two-year college is likely to play an increasing role in post-high school education in the United States. The social forces which created it will be no less operative in the future than they have been in the past. No one expects a lessening of the onslaught of technology or a simplification of the social, economic, and political complexities of life. Drastic changes in the occupational structure and the way of life will continue with resulting implications for specialized and general education. There is reason to believe that an increasing percentage of people of all ages will seek education beyond the high school and will continue to believe that educational opportunities should be equalized.

The spectacular growth and acceptance of the two-year college is a testimony to its vitality and to society's need for it. With the public two-year colleges enrolling approximately one-fifth of all students in public higher institutions, their significance is readily apparent. Allowing for no major political or economic world disaster, a rapid expansion of the two-year college in the decade ahead can be easily predicted. Beyond that, it should be useful to inquire into the conditions under which the junior college can achieve that expansion. A review of those conditions means an examination of issues and problems. The issues are either external, lying beyond the scope and control of individual two-year colleges, dependent on what society considers to be the proper nature and functions of the two-year college, or internal, lying within the sphere of control of the individual college.

EXTERNAL FACTORS

The future of the public junior college movement depends on certain choices the public must make. As each state faces the unprecedented task of providing opportunities for a college population predicted to double in the next 10 years, it must decide whether to expand the capacities of four-year colleges or to decentralize higher education by two-year colleges, or both. To date, in all but a few of the sparsely settled states, the recommendations of various study commissions have called for some type of decentralized plan, usually a system of local junior colleges or a system of extension centers or branches of existing institutions. Interviews and conferences throughout the country brought out few differences of opinion on whether educational opportunity would and should be expanded to additional local communities. The differences of opinion, where they existed, centered on the question of how the expansion should be made.

The alternatives are not, however, as simple—or at least they should not be—as merely determining the easiest method of increasing collegiate facilities to accommodate the greatest number of students. Numerous value judgments become important in the choices. Any decision on the further expansion of two-year colleges should take into consideration the possible advantages of these colleges in (1) equalizing opportunity by making the college available closer to the homes of potential students, (2) making possible greater diversity of programs, particularly for students who cannot or perhaps should not aim at a baccalaureate degree, and (3) providing special services and educational opportunities for adults in local communities.

Another value concept of the junior college—advanced earlier by Tappan, Folwell, and others but not until recently highlighted again—is that they enable universities to discharge their own functions better. Recently, Conant in *The Citadel of Learning* reemphasized this idea when he wrote:

If they [two-year colleges] were vigorously supported and expanded as the wave of increased numbers hit the universities, the distribution of youth among the various types of educational institutions might be radically altered without diminution of the percentage of youths receiving an advanced education. If this were done, the composition of the student bodies in the universities would change without any reduction in size; the emphasis would shift toward professional education. That such a shift would be beneficial for those universities now aiming at becoming first-rate scholarly institutions few would question. On the other hand, if some such development does not occur, the pressure of applicants on the tax-supported universities will force a rapid and enormous increase in the teaching staff. The quality of the faculty is bound to deteriorate and more than one promising center of research and professional education will become a training institution.[1]

Conant continued by recommending that:

There would seem to be great advantages, therefore, in preparing now for the time, only a few years hence, when the flood of college students will be at hand. And those preparations, to my mind, should consist primarily in the establishment of many local two-year colleges. They should be planned to attract the large majority of the youths who now enter a four-year college or university with little intention of completing a four-year course of study.[2]

Much the same point of view was expressed many times by Robert Gordon Sproul during his presidency of the University of California. Indicative of his philosophy is the following quotation from an address in 1957:

The growth of the junior college in California has affected in marked degree both the size and the distribution of the university's enrollment. In the fall of 1954, 27 per cent of the undergraduates (on the Berkeley and Los Angeles campuses) were senior students and 20 per cent were freshmen, whereas in years before the junior colleges became well established, the characteristic distribution was 15 per cent seniors and 36 per cent freshmen. This decrease in lower-division enrollment means, of course, that the physical facili-

[1] James B. Conant, *The Citadel of Learning*, Yale University Press, New Haven, Conn., 1956, p. 71.
[2] *Ibid.*, pp. 71–72.

ties—libraries, laboratories, and classrooms, as well as the available faculty—can be used more efficiently and effectively for the special purposes that universities are uniquely designed to serve, a consummation devoutly to be wished.[3]

Doubtless many university presidents would agree with Conant and Sproul, at least in theory. The real test of their agreement, however, lies in their willingness to take an active lead in their own states for a system of junior colleges supported in part from state funds. It is generally conceded that the large-scale development of the junior college in California was partly the result of the favorable attitude toward it by the University of California.

Relative Costs

Decisions in higher education will rest on theoretical and practical conisderations. Among the latter will be the relative costs of two-year and four-year colleges.

Many persons believe that it costs less to educate students in a junior college than it does in a four-year college. Data collected in connection with the restudy of higher education in California[4] showed that when only *teaching* expenses (total salaries paid for actual teaching after deducting salaries for faculty research and services, plus other teaching expenses such as clerical salaries and supplies) were considered, the cost per student credit hour in some junior colleges was as high or higher than it was at the lower-division level in the state colleges and at the larger campuses of the state university. Two factors may operate to make teaching costs in two- and four-year colleges somewhat similar. First, in technical-vocational courses of junior colleges a relatively small number of students are often in classes for long periods of time thus raising the unit cost above that for academic subjects. Second, on a larger university campus much teaching in the lower division is done by graduate students employed as teaching assistants at a low rate.

Although lower-division unit costs, computed by considering

[3] Robert Gordon Sproul, "Many Millions More," *The Educational Record,* American Council on Education, Washington, vol. 39, no. 2, pp. 101–102, April 1958.

[4] T. R. McConnell et al., *A Restudy of the Needs of California in Higher Education,* California State Department of Education, Sacramento, 1955, table 54, pp. 430–431.

teaching expenses only, may not differ too greatly in two-year and four-year institutions, the story is different when all educational and general expenses are considered. In the California restudy, student-hour costs, computed by using all educational and general expenses, were not ascertained for the lower division in the different types of colleges. They were, however, computed for the institutions as a whole and when that was done, the student credit-hour cost in half of the junior colleges fell below the student credit-hour cost in any of the state colleges, and all junior colleges were far below that of the university.[5] It would be grossly unfair to generalize on these comparisons or to suggest that the differences in costs would apply to the same degree at the lower-division level. Upper-division and graduate education is more costly than lower-division instruction. Besides, one of the important functions of a university is to encourage research in a way that will extend the boundaries of knowledge and the university's services to society. The California restudy data showed that at the two large university campuses at Berkeley and Los Angeles about 70 per cent of the time of the full-time-equivalent departmental faculty in 1953–54 was taken up by teaching and the rest by research, services, and administration.[6] Hence the total cost of instruction in an institution with upper-division, graduate, and research responsibilities would necessarily be higher than in an institution which has only a lower division.

A question arises, however, in determining the most economical way to expand lower-division collegiate facilities in a state. If it is decided that state universities should be the principal means of serving the increasing numbers of freshmen and sophomores and if, in adding to the university staff, the now customary proportion of nonteaching time is retained, then the total cost of education will inevitably be higher than if these students were served by institutions with faculties teaching full time. Even in state colleges where research is not a part of normal duties, the lower-division unit cost may, for comparable subjects, be higher than in junior colleges because teaching loads in state colleges are normally lower than in junior colleges. To be considered also are the differences in expenditures required for housing students in residential colleges in

[5] *Ibid.*, table 53, pp. 426–427.
[6] *Ibid.*, table 57, p. 438.

comparison with the situation in junior colleges where students live at home.

Unfortunately, information on unit costs in different types of institutions is hardly available, and great care is necessary in interpreting any data that are collected. More research on relative institutional unit costs is needed.

If it is educationally and financially advantageous to use two-year colleges, as has been suggested, and if the population distribution and other characteristics of the state make a two-year college system feasible, the choice of state legislatures should not be difficult. Certainly, the need for economy in higher education will be greater in the next 10 years than it has ever been. To the extent that more people can be served more economically by the two-year college, its further development should be considered.

Other State Responsibilities

A state, in deciding to use a two-year college system assumes certain responsibilities. Bogue spelled out three of these responsibilities as they pertain to planning for community colleges:

1. Each state as a whole should be concerned about a comprehensive plan for a state-wide system of higher education.

2. There should be well-defined authority placed by legal enactment in a central agency of the state for determining where community colleges should be located and for advising communities relative to the creation of community college districts.

3. Legislation should be enacted to (a) authorize the establishment of community colleges, (b) authorize the creation of community college districts whose population and wealth are large enough to justify the establishment of a community college, (c) set limits on tax rates which may be levied for capital and current finances, (d) determine the amount of support from the state and the formula under which payments will be made for current and capital expenditures, (e) set the limits of tuition and fees which may be charged, if any at all, (f) designate the authority and the manner to issue bonds, (g) set forth the legal methods by which community college districts may be created, and (h) authorize or require school districts without community colleges to pay charges for their students to attend in districts which have colleges.[7]

[7] Jesse P. Bogue, *The Development of Community Colleges*, American Association of Junior Colleges, Washington, 1957, pp. 9–10.

Bogue's point that a state should be concerned about an over-all plan for higher education would, of course, be logical even if no junior colleges existed. Unfortunately, the presence of an over-all state plan is now more the exception than the rule among states. Undoubtedly, there will have to be more planning and coordination at the state level in the future than there has been in the past. When a two-year college system is part of the plan, its place in the state's system of higher education should be clearly defined. No doubt should be left about its functions. In fact, its distinctive purposes and its role in the state system should be so explicit that there will not be pressures to convert junior colleges into four-year colleges. The legitimacy of the two-year college should be made clear. If it is to have purpose and dignity in the state system, it cannot be considered less important than other institutions.

Secondary or Higher Education? In defining the role of the junior college in a state the question must be faced whether to classify it as secondary or higher education. This question has been much debated. Those who have criticized the close connection of the local junior college with the secondary school have often contended that the association has caused the junior college to become a "glorified high school." The possibility that students attending junior colleges closely associated with high schools would not be given new experiences and stretched intellectually was raised by David Riesman when he said: "The junior college which grows up from below, without an academic board of its own but bound to the secondary school system, may share the vulnerabilities of the latter and not create for the students who go there any sharp increase in illumination."[8] Still, one could cite many instances where the atmosphere and expectations of the junior college even in a unified system are greatly different from that of the high school. A separate governing board for the junior college does not automatically result in greater intellectual demands on the students. Nevertheless, Riesman points to an ever-present danger that the junior college may become too much like the high school.

On the other hand, it is also possible for the junior college to become too much like the traditional four-year college. The fact that many junior college staff members reflect the attitudes of four-

[8] David Riesman, *Constraint and Variety in American Education*, University of Nebraska Press, Lincoln, Neb., 1956, p. 123.

year college teachers became apparent in the study of faculty attitudes discussed in Chapter 7. The junior college should be like
neither the high school nor the standard four-year college. Whether
it is classified legally as an extension of a state's public school system or as part of a system of higher education makes little difference so long as it assumes the multiple responsibilities expected of
it. The fact that it serves a post-high school function automatically
puts it in the category of higher education, as higher education is
conceived in the United States, regardless of legal interpretation.
California serves as an example of a state where the public school
system was extended to include the junior college; yet the more
than 91,000 full-time freshman and sophomore students enrolled in
California junior colleges, constituting approximately 73 per cent
of the lower-division enrollment in all public higher institutions in
the state, certainly make the California junior colleges an important
segment of higher education in the state. They are considered along
with the state colleges and the university system as part of the
state's tripartite system of higher education, and are fully considered in the state's informal machinery for coordinating higher
education.

   Coordination at the State Level. The specific state agency responsible for two-year college planning and supervision varies
among the states according to legislation and the philosophical context in which the two-year college is placed. Where the junior college is fully state-supported and controlled, the responsibility lies
with some type of state board for higher education, frequently the
state department of education. Of the eleven states described in
Chapter 8, in which the local junior college is the dominant pattern,
nine vest the state supervisory responsibility in the state department
of education and two in boards of higher education. Mississippi affords an example of further extension of the planning process.
There, a junior college commission composed of representatives
from the state department of education, the public universities, and
the junior colleges is responsible for determining where and under
what conditions junior colleges shall be established, operational
standards, and similar matters. Other states are also adopting new
organization patterns. By 1959 legislation, Wyoming placed its community colleges under a separate state board entirely independent
of the state department of education. Such a separate board has
also been recommended for Arizona.

The success of the junior college of the future will depend to a considerable extent on the leadership at the state level. In a few states positive leadership at this level is unfortunately not given the two-year colleges now in existence; in those states no state agency concerns itself with the potential role of an expanded system of two-year colleges. In other states well-qualified persons in a state agency devote full time to (1) working with existing junior colleges on curricula, finances, building programs, and legislation, (2) working with communities interested in or planning to establish junior colleges, and (3) assisting in the coordination of junior college education with other segments of education in the state. No matter how great the degree of autonomy of individual junior colleges in a state may be, it seems inconceivable that they can be maximally effective without over-all leadership of this type. Furthermore, as the demand for close coordination of all higher education becomes more necessary, the state must rely on someone as its principal liaison officer with junior colleges and between junior colleges and other segments of higher education.

Financing Junior Colleges. A state that uses two-year colleges must also assume responsibility for financing them adequately. The complexity of this task varies according to the types of colleges. The problem of financing extension centers or branches of universities is simple because the finanical policies and practices are established by the universities. Support of state junior colleges is in a sense simpler than that of local junior colleges because the state is totally responsible for them and only one board determines policy.

Since the local junior college is the predominant pattern of the two-year college movement, special consideration needs to be given to the state's responsibility for ensuring an adequate financial base for their colleges. At present states vary widely in the sources of support for the colleges and in the adequacy of their support. The principal sources of funds are local taxes, state aid, and student tuition.

Martorana reported that nationally more than 50 per cent of operating income for local junior colleges comes from local taxes, about 25 per cent from state aid, about 10 per cent from student charges, and the rest from miscellaneous sources.[9] States vary in all three sources, especially in student tuition and state aid. In

[9] S. V. Martorana, "Patterns of Organization and Fiscal Support in Public Two-year Colleges," *Higher Education*, vol. 14, no. 9, May, 1958.

California to charge for tuition is not legal; in Mississippi tuition charges may be made only for residents of the district maintaining the junior college. In a few states in the Middle West, including Missouri, Oklahoma, Kansas, and Nebraska, state support is either negligible or nonexistent. In New York the state contributes one-third of the operating cost. Some states have set specific amounts for state aid for each full-time student; e.g., Illinois pays approximately $230 per student, Iowa $180, Minnesota $250, Michigan $200. In Mississippi and Texas, the amount of the state's contribution is determined by a biennial appropriation based on the anticipated number of students. Florida and Washington base state aid on an equalization formula. In Washington the state's contribution has amounted to as much as two-thirds of the total operating costs. California also has an equalization formula, but in addition provides $125 per unit of average daily attendance. Not all districts maintaining junior colleges in California qualify for equalization aid. In Texas and North Carolina, only that part of the junior college program that is transferable to a higher institution is eligible for financial assistance from the state.

Only a few states, notably New York, Florida, North Carolina, and Washington, provide substantial aid to the community for the construction of the college plant and other capital outlays. The fact that this practice is so limited is considered to be a serious deterrent to the establishment of new junior colleges.

The task of adequately financing the two-year college program is not to be minimized. It is closely related to the problem of financing all public post-high school education—indeed, all public education—in a time when the cost of education and the numbers to be educated are increasing. In many states an antiquated tax structure, a resistance to new and additional taxes, and an excessive drain on state revenues have already resulted in insufficient funds to meet adequately the mounting costs of the next biennium. Moreover, the cost of higher education in general will increase rapidly during the next decade, primarily because of increased enrollments and the necessity for higher faculty salaries. It would be unfortunate if in the years ahead junior colleges were to be caught in the middle, as local and state revenues are allocated to educational institutions. To the extent that they absorb a share of the load of post-high school enrollments, it is as necessary to support them as it is to provide operating and capital funds for other types of higher institutions.

Private junior colleges also have serious financial problems. New and additional means will have to be found for financing many of them. This necessity, however, is a part of the larger problem of financing all higher education and is beyond the scope of this report.

Patterns of Organization

Should the future public two-year college be organized as a local institution, as a state institution, or as a branch of a university? A review of recent developments throughout the nation affords some clues to trends in pattern and structure.

Since early 1956 probably more state studies of higher education have been undertaken than in any other comparable period in the history of higher education. S. V. Martorana analyzed the statewide studies of higher education that were made between 1950 and 1957 and identified 27 studies which gave some attention to the two-year college. He classified 20 of the studies as favoring two-year colleges by some specific and positive declaration. In the remaining studies judgment was either reserved or the studies were of such nature that recommendations were not in order.[10] The recommendations in many of these studies have given rise to new legislation in several states, and in other states to legislative action leading to substantial increases in state support for two-year colleges. In other states branch systems of universities have been either initiated or expanded.

Of the three basic patterns, the fully state-controlled and state-supported plan has been least considered by those states which have recently been establishing or strengthening a junior college system. Only in Massachusetts and Rhode Island have major legislative studies recommended the establishment of a community college system under the direct control of a state governing board and, except for fees from student tuition, entirely financed by the state. The study commissions in each of these states based their recommendations for state junior colleges partly on the fact that a local

[10] S. V. Martorana, "Consideration of Two-year Colleges in Recent State-wide Studies of Higher Education," parts 1 and 2 of *Higher Education*, Washington, October, 1957, pp. 23–27; November, 1957, pp. 46–50.

junior college system did not fit well with the local school district organization and its ability to support education beyond high school. The state junior college plan also had reemphasis in Georgia where, despite new legislation permitting the establishment of local junior colleges, the state has added three institutions to its system of state junior colleges.

The use of university branches for decentralizing higher education has recently received considerable attention. State universities, including Pennsylvania State University, Indiana University, and the University of Wisconsin, which for some time have maintained several freshman-sophomore centers, have reexamined their plans to determine the advisability and means of expanding and strengthening them. Presumably, in those states an increasing share of lower-division students are to be accommodated by existing and additional extension centers. Branch colleges have also been established in other states, particularly in Ohio, Virginia, and New Mexico.

Of the three basic organizational patterns, the locally controlled community college has received the greatest attention. Legislation for establishing or expanding this type has been enacted in Florida, Oregon, North Carolina, Wyoming, and Georgia. Study commissions have strongly recommended its expansion in Michigan, Illinois, Minnesota, New York, California, and Washington. The marked increase in state aid for local colleges and the rapidity with which such colleges have been established in many states, including Illinois, California, Florida, and New York, is indicative of the current emphasis on this type of institution.

These developments suggest that the public two-year college movement will likely be expanded by all three methods but that the local public junior college will continue to be the dominant pattern. Public education being a state responsibility, each state must decide for itself the best means of providing college opportunities. This it will do in consideration of such factors as the existing educational system, the magnitude of the problem, the financial resources at hand, and, unfortunately in some cases, political expediency.

Extension Centers versus Junior Colleges. Among the issues concerning the organizational pattern of two-year colleges, the question of the relative merits of university extension centers or branches as compared with local junior colleges is receiving much attention. Proponents of the extension center plan contend that the experience of the university in organizing and administering a college program results in higher and more uniform standards than is possible when the responsibility rests with local authorities in different communities. Those who recommend local junior colleges point to the fact that the close relationship of these colleges to the community enable them to meet a wider variety of local needs than an extension center controlled primarily by the parent campus at a distant location.

In evaluating the two plans, comparative information is necessary on such matters as the breadth of program, procedures for curriculum making and improving instruction, characteristics and attitudes of the staff, financial support and stability, admission policies, and cost of attendance to the student.

A review of the facts reported in Chapters 7 and 8, together with additional subjective evaluations growing out of visits to institutions of both types and of interviews, leads to this conclusion: the advantages and disadvantages of extension centers as compared with those of local junior colleges are not easily placed in an "either-or" context. Each system has certain strengths and certain weaknesses. However, there is evidence to support the following generalizations on a comparison of the two plans:

1. The curriculum in extension centers is generally narrower than in junior colleges. With two exceptions, the freshman-sophomore program of the extension centers included in the study was restricted to traditional transfer courses. One exception is in several centers maintained by Pennsylvania State University in which the offering of an associate degree program represents an effort to organize curricula to serve terminal students. The other exception is in the four centers maintained by Purdue University which offer high-level technical programs. No terminal courses are offered in extension centers in Wisconsin, in the nine centers maintained by Indiana University, or in the university branches in Ohio. Although many junior colleges offer only a limited number of vocational-technical curricula and are subject to numerous problems in connection with such instruction, they still have a much more diversified program than most extension centers.

Authorities in Wisconsin suggest that the needs of terminal

students are met by the state's vocational schools. This, however, introduces the question of whether two types of institutions are more effective than comprehensive colleges. This question is considered later in this chapter.

If, however, it is desirable for the two-year college to be comprehensive, the point of view expressed by the staff in extension centers would make it difficult for the centers to achieve this end. As reported in Chapter 7, the respondents from the various extension centers did not subscribe to the various indices of comprehensiveness to nearly so great an extent as did the staff in local junior colleges.

2. The dominance of the parent university over its centers is not necessarily in the best interest of higher education. It should be said that there was evidence that universities maintaining branches were exceedingly zealous in their efforts to make the standard of work in the branches comparable to that on the campus. The leadership on the campus and in the branches was dedicated to this end and appeared to be exerting every means to bring it about. It is true that the supervision by the campus teaching departments of curriculum and instruction in the branches results in close coordination between branches and campus, and this benefits the transfer students, but the same advantage is not necessarily applicable to students who may wish to transfer to colleges other than the parent campus. In many ways the strong arm of the parent campus seems excessive to the point of leaving only minimum opportunity for the branch to exercise a personality of its own. A question thus is raised as to whether a state should have a network of two-year institutions under the aegis of a university and performing essentially the same lower-division functions as the parent organization, or a system of autonomous two-year colleges free to experiment and to adjust to individual community needs. That university control is not necessary to guarantee the success of transfer students is evident from the studies which show the good record of transfer students from junior colleges which have no legal connection with a university.

3. For the most part, extension programs lack the financial stability and adequacy of support enjoyed by most junior colleges. The tendency for the universities to require the centers to be either wholly or substantially self-supporting by means of tuition and fees

results in either excessive fees—in some states considerably higher than those charged students attending classes on the main campus —or restricted budgets. Except in Indiana, the universities require that the branch facilities be donated by the local community. In Wisconsin these facilities may be financed by a special county tax, but even in some Wisconsin communities and in other states the buildings are furnished by local schools or are erected from funds raised by gifts or subscriptions. The Indiana University practice of raising money for building purposes by increasing tuition charges produces campuses and buildings, but does so at the full expense of the students. In contrast to this is the system whereby local junior colleges are financed by a structured tax system which produces more funds with greater certainty.

4. Extension centers as presently operated do not democratize higher education at the lower-division level to the same extent that junior colleges do. Tuition charges in all university centers are high. In the four states in which centers were studied, tuition was approximately $385 per year per full-time student (ranging from $300 to $500). In comparison, California, Illinois, and Mississippi do not charge tuition for junior college students. The range in tuition in the public junior colleges in the other states studied was from $60 to $225 per year. These differences indicate a much greater probability that young people from low-income families will be able to continue their education when junior colleges are available than when extension centers are used.

As a further factor of democratization, any high school graduate may be admitted in most public junior colleges and has the opportunity of demonstrating his ability to carry on a program which he and his counselors consider appropriate for him. To the extent that a state university is not selective essentially the same condition prevails, but since admission practices in branches are the same as those at the parent campus, admission in the centers may become restricted by university policy. In the Pennsylvania centers, for example, only students in the upper two-fifths of their high school classes are admitted to courses leading to a baccalaureate degree and only those in the upper three-fifths of their classes are admitted to terminal programs. Such policies leave unanswered the question of what educational opportunities should be available to students who do not qualify for admission to the centers.

Two additional observations are relevant in comparing extension centers and local junior colleges. One is the theory that technicians and other high-level semiprofessional workers can best be prepared by making the training program a part of a multipurpose college rather than by placing it in a more restricted institution. Granted, the extension center *can* be a comprehensive institution, but, to date, except in Pennsylvania, it has not been so. Since it has not, the comprehensive community college stands in a position better to serve one of society's growing manpower needs.

The other observation relates to the close identity of the local college to its community. This identity is often characterized by large numbers of special and adult students, cooperative projects between the college and the community, an enthusiastic attitude in the community about the college, and campuses and buildings that evoke the pride of the community. All this does not usually transpire to the same degree in extension centers.

The direction which the two-year college takes in each state depends to some extent on local factors. However, the determination of its pattern should be based on what is best for the youths and adults to be served. State university tendencies to persist in state-wide or regional expansion through a system of branches—as a means of adding to its prestige and total enrollment, or as a means of eliminating a system of two-year colleges which would be a potential competitor—are likely not in the best interests of the state.

If Local Junior Colleges—How Best Organized? Where a state's two-year college plan consists of a system of local junior colleges, the question remains whether separate districts or unified districts are preferable. There is no general agreement on this question. Arguments in favor of maintaining the junior college as part of a high school or unified district center on the greater opportunity for vertical integration of curriculum and student personnel services throughout the school system (including the advancement of students in relation to their achievement), and economies resulting from one central administration, centralized purchasing, and like matters. Those who argue in favor of maintaining the junior college by a separate district point to the possibility for a more adequate tax and population base on which to support a desirable program; and the possibility that a separate board of control and a separate top administration are more free, as well as more likely, to devote adequate time to the affairs of the junior college.

If a unified district has a sufficient assessed valuation and enough students in high school to ensure an adequately supported college enrolling enough students to justify an enriched and diversified program, it is logical that the local junior college be a part of such a district. The logic breaks down, however, if the junior college becomes the stepchild of the system; and, unfortunately, according to the report obtained by interviews with junior college staff members in several unified districts, it does. Those interviewed deplored the fact that where a separate accounting of funds is not legally required, the district often does not spend on the junior college all the revenue collected for junior college purposes. They were critical, too, of red tape and the consequent delays in central purchasing, requisitioning of supplies and audio-visual equipment, and the like. They complained that the general lack of understanding of what a junior college is resulted in its conformity with rules and regulations applicable to the high schools. There were also some complaints that the junior college was not provided with the buildings and other campus facilities to make it distinctive and appealing.

The same type of response was elicited in the faculty questionnaire reported in Chapter 7. When asked whether they thought a junior college should be autonomous, two-thirds of the staffs in junior colleges in unified districts said "yes." An even greater percentage of the staffs in separate districts registered the same opinion, but this was no surprise because they presumably would be reluctant to surrender the autonomy under which they work.

Undoubtedly there are many large unified districts, including large cities and districts organized on a county basis, where the inclusion of a junior college as a part of the system is desirable, *provided* the governing board and the superintendent of schools are able to give the junior college the attention and resources it must have. Otherwise, it has little opportunity to operate with maximum effectiveness.

There are many situations where more effective financial and community support for the junior college could be achieved by creating a separate district for its maintenance. The primary service area of many junior colleges extends well beyond the immediate location, in which case some plan of district expansion is undoubtedly desirable. The argument is sometimes advanced that incentives should be made for the enlargement of school districts through unification or consolidation to the point where a junior college is feasible. The ideal is worthy but history shows how slowly school districts are enlarged. In some states legislation permits a cooperative arrangement between contiguous districts for maintaining and administering the junior college. Such a plan has merit, but it needs more experimentation. At best the clumsiness of the arrangement works against the plan.

Most states will undoubtedly profit by legislation permitting local junior colleges to be maintained either by a regular school district or by a separate district created for junior college purposes. This affords flexibility by enabling those regular districts of sufficient size and interest to establish colleges yet makes it possible for special junior college districts to be created.

INTERNAL FACTORS

The junior college's potential contribution to higher education depends to a great extent on its inner strengths. Those responsible for its internal affairs, including its nature and quality, must consider the demands that will be made on this type of college and then proceed to work out a plan for meeting them.

The diversity that has characterized the junior college student body is almost certain to become even greater in the next few years. As higher education becomes more universal, an increasing proportion of high school graduates will seek admission to some type of post-high school institution. If the current trend toward greater selectivity by the four-year colleges continues, an increasing number of high school graduates will subsequently be advised to enroll in a two-year college for their freshman and sophomore years. These situations suggest that the two-year college will continue to enroll students of varying abilities and interests and that the number of students who today might enter a four-year college may tomorrow attend a junior college. In fact, the future may well bring to the junior college an increasing number of graduates who are bona fide transfer students.

The growing number and increasing diversity of students have numerous implications for the two-year college of the future. Among them are (1) the degree of comprehensiveness that must characterize the junior college program, and (2) the academic standards that should prevail.

Comprehensive Institutions

The diversity of students to be served suggests that the public two-year college of the future must be even more comprehensive than it has been in the past. This means that its curriculum and methods of instruction must be realistically geared both to students who will and will not transfer and that its guidance program must implement its dual function. Implied also is its definite responsibility for community service and adult education.

An alternative, as some have suggested, is to establish two types of institutions—one for vocational-technical students and the other for students expecting to transfer. Though this is a possibility, there are both philosophical and practical reasons why the comprehensive college, despite the difficulties in connection with its operation, is to be preferred. High school graduates do not divide themselves into two discrete groups, one destined for the baccalaureate degree and the other marked for immediate employment. Even the students who feel sure about their future often change their plans during and after junior college as evidence on the would-be transfer students presented in other chapters has indicated. Certainly no division of students would be possible on the basis of ability alone since many vocational-technical programs demand students who have abilities as high as would be required for a transfer program. By serving all students in the same institution provision can be made for changes or modification of vocational and educational goals in an orderly, nonwasteful, and nonembarrassing way.

Opinion inside and outside the two-year college is in favor of the comprehensive institution, as is evident from this report. The unusually large percentage (almost 80 per cent) of the staff who, as reported in Chapter 7, indicated they did not favor dividing the junior college into two parts speaks for the opinion of the staff. Though the success of the technical institutes in New York State in implementing a technical program is often pointed to, all recently established two-year institutions in the state are comprehensive and legislation now permits the older units to become comprehensive. Information gathered from interviews across the country made clear that public pressure will be exerted on any two-year college, established either as a preparatory institution or as a terminal institution, to move toward the dual function.

If a two-year college has a comprehensive program, the question of differentiation of its students according to programs arises. How much overlap in the curriculum for presumed terminal and presumed transfer students is desirable? Is a "two-track" plan desirable or feasible? The separation of students is more naturally pronounced in some terminal programs than it is in others. Students in cosmetology and auto-mechanics programs, for example, are readily identifiable and spend much time in school learning skills that have little application to other fields. But even they have statutory and local graduation requirements to meet in subjects such as English and the social sciences. Should these students be confined to special courses organized for terminal students or should they be admitted to courses that carry transfer credit, provided they meet the prerequisites for such courses?

The question becomes more acute for students enrolled in high-level technical or semiprofessional areas, such as electronics, engineering, nursing, and business, where the student spends much time on allied subjects, many of which are in academic fields. There is not a sharp differentiation here between what the student may transfer and what not. The experience of the New York technical institutes has been that about 20 per cent of their graduates have moved into four-year colleges.

It is suggested that the comprehensive two-year college may do well to de-emphasize "tracks" as such and simply consider students as individuals working toward certain goals. Students should be aided by counselors in selecting courses beyond those required by their specialty, and should be held responsible by instructors for performing at requisite levels. Certainly the way should be open for students to change from one goal to another without undue penalty. Certainly, too, the creation of a status difference between terminal and preparatory students is to be avoided at all costs.

Realistic Standards

The second major implication of future enrollment demands is that the junior college must set and maintain realistic standards for itself and its students. In one sense the junior college is caught in the middle by the recent acceleration of academic standards at the college level. It accepts students of all abilities, not all of whom will have been subjected to rigorous standards in high school, yet it must pass its graduates on to the four-year colleges or to industry well able to measure up to current performance expectations. As many colleges and universities enroll fewer freshmen and sophomores but select them carefully, the junior college transfer will increasingly have to compete with a small but exceptionally able native group. This condition may well mean that whereas the junior college has in the past been thought of as a "distributing agency," admitting students of great diversity and helping each to reach an appropriate destination, it may now, so far as its preparatory function is concerned, become a screening agency for the four-year colleges. The extent to which this becomes true will depend on how selective society allows higher education to become and to what degree the survival of the fittest should come to apply to the attainment of a baccalaureate degree.

It is inevitable, however, that the junior college must screen students enrolling in certain courses in which such skills as writing and mathematics are involved. Screening does not necessarily mean a hard-and-fast set of criteria for determining whether a student may be considered a potential transfer, or even whether he may be admitted to a curriculum leading to a baccalaureate degree. The term does imply that students must have the background and ability, as measured by various objective means, to perform adequately in certain subjects known to be acceptable by higher institutions. Students may be able to perform well in some subjects, less well in others.

Although high academic standards must be maintained in courses leading to transfer, the junior college staff must guard against the adoption of standards that are unrealistic for all its students. If the junior college is to continue as the one agency which democratizes post-high school education, the staff must realize that not all students can perform alike. Consideration must continue to be given to the students who need remedial help and to those who perform normally. In no sense is this to suggest that the junior college should be a custodial institution. The needs and values of society and the task of properly educating those who can profit from collegiate education are as foreign to the custodial function as they are demanding that talents of all kinds and levels be used.

The authors of the Rockefeller report on education recognized the problem of standards for people of various abilities when they wrote: "Fortunately, the demand to educate everyone up to the level of his ability and the demand for excellence in education are not incompatible. We must honor both goals. We must seek excellence in a context of concern for all."[11]

There are countless other internal decisions which those responsible for two-year colleges must make—decisions on how and what to teach, who should teach, how to organize a student personnel program, and many others. These decisions will have to be made in the context of sweeping social and industrial development. For example, in the next 10 years there will likely be more dramatic changes in the nation's occupational structure than have occurred in any previous decade. Such changes will completely revamp the occupational training responsibilities of the two-year college and will have serious implication for general education, services to adults, and counseling.

If all internal problems are to be met and if, in addition, the two-year college is to be represented in the deliberations of the persons and agencies which shape the external factors affecting it, the absolute necessity for able leadership is apparent. The increasing scope and complexity of this institution not only demand new administrators to fill new openings but also demand that these administrators be men and women with far-reaching educational vision; capable of interpreting society's needs and expectations; committed to the types of students this in-between institution serves; adept at working with faculties, governing boards, community groups, as well as with representatives of other segments of education; and possessing the integrity that commands the respect of lay and professional people. The finding and development of such leaders is an immediate task. If the task seems complex, it is only because the institution these leaders are to serve is complex.

Needless to say, another immediate task is the procurement and training of teachers and counselors for the two-year college. This will not be accomplished easily, either quantitatively or qualita-

---

[11] *The Pursuit of Excellence*, Rockefeller Brothers Fund, Special Studies Report 5, Doubleday & Company, Inc., New York, 1958, p. 22.

tively. One of the difficulties will be to find and prepare teachers whose image of themselves as staff members of a two-year college is in harmony with the distinctive purposes of this type of college rather than with some other type. Even the most adequate preparation of teachers is incomplete if their attitudes toward the junior college are incompatible with its purposes.

It will soon be a hundred years since the two-year college was conceived. There were realistic expectations that have been fulfilled, and there were also overexpectations. The next ten years will sharpen and identify whatever role it is to have in the future.

Appendixes

APPENDIX A. Fresno State College, California
APPENDIX B. San Jose State College, California
APPENDIX C. University of California
APPENDIX D. University of Southern California
APPENDIX E. University of Georgia
APPENDIX F. University of Illinois
APPENDIX G. The Public Higher Institutions in Iowa
APPENDIX H. The Public Higher Institutions in Kansas
APPENDIX I. University of Michigan
APPENDIX J. Michigan State University
APPENDIX K. University of Mississippi
APPENDIX L. University of Texas
APPENDIX M. Cooperating Two-year Colleges
APPENDIX N. Cooperating Four-year Colleges
APPENDIX O. Cooperating Officials in State Agencies and Universities

APPENDIX A
Fresno State College
California

The native students included in the Fresno study had completed 60 to 64 semester units. Excluded from the native category were those who after entering Fresno State College returned to junior college for additional work, and then returned to Fresno. The junior college transfers included those who had completed at least 60 and not more than 64 units at the time of transfer and were eligible for junior classification.

Table A-1. Performance and Persistence of Native Students and Junior College Transfers with Beginning Junior Classification at Fresno State College, Fall, 1953

	Fall, 1953	Spring, 1954	Fall, 1954	Spring, 1955
Number of native students.................... 171	164	155	147
Per cent persisting...............................	96	91	86
Median grade-point average*................ 1.63	1.71	1.71	1.81
Number and per cent receiving degrees by end of fourth semester after junior classification.. 132, or 77 per cent			
Number and per cent receiving degrees after fourth semester of attendance following junior classification.................... 11, or 7 per cent			
Total number and per cent receiving degrees.................. 143, or 84 per cent			
Number of junior college transfers................ 116	105	90	86
Per cent persisting...............................	91	78	74
Median grade-point average................ 1.40	1.33	1.50	1.71
Number and per cent receiving degrees by end of fourth semester after transfer.. 45, or 39 per cent			
Number and per cent receiving degrees after fourth semester of attendance following transfer............................. 18, or 15 per cent			
Total number and per cent receiving degrees.................. 63, or 54 per cent			

* Grade-point average based on a 3-point scale.

San Jose State College
California

The native students had completed between 90 and 111 quarter units, and the transfer students between 90 and 96 quarter units. Since cumulative grade-point averages were more easily obtained from the San Jose State records, the median cumulative grade-point average rather than the median for each quarter is reported.

Table B-1. Performance and Persistence of Native Students and Junior College Transfers Enrolling as Juniors at San Jose State College, Fall, 1953

	Beginning sample	Fall, 1953	Winter, 1954	Spring, 1954	Fall, 1954	Winter, 1955	Spring, 1955
Number of native students..........	288	278	271	270	253	253	243
Per cent persisting...................		96	94	94	88	88	84
Median cumulative grade-point average*		1.70	1.74	1.70	1.73	1.73	1.72
Number and per cent receiving degrees by end of fourth semester after junior classification... 207, or 72 per cent							
Number of junior college transfers...	233	230	211	203	173	169	161
Per cent persisting...................		99	91	87	74	72	69
Median cumulative grade-point average..		1.57	1.64	1.65	1.68	1.68	1.71
Number and per cent receiving degrees by end of fourth semester after transfer.. 121, or 52 per cen							

* Grade-point average based on a 3-point scale.

Table B-2. Date of Graduation of Native and Junior College Transfer Students Classified as Juniors in Fall, 1953, at San Jose State College

	Native students					
	Men (N = 102)		Women (N = 186)		Total (N = 288)	
	No.	Per cent	No.	Per cent	No.	Per cent
By June, 1955	62	60.8	145	78.0	207	71.9
By February, 1957	22	21.6	16	8.6	38	13.2
Nongraduates	18	17.6	25	13.4	43	14.9
Total	102	100.0	186	100.0	288	100.0
	Junior college transfers					
	(N = 105)		(N = 128)		(N = 233)	
By June, 1955	48	45.7	73	57.0	121	51.9
By February, 1957	23	21.9	17	13.3	40	17.2
Nongraduates	34	32.4	38	29.7	72	30.9
Total	105	100.0	128	100.0	233	100.0

APPENDIX C

University of California
Berkeley and Los Angeles

The University of California compared the performance and persistence of native and junior college transfer students enrolling as juniors in fall, 1953, on the Berkeley and Los Angeles campuses. Transfer students were studied in two groups: (1) those eligible for admission to the university at the time of high school graduation, and (2) those ineligible for admission to the university at the time of high school graduation but qualifying for transfer through their junior college work or their combined high school and junior college records.

Table C-1. Persistence of Native Students and Junior College Transfers Enrolling as Juniors at University of California, Fall, 1953

	Enrolled fall, 1953	Consecutively attending through spring, 1955	Total persisting spring, 1955	Not graduating June, 1955	Nongraduated continuing fall, 1955
Berkeley					
Number of native students	864	689	746	161	129
Per cent persisting		80	86	19	15
Number of eligible junior college transfers	184	141	150	34	30
Per cent persisting		77	81	18	16
Number of ineligible junior college transfers	213	119	127	37	28
Per cent persisting		56	60	17	13
Los Angeles					
Number of native students	587	471	486	140	122
Per cent persisting		80	83	24	21
Number of eligible junior college transfers	141	89	95	42	36
Per cent persisting		63	67	30	26
Number of ineligible junior college transfers	288	177	192	78	67
Per cent persisting		62	67	27	23

Table C-2. Comparative Performance in Consecutive Semesters in the University of California of Native Students and Junior College Transfers Entering Berkeley and Los Angeles as Juniors, Fall, 1953

	Berkeley						Los Angeles					
	Fall, 1953	Spring, 1954	Fall, 1954	Spring, 1955	Fall, 1955	Spring, 1956	Fall, 1953	Spring, 1954	Fall, 1954	Spring, 1955	Fall, 1955	Spring, 1956
Number of native students	864	809	741	689	129	50	587	552	499	471	122	26
Per cent persisting		94	86	80	15	6		94	85	80	21	4
Units per semester	14.69	14.79	14.84	14.47	13.00	12.37	14.97	15.16	15.12	14.34	12.84	12.71
Grade-point average	1.63	1.68	1.71	1.78	1.60	1.54	1.68	1.71	1.74	1.88	1.74	1.86
Number of eligible junior college transfers	184	168	148	141	30	12	141	124	96	89	36	9
Per cent persisting		91	80	77	2	0.07		88	68	63	26	6
Units per semester	14.98	15.18	14.98	14.37	13.12	12.75	14.73	14.95	15.03	15.91	12.28	12.90
Grade-point average	1.45	1.62	1.68	1.84	1.42	1.26	1.43	1.53	1.60	1.75	1.71	1.81
Number of ineligible junior college transfers	213	185	139	119	28	14	288	250	200	177	67	27
Per cent persisting		87	65	56	13	7		87	69	62	23	9
Units per semester	14.63	14.11	14.27	13.90	12.57	12.54	14.34	14.24	14.04	14.10	11.89	10.81
Grade-point average	1.07	1.26	1.38	1.60	1.40	1.30	1.10	1.32	1.45	1.60	1.58	1.71

Table C-3. Comparison of Bachelor Degrees* Earned by Native Students and
Junior College Transfers Entering University of California as Juniors,
Fall, 1953, Berkeley and Los Angeles

	Berkeley				Los Angeles			
	Enrolled fall, 1953	Degree by June, 1955	Degree by June, 1956	Degree by Jan., 1957	Enrolled fall, 1953	Degree by June, 1955	Degree by June, 1956	Degree by Jan., 1957
Number of native students.... 864	493	178	27	587	285	170	15
Per cent.....................	57	21	3		48	30	2
Total number and per cent receiving degrees by January, 1957...... 698, or 81 per cent				.... 470, or 80 per cent				
Number of eligible junior college transfers......... 184	105	33	2	141	39	43	3
Per cent.....................	57	18	1		28	30	2
Total number and per cent receiving degrees by January, 1957...... 140, or 76 per cent				.... 85, or 60 per cent				
Number of ineligible junior college transfers......... 213	75	34	7	288	76	88	10
Per cent.....................	35	16	3		26	31	3
Total number and per cent receiving degrees by January, 1957...... 116, or 54 per cent				.... 174, or 60 per cent				

* Figures refer to degrees received on campus only; equivalent degrees in off-campus
professional schools are not included.

Table C-4. Performance and Persistence by Selected Colleges of Native Students and Junior College Transfers Enrolling as Juniors at University of California, Fall, 1953

	Berkeley				Los Angeles			
	Fall, 1953	Spring, 1954	Fall, 1954	Spring, 1955	Fall, 1953	Spring, 1954	Fall, 1954	Spring, 1955
Letters and Science:								
Number of native students	635				316			
Per cent persisting		88	79	71		91	81	76
Grade-point average*	1.64	1.69	1.71	1.82	1.70	1.76	1.80	1.97
Number of eligible junior college transfers	101				79			
Per cent persisting		90	72	68		85	66	60
Grade-point average	1.49	1.59	1.69	1.87	1.35	1.56	1.60	1.74
Number of ineligible junior college transfers	139				152			
Per cent persisting		86	64	51		85	64	55
Grade-point average	1.11	1.28	1.43	1.59	1.10	1.29	1.47	1.63
Business Administration:								
Number of native students	72				66			
Per cent persisting		92	86	79		96	94	92
Grade-point average	1.43	1.66	1.50	1.59	1.60	1.59	1.64	1.73
Number of eligible junior college transfers	14				12			
Per cent persisting		79	71	64		92	83	83
Grade-point average	1.27	1.71	2.00	1.71	1.35	1.39	1.47	1.49
Number of ineligible junior college transfers	22				39			
Per cent persisting		83	55	41		80	77	64
Grade-point average	0.84	1.21	1.17	1.60	0.91	1.33	1.39	1.51
Engineering:								
Number of native students	75				52			
Per cent persisting		97	89	88		92	83	79
Grade-point average	1.57	1.62	1.73	1.77	1.60	1.64	1.71	1.87
Number of eligible junior college transfers	47				22			
Per cent persisting		85	77	74		82	54	45
Grade-point average	1.43	1.75	1.74	1.87	1.52	1.34	1.82	1.90
Number of ineligible junior college transfers	32				27			
Per cent persisting		75	62	41		82	59	59
Grade-point average	1.10	1.32	1.34	1.75	1.07	1.28	1.38	1.46

*Grade-point average based on a 3-point scale.

Table C-5. Comparison of Percentages of Native and Transfer Students Earning Bachelors' Degrees in Selected Colleges at University of California

	Native students			Junior college—eligible			Junior college—ineligible		
	No. enrolling fall, 1953	Per cent degrees by June, 1955	Per cent degrees by January, 1957	No. enrolling fall, 1953	Per cent degrees by June, 1955	Per cent degrees by January, 1957	No. enrolling fall, 1953	Per cent degrees by June, 1955	Per cent degrees by January, 1957
Berkeley									
Letters and science	646	56	71	104	61	65	145	39	50
Business administration	98	61	84	17	59	71	25	36	48
Engineering	76	29	82	50	38	78	33	18	49
Los Angeles									
Letters and science	317	48	75	79	23	53	152	24	51
Business administration	76	47	77	13	31	69	42	31	67
Engineering	41	44	95	22	27	50	28	32	61
Applied arts	140	49	79	27	37	74	68	26	60

APPENDIX D

University of Southern California

Table D-1. Performance and Persistence of Native Students and Junior
College Transfers Enrolling as Juniors at University of
Southern California, Fall, 1953

	Fall, 1953	Spring, 1954	Fall, 1954	Spring, 1955
Number of native students*	495	469	435	395
Per cent persisting		95	88	80
Median grade-point average†	2.43	2.53	2.54	2.57
Number and per cent receiving degrees by end of fourth semester after junior classification				332, or 67 per cent
Number and per cent continuing in professional schools but not receiving degrees in four semesters				25, or 5 per cent
Total number and per cent receiving degrees in four semesters or continuing in professional schools				357, or 72 per cent
Number of junior college transfers	321	301	268	235
Per cent persisting		94	83	73
Median grade-point average	2.27	2.40	2.50	2.55
Number and per cent receiving degrees by end of fourth semester after transfer				155, or 48 per cent
Number and per cent continuing in professional schools but not receiving degrees in four semesters				48, or 15 per cent
Total number and per cent receiving degrees in four semesters or continuing in professional schools				203, or 63 per cent

* Out of a total of 2,148 students entering as freshmen, September, 1951.
† Grade-point average based on a 3-point scale.

University of Georgia

Native students were compared with three groups of transfer students, those from junior colleges in the Georgia university system, those from other junior colleges in Georgia, and those from junior colleges outside the state.

Table E-1. Performance and Persistence of Native Students and Junior College Transfers with Beginning Junior Classification, University of Georgia, Fall, 1954

	Fall, 1954	Winter, 1955	Spring or summer, 1955	Fall, 1955	Winter, 1956	Spring or summer, 1956
Number of native students..........	321	309	300	277	275	270
Per cent persisting...................		96	93	86	86	84
Average grade......................			80			82

Number and per cent receiving degrees within two years after junior classification... 241, or 75 per cent

Number of transfers from junior colleges in university system.......	57	51	51	49	48	48
Per cent persisting...................		89	89	86	84	84
Average grade......................			81			83

Number and per cent receiving degrees within two years after transfer.. 46, or 81 per cent

Number of transfers from other junior colleges in Georgia...........	37	35	35	30	30	29
Per cent persisting...................		95	95	81	81	78
Average grade......................			80			82

Number and per cent receiving degrees within two years after transfer.. 23, or 62 per cent

Number of transfers from out-of-state junior colleges................	33	33	33	30	29	29
Per cent persisting...................		100	100	91	88	88
Average grade......................			78			80

Number and per cent receiving degrees within two years after transfer.. 25, or 76 per cent

Total number of transfers...........	127	119	119	109	107	106
Per cent persisting...................		94	94	86	84	83
Average grade......................			80			82

Number and per cent receiving degrees within two years after transfer.. 94, or 74 per cent

APPENDIX F

University of Illinois

The University of Illinois study involved an investigation of the persistence and performance of 168 junior college transfer students and 1,040 native students, all of whom entered the junior year in the fall of 1952 with at least 60 semester hours of credit.

Table F-1. Performance and Persistence of Native Students and Junior College Transfers Enrolling as Juniors in the University of Illinois, Fall, 1952

	Fall, 1952			Spring, 1953			Fall, 1953			Spring, 1954		
	Men	Women	Total	Men	Women	Total	Men	Women	Total	Men	Women	Total
Number of native students......	728	312	1040	697	283	980	648	261	909	635	256	891
Per cent persisting............				96	91	94	89	84	87	87	82	86
Median grade-point average*..	3.58	3.76	3.64	3.63	3.84	3.69	3.64	4.02	3.75	3.76	4.02	3.83

Per cent receiving degrees:

	Men	Women	Total
At end of fourth semester after junior classification.........	56	72	61
After fourth semester following junior classification.........	25	4	19
Total........	81	76	80

	Fall, 1952			Spring, 1953			Fall, 1953			Spring, 1954		
Number of junior college transfers.	141	27	168	118	23	141	91	20	111	82	19	101
Per cent persisting..........				84	85	84	64	74	66	58	70	60
Median grade-point average..	3.17	3.31	3.20	3.48	3.50	3.50	3.54	3.81	3.61	3.55	4.33	3.69

Per cent receiving degrees:

	Men	Women	Total
At end of fourth semester after transfer......	36	59	40
After fourth semester following transfer......	7	11	14
Total........	51	70	54

* Grade-point average based on a 5-point scale.

Table F-2. Median Grade Points by Sex for Native and Transfer Students Enrolling as Juniors at University of Illinois, Fall, 1952

College of enrollment	Fall, 1952				Spring, 1953				Fall, 1953				Spring, 1954				Per cent degrees spring, 1954	Per cent degrees spring, 1955
	Men		Women		Men		Women		Men		Women		Men		Women			
	No.	GPM	No.	GPM	No.	GPM	No.	GPM	No.	GPM	No.	GPM	No.	GPM	No.	GPM		
Agriculture:																		
Native	92	3.72	51	3.68	91	3.79	50	4.02	87	3.84	49	4.17	83	3.94	48	4.15	76.6	88.3
Transfer	9	3.90	1	—	9	3.65	1	—	7	4.05	0	—	7	4.55	0	—	66.7	66.7
Commerce:																		
Native	134	3.43	17	3.85	131	3.48	16	3.60	126	3.53	15	4.28	118	3.64	12	4.10	57.0	79.6
Transfer	34	3.03	3	2.85	29	3.32	3	3.25	21	3.54	2	3.55	21	3.52	2	3.95	47.4	55.3
Div. of special service:																		
Native	2	3.85	0	—	2	3.50	0	—	0	—	0	—	0	—	0	—	67.7	67.7
Transfer	1	—	0	—	1	—	0	—	1	—	0	—	1	—	0	—	50.0	50.0
Education:																		
Native	7	3.35	41	4.09	7	3.58	41	4.09	4	3.90	37	4.31	5	3.25	31	4.45	63.6	70.9
Transfer	2	4.10	5	3.65	2	3.85	4	3.90	2	4.55	4	4.00	2	4.20	4	4.55	71.4	85.7
Engineering:																		
Native	132	3.84	0	—	126	3.77	0	—	120	3.80	0	—	118	4.00	0	—	43.3	88.8
Transfer	31	3.17	0	—	27	3.32	0	—	21	3.35	0	—	20	3.30	0	—	24.2	54.1
Fine arts:																		
Native	50	3.50	32	3.75	47	3.54	28	3.90	45	3.72	27	4.23	40	3.97	27	4.15	39.8	64.1
Transfer	10	3.10	0	—	9	3.17	0	—	9	3.09	0	—	7	3.45	0	—	—	40.0

Table F-2. Median Grade Points by Sex for Native and Transfer Students Enrolling as Juniors at University of Illinois, Fall, 1952 (Continued)

College of enrollment	Fall, 1952				Spring, 1953				Fall, 1953				Spring, 1954				Per cent degrees spring, 1954	Per cent degrees spring, 1955
	Men		Women		Men		Women		Men		Women		Men		Women			
	No.	GPM	No.	GPM	No.	GPM	No.	GPM	No.	GPM	No.	GPM	No.	GPM	No.	GPM		
Journalism:																		
Native	28	3.60	19	4.02	28	3.73	18	4.00	26	3.87	18	4.05	27	3.82	13	3.85	64.7	74.5
Transfer	7	3.45	0	—	6	3.90	0	—	5	4.05	0	—	5	3.85	0	—	50.0	75.0
Liberal arts, sciences:																		
Native	173	3.85	87	3.79	167	3.87	81	3.89	137	3.69	73	4.06	129	3.92	64	4.09	69.9	79.7
Transfer	41	3.35	14	3.40	33	3.69	11	3.55	21	3.65	10	4.00	18	3.73	9	4.32	42.1	47.4
Physical education:																		
Native	23	3.38	11	3.57	21	3.35	10	3.60	20	3.75	10	4.20	20	3.80	8	4.05	46.5	69.8
Transfer	0	—	2	3.10	0	—	2	3.10	0	—	1	—	0	—	1	—	50.0	50.0
Veterinary medicine:																		
Native	6	3.50	0	—	6	4.10	0	—	6	4.15	0	—	6	4.10	0	—	85.7	100.0
Transfer	1	—	1	—	1	—	0	—	0	—	0	—	0	—	0	—	50.0	50.0

The Public Higher Institutions in Iowa

A study was made of almost seventeen hundred students who transferred from different types of colleges to the State University of Iowa, Iowa State Teachers College, and Iowa State College from June, 1953, to March, 1955. No comparison was made between the record of transfer students and native students. To be compared are the performance of transfer students before and after transfer, and the performance after transfer of students from the different types of colleges.

Table G-1. Performance and Degrees Received by Transfer Students to the Three Public Higher Institutions in Iowa, June, 1953, to March, 1955

	From private senior colleges	From public senior colleges	From private junior colleges	From public junior colleges
Number of transfers	763	460	153	312
Mean academic average at transfer	2.38	2.19	2.56	2.52
Mean average at three public higher institutions*	2.27	2.38	2.26	2.23
Per cent receiving degrees	38	40	44	41

*Grade-point average based on a 4-point scale.

Table G-2. Performance and Degrees Received by Transfer Students to State University of Iowa, June, 1953, to March, 1955

	From private senior colleges	From public senior colleges	From private junior colleges	From public junior colleges
Number of transfers	423	258	50	107
Average number of semesters enrolled	4.3	5	3.8	4
Mean academic average at transfer	2.33	2.29	2.68	2.20
Mean average at S.U.I.	2.12	2.36	2.25	2.06
Per cent receiving degrees	43	48	46	46

The Public Higher Institutions in Kansas

Table H-1. Performance and Persistence of Native and Junior College Transfer Students Enrolling as Juniors in Three Public Colleges in Kansas, Fall, 1953

	Fort Hays Kansas State College (Hays)				Kansas State Teachers College (Pittsburg)				Kansas State Teachers College (Emporia)			
	Fall, 1953	Spring, 1954	Fall, 1954	Spring, 1955	Fall, 1953	Spring, 1954	Fall, 1954	Spring, 1955	Fall, 1953	Spring, 1954	Fall, 1954	Spring, 1955
Number of native students	150	138	109	90	111	104	88	78	173	153	116	103
Per cent persisting		92	73	60		94	79	70		88	67	60
Median grade-point average*	1.80	1.87	1.93	1.82	1.60	1.97	2.00	1.89	1.77	1.82	1.86	2.00
Number and per cent receiving degrees by end of fourth semester after junior classification	88, or 59 per cent				45, or 41 per cent				79, or 46 per cent			
Number of junior college transfers	11	11	9	7	68	62	46	43	30	29	19	18
Per cent persisting		100	82	64		91	68	63		97	63	60
Median grade-point average	2.03	2.07	2.07	2.02	1.60	1.79	1.77	2.00	1.67	1.88	2.34	1.97
Number and per cent receiving degrees by end of fourth semester after transfer	6, or 55 per cent				30, or 44 per cent				13, or 43 per cent			

* Grade-point average based on a 3-point scale.

Table H-2. Performance and Persistence of Native and Junior College Transfer
Students Enrolling as Juniors at the University of Kansas and
Kansas State College at Manhattan, Fall, 1953

	University of Kansas (Lawrence)				Kansas State College* (Manhattan)			
	Fall, 1953	Spring, 1954	Fall, 1954	Spring, 1955	Fall, 1953	Spring, 1954	Fall, 1954	Spring, 1955
Number of native students....	455	437	423	420	30	26	25	21
Per cent persisting...............		96	93	92		86	83	70
Median grade-point average..............	2.72	2.77	2.80	2.87	1.57	1.50	1.47	1.77
Number and per cent receiving degrees by end of fourth semester after junior classification.........	298, or 65 per cent				11, or 37 per cent			
Number of junior college transfers...............	81	73	68	66	30	28	25	24
Per cent persisting...............		90	84	82		93	83	80
Median grade-point average...............	2.26	2.43	2.48	2.59	1.28	1.64	1.68	1.94
Number and per cent receiving degrees by end of fourth semester after transfer..................	34, or 41 per cent				16, or 53 per cent			

* Data are a sampling of native and transfer students matched by sex and curriculum.

University of Michigan

The University of Michigan compiled certain data on all juniors (including transfer students) carrying 12 or more hours of work in the school years 1953–54 and 1954–55. Data were also compiled on the junior college transfers who entered the university with at least 60 or more hours of advanced credit in September, 1953. Their record for both the junior and senior years is presented; only their performance for 1953–54 can be compared with that of all juniors for the same year.

Table I-1. Comparison of Performance of Junior College Transfers Enrolling as Juniors with All Junior Students Enrolling at University of Michigan, Fall, 1953

	Fall, 1953	Spring, 1954	Fall, 1954	Spring, 1955
All students classified as juniors........... 1,556		1,556	1,733	1,733
Median grade-point average* for year...........		2.72		2.72
Number of junior college transfers......... 129		123	113	108
Per cent persisting...........................		95	88	84
Median grade-point average.......... 2.4		2.6	2.8	2.8
Number and per cent receiving degrees by end of fourth semester after transfer... 76, or 59 per cent				
Number and per cent receiving degrees by end of eighth semester after transfer.. 101, or 78 per cent				

* Grade-point average based on a 4-point scale.

APPENDIX J

Michigan State University

Table J-1. Performance and Persistence of Native and Transfer Students Enrolling as Juniors in Michigan State University, Fall, 1953

	September, 1953	Fall, 1953	Winter, 1954	Spring, 1954	Fall, 1954	Winter, 1955	Spring, 1955
Number of native students*...	1,336	1,269	1,026	999	975	936	908
Per cent persisting...............		95	77	75	73	70	68
Median grade-point average†.....		2.53	2.56	2.56	2.59	2.59	2.60

Number and per cent receiving degrees by end of sixth term after junior classification... 906, or 68 per cent

Number of junior college transfers	124	123	115	113	102	98	97
Per cent persisting...............		99	93	91	82	79	78
Median grade-point average......		2.23		2.45	2.43		2.75

Number and per cent receiving degrees by end of sixth term after transfer.. 65, or 53 per cent

* Out of a total of 2,148 students entering as freshmen, September, 1951.

† Grade-point average based on a 4-point scale.

University of Mississippi

Table K-1. Performance and Retention of Native Students, Four-year College
Transfers, and Junior College Transfers Enrolling as Juniors
at the University of Mississippi, Fall, 1953

	At point of junior classification	Fall, 1953	Spring, 1954	Fall, 1954	Spring, 1955	Per cent degrees spring, 1955
Native students:						
Men	161	157	149	140	131	
Women	39	37	37	34	31	
Total	200	194	186	174	162	74.5
Per cent persisting	100	97.0	93.0	87.0	81.0	
Median GPA:*						
Men	3.00	3.20	3.48	3.50	3.66	
Women	3.51	3.77	3.87	4.06	4.23	
Total	3.08	3.33	3.50	3.61	3.76	
Four-year transfers:						
Men	66	65	59	52	47	
Women	40	40	36	31	29	
Total	106	105	95	83	76	70.8
Per cent persisting	100	99.1	89.6	78.3	71.7	
Median GPA:*						
Men	3.17	3.00	3.19	3.46	3.37	
Women	3.46	3.75	3.68	3.98	4.09	
Total	3.28	3.33	3.37	3.81	3.80	
Junior college transfers:						
Men	59	59	56	47	39	
Women	29	29	28	18	17	
Total	88	88	83	65	56	60.2
Per cent persisting	100	100	94.3	73.9	63.6	
Median GPA:*						
Men	3.45	3.26	3.33	3.04	3.48	
Women	4.18	3.85	3.85	3.90	4.09	
Total	3.64	3.33	3.50	3.49	3.65	

* Grade-point average (GPA) based on a 5-point scale.

Table K-2. Performance and Persistence by Departments of Native Students,
Four-year College Transfers, and Junior College Transfers Enrolling
as Juniors at University of Mississippi, Fall, 1953

	Spring, 1953	Fall, 1953	Spring, 1954	Fall, 1954	Spring, 1955
Commerce:					
Number of native students	69	65	62	57	54
Per cent persisting		94	90	83	78
Median grade-point average	3.10	3.32	3.36	3.58	3.63
Number of four-year transfers	38	38	35	29	29
Per cent persisting		100	92	76	76
Median grade-point average	3.08	3.00	3.37	3.50	3.22
Number of junior college transfers	38	38	36	34	32
Per cent persisting		100	95	89	84
Median grade-point average	3.68	3.71	3.58	3.56	3.64
Education:					
Number of native students	34	33	31	28	27
Per cent persisting		97	91	82	79
Median grade-point average	2.58	3.04	3.48	3.60	3.98
Number of four-year transfers	12	12	11	11	10
Per cent persisting		100	92	92	83
Median grade-point average	3.01	3.62	4.00	3.92	4.08
Number of junior college transfers	9	9	9	5	5
Per cent persisting		100	100	56	56
Median grade-point average	3.57	3.29	3.66	3.75	3.88
Engineering:					
Number of native students	20	19	19	19	19
Per cent persisting		95	95	95	95
Median grade-point average	3.32	3.58	3.50	3.78	3.86
Number of four-year transfers	7	6	6	5	5
Per cent persisting		86	86	71	71
Median grade-point average	3.02	2.62	2.61	4.00	3.84
Number of junior college transfers	7	7	7	4	3
Per cent persisting		100	100	57	43
Median grade-point average	3.53	2.69	1.71	2.40	3.07
Liberal Arts:					
Number of native students	57	57	54	50	42
Per cent persisting		100	96	89	75
Median grade-point average	3.31	3.60	3.72	3.68	3.54

Table K-2. Performance and Persistence by Departments of Native Students, Four-year College Transfers, and Junior College Transfers Enrolling as Juniors at University of Mississippi, Fall, 1953 (Continued)

	Spring, 1953	Fall, 1953	Spring, 1954	Fall, 1954	Spring, 1955
Liberal Arts:					
Number of four-year transfers	42	42	36	31	25
Per cent persisting		100	86	74	60
Median grade-point average	3.34	3.48	3.33	3.84	3.90
Number of junior college transfers	27	27	24	15	11
Per cent persisting		100	89	56	41
Median grade-point average	3.84	3.34	3.44	3.40	3.76
Pharmacy:					
Number of native students	20	20	20	20	20
Per cent persisting		100	100	100	100
Median grade-point average	2.98	3.32	3.54	3.40	3.86
Number of four-year transfers	7	7	7	7	7
Per cent persisting		100	100	100	100
Median grade-point average	3.41	2.89	3.21	3.12	3.82
Number of junior college transfers	7	7	7	7	5
Per cent persisting		100	100	100	71
Median grade-point average	3.65	3.44	3.56	3.13	3.60

APPENDIX L

University of Texas

Table L-1. Performance and Persistence of Native Students and Junior College Transfers Enrolling as Juniors at University of Texas, Fall, 1953

	Fall, 1953	Spring, 1954	Fall, 1954	Spring, 1955
Number of native students........... 546		531	529	519
Per cent persisting........................		97	97	95
Median grade-point average*...... 1.50		1.59	1.60	1.67
Number and per cent receiving degrees by end of fourth semester after junior classification....................................... 467, or 86 per cent				
Number of junior college transfers..... 197		192	153	142
Per cent persisting........................		97	78	72
Median grade-point average....... 1.20		1.38	1.40	1.50
Number and per cent receiving degrees by end of fourth semester after transfer.. 130, or 66 per cent				

* Grade-point average based on a 3-point scale.

Cooperating Two-year Colleges

Institution	Location	Chief Administrator*
California:		
Bakersfield College	Bakersfield	Ralph Prator, President
City College of San Francisco	San Francisco	Louis G. Conlan, President
College of San Mateo	San Mateo	Julio L. Bortolazzo, President
East Contra Costa Junior College (now Diablo Valley College)	Concord	Karl O. Drexel, Director
Fresno Junior College	Fresno	Stuart M. White, President
Los Angeles Harbor Junior College	Wilmington	Raymond J. Casey, Director
Los Angeles Valley Junior College	Van Nuys	Walter Coultas, Director
Menlo College	Menlo Park	William E. Kratt, President
Modesto Junior College	Modesto	Roy C. McCall, President
Orange Coast College	Costa Mesa	Basil H. Peterson, President
Palomar College	San Marcos	John W. Dunn, President
Pasadena City College	Pasadena	W. B. Langsdorf, President
Reedley College	Reedley	Stephen E. Epler, President
San Bernardino Valley College	San Bernardino	John L. Lounsbury, President
Shasta College	Redding	G. A. Collyer, President

* At the time the study was made.

Cooperating Two-year Colleges (Continued)

Institution	Location	Chief Administrator*
West Contra Costa Junior College (now Contra Costa College)	San Pablo	Joseph P. Cosand, Director
Georgia:		
Abraham Baldwin Agricultural College	Tifton	George P. Donaldson, President
Armstrong College of Savannah	Savannah	Foreman M. Hawes, President
South Georgia College	Douglas	William S. Smith, President
Young L. G. Harris College	Young Harris	Charles R. Clegg, President
Illinois:		
Chicago City Junior College		
Wright and Wilson Branches	Chicago	Peter Masiko, Jr., Dean
Elgin Community College	Elgin	G. I. Renner, Dean
Joliet Junior College	Joliet	E. W. Rowley, Dean
La Salle-Peru-Oglesby Junior College	La Salle	F. H. Dolan, Superintendent
Monticello College	Alton	Russell T. Sharpe, President
Springfield Junior College	Springfield	Andrew A. O'Laughlin, Dean
Iowa:		
Clarinda Junior College	Clarinda	Paul C. Larsen, Dean
Fort Dodge Junior College	Fort Dodge	Paul Seydel, Director
Graceland College	Lamoni	W. S. Gould, Vice President
Mason City Junior College	Mason City	Clifford H. Beem, Dean
Massachusetts:		
Bradford Junior College	Bradford	Dorothy M. Bell, President

Cooperating Two-year Colleges (Continued)

Institution	*Location*	*Chief Administrator* *
Holyoke Junior College	Holyoke	G. E. Frost, Director
Nichols Junior College	Dudley	James L. Conrad, President
Worcester Junior College	Worcester	Harold Bentley, Director
Minnesota:		
Concordia College	St. Paul	W. A. Poehler, President
Rochester Junior College	Rochester	Charles E. Hill, Dean
Virginia Junior College	Virginia	Floyd B. Moe, Dean
Mississippi:		
Copiah-Lincoln Junior College	Wesson	F. M. Fortenberry, President
Hinds Junior College	Raymond	G. M. McLendon, President
Jones County Junior College	Ellisville	J. B. Young, President
Meridian Junior College	Meridian	J. O. Carson, Director
New York:		
Briarcliff Junior College	Briarcliff Manor	Clara M. Tead, President
Erie County Technical Institute	Buffalo	Laurence E. Spring, President
New York City Community College of Applied Arts and Sciences	Brooklyn	Otto Klitgord, President
Orange County Community College	Middletown	Edwin H. Miner, President
State University of New York, Agricultural and Technical Institute	Morrisville	Malcom B. Galbreath, Director
Westchester Community College	White Plains	Philip C. Martin, President
North Carolina:		
Asheville-Biltmore College	Asheville	Glenn L. Bushey, President

Cooperating Two-year Colleges (Continued)

Institution	Location	Chief Administrator*
Charlotte College	Charlotte	Bonnie Cone, Director
Mars Hill College	Mars Hill	R. M. Lee, Dean
St. Mary's Junior College	Raleigh	Richard G. Stone, President
Wilmington College	Wilmington	W. M. Randall, Dean
Ohio:		
Ohio Mechanics Institute	Cincinnati	Kenneth R. Miller, President
Oklahoma:		
Eastern Oklahoma A. & M. College	Wilburton	E. T. Dunlap, President
Northern Oklahoma Junior College	Tonkawa	V. R. Easterling, President
Poteau Junior College	Poteau	G. E. Evans, Superintendent
Oregon:		
Multnomah College	Portland	John S. Griffith, President
Oregon Technical Institute	Oretech	Winston D. Purvine, Director
Pennsylvania:		
Hershey Junior College	Hershey	Varnum Fenstermacher, Dean
Keystone Junior College	LaPlume	Blake Tewksbury, President
Pennsylvania State University Altoona Undergraduate Center	Altoona	Robert E. Eiche, Administrative Head
Pennsylvania State University Erie Undergraduate Center	Erie	Irvin H. Kochel, Administrative Head
Pennsylvania State University York Undergraduate Center	York	Edward M. Elias, Administrative Head
York Junior College	York	J. F. Marvin Buechel, President

Cooperating Two-year Colleges (Continued)

Institution	Location	Chief Administrator*
Texas:		
Amarillo College	Amarillo	A. M. Meyer, President
Del Mar College	Corpus Christi	E. L. Harvin, President
Howard County Junior College	Big Spring	W. A. Hunt, President
Lee Junior College	Baytown	Walter Rundell, Dean
Lon Morris College	Jacksonville	H. V. Robinson, Dean
San Angelo College	San Angelo	R. M. Cavness, President
San Antonio College	San Antonio	Wayland Moody, President
Schreiner Institute	Kerrville	Andrew Edington, President
Tyler Junior College	Tyler	H. E. Jenkins, President
Wisconsin:		
University of Wisconsin Racine Extension Center	Racine	A. E. May, Director
Wausau Extension Center	Wausau	Henry C. Ahrnsbrak, Director

APPENDIX N

Cooperating Four-year Colleges

Institution	*Coordinator of Study*

California:
  Fresno State College — Leo Wolfson, Dean of Students
  San Jose State College — L. D. Edmison, Test Officer
  University of California — Grace V. Bird, Associate Director, Office of Relations with Schools
  University of Southern California — Bernard L. Hyink, Dean of Students
Georgia:
  University of Georgia — R. T. Osborne, Director, Guidance Center

Illinois:
  University of Illinois — Raymond J. Young, Associate Professor, Bureau of Educational Research

Iowa:
  Iowa State College — Arthur M. Gowan ⎱
  Iowa State Teachers College — Marshall R. Beard ⎰ Committee of Registrars
  State University of Iowa — Ted McCarrel
Kansas:
  Fort Hays State College ⎱
  Kansas State College — Rees H. Hughes, President Emeritus (Pittsburg), Coordinator
  Kansas State Teachers College of Emporia and Pittsburg ⎰
  University of Kansas
Michigan:
  University of Michigan — John E. Milholland, Chief, Evaluation and Examination Division
  Edward G. Groesbeck, Director, Office of Registration
  Michigan State University — Kermit H. Smith, Registrar
Mississippi:
  University of Mississippi — John B. Morris, Director, Institutional Research

Texas:
  University of Texas — Byron Shipp, Registrar

350

APPENDIX O

Cooperating Officials in State Agencies and Universities*

California:
> Hugh G. Price, Chief, Bureau of Junior College Education, State Department of Education, Sacramento

Florida:
> James L. Wattenbarger, Director, Division of Community Junior Colleges, State Department of Education, Tallahassee

Georgia:
> Harmon Caldwell, Chancellor, University System of Georgia, Atlanta

Illinois:
> Ward N. Black, Assistant Superintendent of Public Instruction, Springfield

Indiana:
> Hugh W. Norman, Dean, University Extension, Indiana University, Bloomington

Iowa:
> B. H. Graeber, Junior College Consultant, State Department of Education, Des Moines

Massachusetts:
> John P. Mallan, Executive Secretary, Special Commission on Audit of State Needs, Boston
>
> Stanley F. Salwak, Assistant to the Provost, University of Massachusetts, Amherst

Minnesota:
> Elmer M. Weltzin, Director of Junior Colleges, State Department of Education, St. Paul
>
> Robert J. Keller, Professor of Education, University of Minnesota, Minneapolis

Mississippi:
> B. C. Hill, Supervisor of Junior Colleges, State Department of Education, Jackson

* The individuals listed are those who were especially helpful in gathering and supplying information and in reviewing prepared statements about the two-year college program in their respective states. In addition to this list, numerous other officials in state agencies, universities, and colleges made themselves available for helpful interviews.

New York:

Lawrence L. Jarvie, Executive Dean, State University of New York, Albany

Elbert K. Fretwell, Jr., State Education Department, The University of the State of New York, Albany

North Carolina:

Harris Purks, Director, Board of Higher Education, Raleigh

Ohio:

D. H. Eikenberry, Professor of Education, Ohio State University, Columbus

A. C. Gubitz, Dean, Ohio University, Athens

Oklahoma:

M. A. Nash, Chancellor, Oklahoma State Regents for Higher Education, Oklahoma City

Thomas Sexton, Assistant Chancellor, Oklahoma State Regents for Higher Education, Oklahoma City

Oregon:

John R. Richards, Chancellor, Oregon State System of Higher Education, Eugene

Rex Putnam, Superintendent of Public Instruction, Eugene

Pennsylvania:

E. L. Keller (and staff), Director, General Extension, Pennsylvania State University, University Park

Lester F. Johnson, Supervisor, Higher Education, Department of Public Instruction, Harrisburg

Texas:

B. W. Musgraves, Executive Director, Texas Council of Public Junior Colleges, Texas Education Agency, Austin

Washington:

D. Grant Morrison, Director of Junior College Education, State Department of Public Instruction, Olympia. (Succeeded in office by L. J. Elias)

Wisconsin:

W. M. Hanley, Director, Freshman-Sophomore Center System, University of Wisconsin, Madison

C. L. Greiber, State Director, Vocational and Adult Education, Madison

Index